*Of Course You Love
Homemade French Fries—
But Have You Ever Tried*

- CRAB-STUFFED BAKED POTATOES
- POTATO AND LEEK CASSEROLE
- SESAME POTATO BREAD
- GERMAN SOUR CREAM CAKES
- POMMES MARGUERITE
- YORKSHIRE PUDDING
- CURRIED POTATOES WITH SCALLIONS AND EGGS
- IRISH POTATO CODDLE
- HOT GERMAN POTATO SALAD
- OLD-FASHIONED POTATO PANCAKES

They're all here—plus many more taste-tempting,
nourishing dishes made from that most
reliable and versatile of vegetables, The Potato.
Enjoy!

The Great Potato Cookbook

ALL NEW SOPHIE LEAVITT'S PENNY PINCHER'S
   COOKBOOK
THE ART OF FRENCH COOKING by Fernande Garvin
THE ART OF ITALIAN COOKING by Mario Lo Pinto
THE ART OF JEWISH COOKING by Jennie Grossinger
BAKING BREAD THE WAY MOM TAUGHT ME
   by Mary Ann Gross
BETTER HOMES AND GARDENS® ALL-TIME FAVORITE
   BARBECUE RECIPES
BETTER HOMES AND GARDENS® BLENDER
   COOKBOOK
BETTER HOMES AND GARDENS® HOME CANNING
   COOKBOOK
BETTER HOMES AND GARDENS® NEW COOKBOOK
BLEND IT SPLENDID: THE NATURAL FOODS BLENDER
   BOOK by Stan and Floss Dworkin
THE COMPLETE BOOK OF PASTA by Jack Denton Scott
COOKING WITHOUT A GRAIN OF SALT by Elma W. Bagg
COOKING WITH HERBS AND SPICES by Craig Claiborne
CREPE COOKERY by Mable Hoffman
CROCKERY COOKERY by Mable Hoffman
CUISINE MINCEUR by Michel Guérard
JEANE DIXON'S ASTROLOGICAL COOKBOOK
THE FRENCH CHEF COOKBOOK by Julia Child
GREAT COOKING OUTDOORS by Gale T. Holsman
   and Beverly Holsman
THE GREAT POTATO COOKBOOK by Maria Luisa Scott
   and Jack Denton Scott
LAUREL'S KITCHEN by Laurel Robertson, Carol Flinders
   and Bronwen Godfrey
MADAME WU'S ART OF CHINESE COOKING by Sylvia Wu
MAKE-A-MIX COOKERY by Nevada Harward,
   Madeline Westover and Karine Eliason
MASTERING MICROWAVE COOKING by Maria Luisa Scott
   and Jack Denton Scott
PUTTING FOOD BY by Ruth Hertzberg, Beatrice Vaughan
   and Janet Greene
RICHARD DEACON'S MICROWAVE COOKERY
SOUPS by Jeannette Seaver
SOURDOUGH COOKERY by Rita Davenport
THE UNABRIDGED VEGETABLE COOKBOOK
   by Nika Hazelton
WHOLE EARTH COOKBOOK by Sharon Cadwallader
   and Judi Ohr
THE WORLD-FAMOUS RATNER'S MEATLESS
   COOKBOOK by Judith Gethers and Elizabeth Lefft
YOGURT COOKERY by Sophie Kay

The Great Potato Cookbook

By Maria Luisa Scott
and Jack Denton Scott

BANTAM BOOKS · TORONTO · NEW YORK · LONDON

THE GREAT POTATO COOKBOOK
A Bantam Book / August 1980

ISBN 0-553-13673-9

Published simultaneously in the United States and Canada

Bantam Books are published by Bantam Books, Inc. Its trade-
mark, consisting of the words "Bantam Books" and the por-
trayal of a bantam, is Registered in U.S. Patent and Trademark
Office and in other countries. Marca Registrada. Bantam
Books, Inc., 666 Fifth Avenue, New York, New York 10103.

"Of all books produced since the most remote ages by human talents and industry, those only that treat of cooking are, from a moral point of view, above suspicion. The intention of every other piece of prose may be discussed and even mistrusted; but the purpose of a cookery book is one and unmistakable. Its object can conceivably be no other than to increase the happiness of mankind . . ."

JOSEPH CONRAD

Table of Contents

Foreword

Americans eat four times more potatoes than any other vegetable. The potato appears on more menus more often than any other single food.

And no one can deny that the potato may be our best food buy, our tastiest vegetable, a money-saving, savory stand-in for meat.

Yet too many of us consider the world's most important vegetable a fattening filler, believing it long on starch, fat and carbohydrates, short on protein and vitamins, to be guiltily indulged in only at the risk of widening our waists.

The truth is that we would have to eat 11 pounds of potatoes to put on one pound of weight. We spend only two percent of our food dollar on potatoes, but receive from that small amount more than 25 percent of all our energy and nutrient requirements. It is also a fact that potatoes have 74.5 percent more food energy per acre than wheat, and 77.6 percent higher protein per acre than rice.

Consider that the publicity-poor potato really contains only one percent fat, that ounce for ounce it has no more calories than the touted keep-the-doctor-away apple, and is less caloric than equal weights of pears, avocados, rice or bran flakes. The potato may also be the best of all brain foods.

The United States Department of Agriculture, which knows its potatoes, reports that if a person's entire diet consisted of that vegetable, he would get all of the riboflavin (B2), one-and-a-half times the iron, three to four times the thiamine (B1) and niacin (B3) and more than ten times the amount of vitamin C that the body needs.

These facts were not known to Peru's Inca indians, who first cultivated the potato about 200 B.C., yet those ancient people not only realized long before anyone else that the remarkable plant *Solanum tuberosum* was a wonder food, but also invented freeze-drying to preserve the vegetable for lean days, thus making our own lives easier thousands of years later.

Millions throughout the world are indebted to that culture—and to the Spanish conquistadores who first found the potato high in the Andes and did not realize that it would prove to be more precious than Inca gold.

In 1537, a scouting party of Gonzalo Jiménez de Quesada's expedition entered the Andean village of Sorocota and found, in the homes of the natives who had fled, corn, beans and a strange vegetable ranging in size from a nut to an apple, in color from gold, black, blue and gray to red.

The vegetable had many uses, raw slices were placed on broken bones, rubbed on the head to cure aching, used as heat retainers to relieve the pain of gout, rubbed on the face and body to cure skin disorders, carried to prevent rheumatism; raw slices were also eaten with other food to prevent indigestion.

The Incas had names for the vegetable, a hard potato was called "Knife-Breaker," others were "Human-Head" and "Red Mother." One with red flesh was called "Weeps Blood for the Incas."

Their general name for this miracle plant of 52 varieties was *papa*, meaning tuber. But the Spaniards preferred to call the vegetable *turma de tierra*, or truffle. They found it "floury, of good flavor, a dainty dish even for Spaniards."

They also found that it not only was the staple food of the Incas, but one that they had learned to preserve indefinitely. The *papas* (the potato is still called that in Spain, or sometimes *patata*; the English name "potato" is a corruption of *batata*, West Indian for sweet potato) were taken to 13,000 feet in the Andes, where they froze at night, then thawed in the sunlight. This was repeated until the potatoes were without moisture, hard but very light. Often the vegetable was cooked and cut up before freezing, and sometimes the moisture was stamped out with bare feet. The world's first freeze-dried food was called *chuño*.

When that Inca potato was introduced into Europe some 400 years ago, it immediately became the subject of lies, myths and slander. It was not mentioned in the Bible, thus was unfit for human use. A member of the nightshade family that included several poisonous plants, it was considered dangerous, and because it was not grown from seed it was said to be evil, responsible for leprosy, syphilis and scrofula. French experts claimed it would destroy the soil in which it was planted, and physicians there said it was responsible for several serious illnesses and was also a dangerous aphrodisiac. As late as the 18th century Russian peasants preferred to die of starvation rather than plant the sexually unclean potato.

History gets hysterical about how the vegetable was introduced into Europe, giving both Sir Walter Raleigh and Sir Francis Drake credit. But facts favor the conquistadores, and a Spanish monk, Hieronymus Cardan. Potatoes probably were introduced earlier in Spain, but public attention was focused on them in Seville markets in 1570, and also when they were used there in 1573 to feed hospital patients.

The tubers were first grown in Italy in 1585, then in Germany, Austria and Switzerland, finally in France. As late as 1744, Frederick II of Germany commanded peasants to plant potatoes, which he furnished free and sent soldiers along to see that his order was carried out. In 1764, a Swedish edict forced the Swedes to grow potatoes.

But most of Europe was not overly enthusiastic about the vegetable until France led the way, proving what a taste treat it was. Responsible for this action was French pharmacist Antoine Parmentier, who learned to enjoy potatoes when he was a prisoner of the Germans during the Seven Years' War.

Declaring the French fear of the vegetable nonsense, he invited the famous to his home, among them Benjamin Franklin, and offered them an all-potato menu, often with as many as 20 dishes. He also used a subtle piece of psychology to get the French farmers to plant them. King Louis XVI gave him permission to plant potatoes at Les Sablons, a sandy, barren plot not far from Paris. During the day Parmentier stationed soldiers to stand guard at his potato field. But at night it was unguarded. Curious about plants that were so valuable. Frenchmen stole them and planted them in their own gardens. Today France honors Parmentier by naming some of the best of its potato dishes after him.

It took at least two centuries after its export from South America for the potato to be accepted and developed in Europe. England did not produce them in any quantity until 1796. Earlier though, probably in 1663, England did send potatoes to Ireland where they were promptly planted and appreciated.

The United States got its potatoes in 1719 when a colony of those Irish settled at Londonderry, New Hampshire, and grew them. But potatoes were slow to win favor. As late as 1740, it was a practice with masters to advise apprentices that they were not obliged to use potatoes, which were said to shorten men's lives and make them unhealthy. It was only when a few of the upper class ate them and pronounced them palatable that some people began to lose their suspicion and eat the new vegetable.

It even took nutritionists a long time to rally around the potato, and it is only within the last few years that they began preaching that not only are potatoes a valuable source of essential amino acids (produced by protein foods, usually animal), but also high in potassium, which is necessary for the utilization of protein and the body's retention of nitrogen. The potassium content not only makes the potato highly digestible but valuable in treating digestive disorders.

We need more than three times as much carbohydrates as protein in order to supply energy to the brain, heart, lungs and muscles. The brain alone consumes about 25 percent of all fuel intake and carbohydrates seem to be the only fuel on which the brain can work efficiently. In addition, the potato gives excellent nutritional return for every gram of carbohydrate it contains.

It is such a near-perfect food that the Agricultural Research Service of the United States Department of Agriculture declared that, "A diet of whole milk and potatoes would supply almost all of the food elements necessary for the maintenance of the human body."

In one experiment, a man remained in excellent health with constant body weight for 167 days on a diet of cooked potatoes, a few fruits and only occasionally tea or black coffee with sugar.

In another calorie test, Robert Luescher, a Michigan State graduate student, went on a potato diet for 22 days. He ate four pounds every day, boiling them for breakfast, making salads for lunch and frying them for dinner. No matter how he cooked them the potatoes came to only 1,300 calories a day. To get his intake up to 3,600 daily, Luescher added extra fats, cream, butter and cheese to the potatoes. At the end of that three-week potato spree he had put on exactly four ounces.

Long before that an entire nation ate little else but potatoes for many years. Prior to the famine of the 1840's, caused by the potato blight, the majority of the people of Ireland lived on potatoes and some milk (adults ate eight to ten pounds a day). Not only did they not suffer from protein deficiency or lack of energy, but they remained in vigorous health until that cheap and perfect food ran out. Then about one million died, and another million left for other countries, many for America.

The Irish in this country are fond of telling a story that sums up the value of the potato. About to sit down to dinner, a small boy seeing a platter of potatoes and nothing else on the table asked what they were going to have with them. "You'll have the little ones with the big ones, and big ones with the little ones, and thank God we've got 'em," his mother said.

A simple chart calculated on an average-sized boiled potato containing 76 calories places this beneficial personality of the potato into perspective. (The average adult American male requires from 2,600 to 2,800 calories a day, which means that the charted boiled potato accounts for less than three percent of a day's food calories.)

Nutrients of a Medium-sized Potato Boiled in Its Skin

Protein: 2.1 grams; supplies over 3 percent of daily protein need.

Iron: 6 milligrams; 6 percent of daily need.

Thiamine (B1): 90 micrograms; 6 to 7 percent of daily need.

Riboflavin (B2): 40 micrograms; 2 to 3 percent of daily need.

Niacin (B3): 1.5 milligrams; about 10 percent of daily need.

Vitamin C: 16 milligrams; more than 25 percent of daily need.

The powerhouse potato also contains magnesium, phosphorus, calcium, copper and other important minerals, and its sodium level is low, only 3 milligrams, making it valuable in low-sodium diets such as those for high blood pressure. With today's nutritionists urging less animal fat and protein intake and more carbohydrates, the potato takes on added value. Its carbohydrate is 92 to 98 percent usable, the necessary and hard-to-get iron, which the potato has more of than any other vegetable, 93 percent usable, and potato vitamin B1 is more usable than a similar amount of the purified vitamin.

Tuft's University's Dr. Jean Mayer, a onetime Presidential adviser on nutrition, says that people are obsessed with the idea that starchy foods are "horribly" fattening, while the fact is that the potato not only has fewer calories than believed but that each 100 calories contains 10 percent of good quality protein.

Nutritionist R. A. Seelig remarks that when starch, as in potatoes, is substituted for sugar in the diet, appetite is reduced. For this reason, and also the fact that they supply multiple vitamins and minerals along with calories, potatoes are actually valuable in a reducing diet.

One science researcher states that in a 20-year search of accepted nutrition literature, no source has been found in which a responsible scientist has advocated the elimination of the potato from programs for weight control.

When you consider that a pretty large baked potato has only 90 calories, and that one pat of butter, weighing about one-third ounce has 72 calories, and 1½ tablespoons of French dressing on your salad has 100 calories, it is clear that the potato is more victim than villain in this count-your-calories contest that increasingly engages Americans.

This may be true, say the potato's critics, but most of us do add high-caloric foods such as butter, cream and sour cream to mashed and baked potatoes. Don't worry, reply most nutritionists, for by doing so we are also supplying extra calcium, vitamin A and strengthening the B2 intake.

Potatoes thus become a superb nutrition base to which we can add other nutrients necessary to our diet. Although this does add more calories, consider that even a dish of scalloped potatoes with milk and butter contains only 145 calories a portion. This makes up only about five percent of the daily caloric diet, and look what you get in return in the way of benefits.

No one has much to say in favor of fried potatoes, except that they may be the tastiest of all. But ten ½ x ½ x 2-inch fried slices amount to just 137 calories. Compare that with the 300 calories of the popular hot dog and hamburger, 420 for a piece of chocolate cake, 200 for ½ cup of vanilla ice cream, 400 for a sundae, 200 for a single doughnut, even the 225 calories for a cup of cooked rice. Compute the relative food values, and the potato comes out far ahead.

It also does well from a dollar standpoint. Yearly, Americans buy $2 billion worth of fresh and $2.5 billion of processed potatoes grown in every state. Per capita, we eat 122 pounds a year (the Germans eat 374); our total 30 billion pounds, 2 billion of which are French fries.

America may wrongly consider the potato a food that creates fatties, but we have interesting ways with it. We have created more stuffings than anyone, blending the mealy baker with everything from cottage cheese to caviar and salmon. We also hash, mash, mince, cream, fry, steam, boil and roast them; add them to improve soups and chowders; combine them with cheese, onions, butter and milk as a main dish, team them with tuna, couple them with chicken, make croquettes, pair them with leftover meat in a pie, create unique casseroles, put them in stews, pat them into patties, even make delicious doughnuts and chocolate cake with them.

The French who fondly call the potato *pomme de terre,* "apple of the earth," do much more than French fry potatoes. They have over 100 classic recipes, from the dramatic *pommes de terre soufflées,* which puff into hollow golden balls, to the impressive *pommes Anna,* potatoes sliced very thin, baked in sweet butter and turned out like a cake.

The Germans, who may respect the potato most, and have two names for it, *kartoffel,* or truffle, and *erdapfel*, earth apple, use it for noodles, dumplings, pancakes and bread. They imaginatively mix mashed potatoes with applesauce, sugar and vinegar, use potatoes to stuff geese and make a renown hot potato salad. In Russia and Poland, the potato, called *kartofel*, truffle, is the base for many soups. It is stewed in sour cream; patties are stuffed with spicy mushrooms, and both countries make famous potato puddings and ingeniously stuff the vegetable with meat and fish.

The Italians turn the *patate* into their famous *gnocchi*. The Spanish fill a spectacular omelet with *papas*, the Greeks make a superb sauce, *skordalia* with potato, olive oil, garlic and lemon, which they serve with seafood, and the Swiss have created *röesti*, a flat potato cake that has become the national dish.

The world's ways with the poor man's food and the gourmet's delight are endless.

Here, for the first time, is a balanced collection of representative and respected potato recipes from around the globe. Here, too, are the classics, the familiar and the famous, the little known, the innovative and the ingenious. In short, here is *The Great Potato Cookbook*.

Finally, although some of this information may be scattered elsewhere throughout the book, here, for weight-worriers, is a quick calorie reference chart, placing the potato in perspective.

Calorie Comparison Chart

	CALORIES
POTATOES—boiled, ½ cup	45
mashed, milk added	70
½ cup baked, 1 medium	90
potato salad with dressing—½ cup	99
Spaghetti—cooked, ¾ cup	115
Bread—2 slices	120
Whiskey—100 proof, 1 jigger	125

Biscuit—one, 2½ inches diameter	130
Candy—chocolate, 1-ounce bar	150
Rice—cooked, ¾ cup	150
Sweet Potato—baked, 1 medium	155
Milk—whole, 1 glass	165
Peanuts—roasted, 1 ounce	170
Pancakes—3, 4 inches in diameter	180
Pizza—⅛ of a 14-inch pie	180
Macaroni—with cheese, ½ cup	240
Ground beef—3 ounce patty	245
Steak—4 inches x 2½ inches x ½ inch	330
Cake—chocolate, 2-inch section of 10-inch layer cake	420
Milk shake—1, 12-ounce glass	520

Raising Your Own, Varieties, Buying, Storing, Cooking, Microwave Cooking

Raising Your Own

With so many of us digging in the soil these days and with home gardening almost as popular as tennis, it is our pleasure to report that potatoes may not only be the world's perfect food, but probably the easiest to raise. We've raised them and have always found it fun and rewarding. It's difficult to define the personal pleasure received from spading up potatoes planted from seed, feeling them firm and aromatic in your hands, smelling of the good earth, of sun and of rain, an almost pungent, yet exciting, seldom-experienced aroma that above-the-earth vegetables do not have. Another bonus is the surprise at the fecundity of this "apple of the earth," which from a small cut-out piece with two or three "eyes" will produce a whole cluster of offspring.

The professional farmer says all of this more realistically, "Potatoes are a highly productive crop."

There is one drawback however. They do need space. To supply enough potatoes for the needs of one person requires 70 to 100 feet of space. They like somewhat sandy, light soil, and they should be planted about May 1st on the East Coast, but it is wise to check with your local gardeners.

The first decision is the variety you want to grow. With us it is never a problem, we always plant the Russet Burbank, which is the mealy Idaho. They don't have quite that Idaho flavor, imparted by the soil out there probably, but they are superb. (See detail on varieties later on in this chapter.)

After you decide what variety you want, buy "certified" seed stock from your local garden center or from a seed company. Certified means that they are guaranteed to produce and have not been chemically sprayed to stop sprouting. Seed potatoes are sold by the pound. Three pounds will handle a row 25 feet long.

The first step is to cut the seed potatoes into sections, each containing two "eyes"; we use three, an extra one for good luck. When you put them into the soil make sure one eye is staring upward at you, more or less centered in the hole you have dug. They should be planted 12 inches apart, five inches deep, in rows 30 inches apart.

After the plants begin sprouting in about two weeks, cultivate them weekly, hoeing out the weeds, building "hills" around each plant, using the soil from the walking area between the rows. This hilling will protect the growing potatoes from too much sun, which can turn them green and make them taste bitter.

When the plants are 12 inches high they should bear blossoms. This is the signal to start spreading bone meal, compost or manure once around each hill. Don't overdo it or the potatoes may pick up a disease known as the "common scab." One bushel of manure for every 100 feet is a safe limit.

If the season is dry, water the plants well once a week—in the morning. This gives the foliage a chance to dry out during the day and prevent rotting, in case you've watered the leaves more than you have the thirsty tubers underground.

When do you harvest? Easy. Just make sure you finish it before the first frost. Begin harvesting when the plants become very dry and start to tumble over. This should occur in early fall, about four months after the seed stock was planted. Two weeks after the plants become dry pull them up and dig the potatoes.

Each plant should contain its crop of several potatoes in about an 8-inch layer. Don't, however, just start digging or you'll end up spearing potatoes with your spade. Begin from the outside edge, carefully digging straight down, bringing the potato crop up in sections. Carefully turn the soil over and pick out the potatoes.

But, if you don't have the space, time, or inclination to raise your own potatoes, don't feel cheated. Superior potatoes are available in most grocery stores. Not only are they among the best of all food buys, but they come in a variety of shapes, sizes and textures.

Varieties

When buying potatoes, the following information should prove helpful, as much of it comes from one of the leading experts in the country, The Potato Board of Denver, Colorado, which has compiled its useful *The Whole Potato Catalog*.

Although there are different names, some of them local, for potatoes in various sections of the country, basically there are four types: Russet, Long White, Round Red, Round White. These also come in several varieties, each of which has its own champions. For example, some believe that the best Long Whites come from Long Island. Californians disagree; they also have a famous Long White. Many of us agree that the best Russet is that mealy mouthful from Idaho. People in Maine don't agree. They also have a famed Russet baker. Perhaps the most popular Russet is the Russet Burbank; favored in the Round Reds is the Norland and the Red Pontiac; in the Round White, the Superior and the Katahdin.

All types can be bought as "new potatoes" early in the season, but the timing varies regionally. Consequently, as many of us believe, new potatoes are not a variety in themselves. Quite simply, these thin-skinned tasty little morsels are potatoes that come to the market directly from the field and are not placed in storage. Usually they are harvested to be smaller in size, tenderer, with a unique, feathery skin texture and are available all year in limited quantities.

New potatoes are excellent boiled, steamed or in salads. Round Reds are best for oven roasting or boiling; Round Whites and Long Whites are fine for mashing, frying, boiling and roasting. Both Whites are good for salads. Russets are the classic bakers, the fluffiest and mealiest. But there are those among us (including the authors) who feel that Russets from Idaho can be used for anything. They are excellent for potato dumplings and pancakes, also for *gnocchi* and French fries. We also like the Russets baked for four minutes in the microwave oven, then peeled and sliced as steak or country fries.

A good rule of thumb. Bakers are mealy and dry; boilers, moist and firm.

In the recipes that follow mainly we will not specify the variety of potato to use. If you want to know what kind of potato is best for salad, mashed or fried, refer back to this section. But most of us have a favorite all-purpose variety and use it for just about everything. The authors do not want to upset that potato-cart. After all, few of us are such perfectionists that we will complain about a salad because the potatoes have a mealy texture rather than the firm and waxy one the experts claim is right.

Buying

Grading of potatoes is on a voluntary basis, except where required by state law or Federal Marketing Order. The best is U.S. Extra No. 1, which should have no defects, weigh 5 ounces and be 2¼ inches in diameter. The next grade, the U.S. No. 1 must be 1⅞ inches in diameter, with no minimum size.

Best bet in buying is to select loose potatoes that are well formed, smooth, firm, with few eyes, no discoloration, cracks, bruises or soft spots. Firmness is especially important. Red potatoes and some whites are sometimes treated with colored or clear wax to make them appear fresher than they are. Avoid them. The FDA requires that these be plainly marked, but you can tell them by the unnatural waxy feel. Also do not buy potatoes that have even the slightest greenish hue. These have been overexposed to light and will have a bitter, unpleasant flavor.

Storing

Do not wash potatoes before storing, as this hastens decay. Store them in a dry, dark place at 45° to 50° F. They will last for up to three months (if they are firm and reasonably fresh when purchased). If you must store them at warmer temperatures then buy only a week's supply at a time. Higher temperatures cause fast sprouting and shriveling.

Do not store potatoes in the refrigerator. Below 40

degrees, potato starch turns to sugar, making the potato much too sweet. Too-cold storage also causes the potatoes to darken during cooking.

Cooking

Nutrients close to the skin are lost when potatoes are peeled before cooking. Thus, for full value bake, boil or steam potatoes in their skins. If you must peel them for cooking (for frying, etc.), use a vegetable parer and peel as thinly as possible. Also, do not soak peeled potatoes in water to crisp them; some nutrients will dissolve in the water.

Our advice, then, is to cook potatoes in their skins, but we are not going to point this out in each recipe unless it is necessary to that recipe. Some, for example the French, rarely cook potatoes in the skins. So we will stay with the authenticity of each recipe. If it decrees that potatoes should be cooked in the skin we will so state. If we do not make this statement, and if it is possible for you to boil or steam potatoes in their skins, by all means do so. The vitamins and nutrients will be in you, and not be left in the cooking water.

Following is more helpful material from The Potato Board's *The Whole Potato Catalog*; our own experience and our own book, *Mastering Microwave Cooking*.

First, here is a quick reference chart for potato equivalents. One pound of potatoes equals:

Three medium potatoes

Three cups of peeled and sliced

Two-and-one-half cups of peeled and diced

Two cups of mashed

Two cups of French fries

Two pounds of medium potatoes equal:

Six servings of potato salad, averaging one potato per serving.

To Rice

Prepare boiled or steamed potatoes; drain and peel. Force potatoes through a potato ricer or a food mill. They may be tossed with melted butter or margarine before or after ricing.

To Boil

In a heavy saucepan with a tight-fitting lid, cook the potatoes in about 1 inch of boiling salted water until fork-tender: whole, 30 to 40 minutes; cut-up, 20 to 25 minutes. (If the lid doesn't fit tightly, the water may boil away so check occasionally and add more hot water if necessary.)

To Bake

A medium-sized potato (about 3 per pound) will bake in 40 to 45 minutes at 400° F. However, oven temperatures can range from 325° F. to 450° F. so you can bake the potatoes along with whatever else you have in the oven, saving energy. Adjust the timing according to the temperature. Pierce the skin of each potato in several places with the tines of a fork before baking. This allows steam to escape and prevents the potato from bursting. Bake them directly on the oven rack or a cookie sheet. Potatoes are done when they are soft when pinched with mitted hands, or tested with a slim skewer or fork. If soft skins are desired, rub each potato with a little salad oil before baking.

There are two schools of thought on baking potatoes in foil: One claims it makes the potatoes soggy, the other that foil improves flavor, keeps the potatoes warm, and most important, gives a second skin that helps retain nutrients.

We remind you that potatoes offer the best source of vitamin C, next to citrus fruit. Our bodies cannot store this vitamin, so we should replenish it daily. The problem is that much vitamin C is destroyed in cooking, especially at higher temperatures.

In tests conducted by Reynolds to determine the amount of vitamin C retention, potatoes baked in Reynolds Interfolded Sheets were tested against unwrapped potatoes. The results proved that potatoes baked in foil contained 20 percent more vitamin C than potatoes baked without foil. After two hours holding, the foil-wrapped potatoes had 80 percent more vitamin C. And after four hours holding, the foil-wrapped potatoes had a 3½:1 edge in vitamin C content over those that were unwrapped. In another test, foil-wrapped potatoes stayed at serving temperature for 43 minutes after being removed from the oven, 20 minutes longer than those that were unwrapped.

We find foil-wrapped potatoes are also a plus for those who like to eat the skin of a baked potato. It is softer and moister, and, besides being tasty, that skin is a storehouse of nutrients.

The only way to prove all this to your own satisfaction is to run your own tests, draw your own conclusions, and then bake the potatoes the way you like them best. We will say this: Heat vanishes from baked potatoes quickly and they are not at their best unless piping hot. Tightly wrapped in foil there is no doubt that baked potatoes arrive at the table hotter than the unwrapped and are kept hot throughout the meal. We consider baked potatoes so important and popular that we have devoted a chapter to them.

To Mash

Prepare boiled or steamed potatoes; drain and peel. Using a potato masher, electric mixer or ricer, mash the potatoes. Gradually add milk, salt and pepper to taste, and, if you like, a bit of butter or margarine.

Beat until the potatoes are light and fluffy. The texture of the potatoes will depend on the amount of milk used; the more milk, the creamier and thinner the potatoes will be. But too much milk will make them thin and soupy. There are variations on how to mash potatoes. Recipes that follow will explain this in detail.

To Pan Roast

Prepare boiled or steamed potatoes, but cook only 10 minutes; drain and peel. Arrange the potatoes in a shallow pan. Brush them with melted butter, margarine or salad oil. Bake, uncovered, at 400° F., or until fork-tender, turning occasionally and basting with more fat. If roasting with meat, arrange peeled, raw, halved or quartered potatoes around the meat in the roasting pan about 1½ hours before serving. Baste with pan drippings. Turn and baste frequently to brown.

To Steam

This is one of the most effective ways to preserve nutrients. If you don't have a steamer, improvise by placing a wire rack on the bottom of a kettle or large saucepan and add water to just below the level of the rack. Bring the water to a boil, add potatoes and cook over medium heat, tightly covered, until fork-tender: whole, 30 to 45 minutes; cut-up, 20 to 30 minutes. If lid is not tight fitting check occasionally to see if hot water should be added. If you don't have a rack, invert custard cups or crumple aluminum foil to make an elevated platform.

To French Fry

Cut raw potatoes into strips about ¼- to ½-inch thick. Toss the strips into a bowl of ice and water to keep crisp while cutting the remainder. Don't soak as the potatoes will absorb water, prolonging the cooking time and making the potatoes oily and soggy.

Pat the strips dry with paper towels. Heat about 4 inches of vegetable oil to 390° F. in a deep-fat fryer or large heavy saucepan. Place a layer of potato strips in a wire basket and immerse the basket in hot fat; or place the strips, a few at a time, directly into the hot oil. Cook about 5 minutes, or until golden brown and tender. Drain well on paper towels; salt lightly and keep warm in a 300° F. oven until ready to serve. See additional method on page 232.

To Prepare Salad

It is best to use potatoes with a firm, waxy texture; new potatoes are best, but Round Whites or Reds are also excellent. It is a must to cook potatoes in their skins for salad. Most flavor is retained with this method. Salads are also much tastier if the potatoes are peeled hot and the salad dressing added while the slices are warm.

These are conventional cooking tips from The Potato Board. We will also offer variations in the methods of the 350 recipes that follow.

Microwave Cooking

It is one of the marvels of the microwave oven that it can bake a 7-ounce potato in 4 minutes in contrast to an electric or gas oven that takes an hour, more or less. This savings in energy is impressive, but so is the fact that having a baked potato can be a last-minute decision.

Select 7-ounce, blocky potatoes that are uniform in size. If the potatoes have too long a taper, the slender portion will be cooked before the rest of the potato.

Also, if you cook small and large potatoes together, the smaller will be done first. Scrub the potatoes and pierce them in several places with a sharp knife on both sides. If you are cooking one potato, place it in the center, more than one (do not cook more than six at a time), place the potatoes spoke-fashion, at least one inch apart.

It isn't necessary to place the potatoes in a dish. Cook them on double-folded paper towel. The towels will also absorb some of the moisture from the potatoes and prevent oversteaming.

Cooking time, as it does with all food in the microwave oven, depends upon the size and variety of the potato. We have found that a Maine or New York state potato cooks more quickly than the more solid Idaho. Caution: When half of the cooking time has elapsed turn the potato. When we cook a 7-ounce potato for 4 minutes, we set the timer on 2 minutes as a reminder, then turn it and cook it another 2 minutes. We remind you again: Foil is necessary in much microwave cookery. It provides two important functions, keeping the food warm while aiding in the carry-over cooking time. Getting the baked potato to the table hot is a problem for all of us. Foiling solves this. No more cold or lukewarm potatoes.

The following are estimated times. Each microwave cook must experiment with timing (and potatoes) in order to cook a potato to his own taste-satisfaction.

Baking Time for a 7-ounce Potato

1 potato	4 to 5 minutes
2 potatoes	6 to 7 minutes
3 potatoes	8 to 9 minutes
4 potatoes	10 to 11 minutes
6 potatoes	14 to 15 minutes

When cooking anything in the microwave oven remember that the carry-over cooking time is important. We always remove potatoes when they are still firm, thus we cook the short time, 4 rather than 5 minutes, and allow for the carry-over cooking. If potatoes are withered-looking before you remove them from the oven they are overcooked. Don't be discouraged. Trial and error will perfect timing.

If preparing a simple baked potato, then cook the full 4 minutes. But if baking a potato for further cooking, then shave some time, looking ahead to the additional cooking that will be necessary. For example, if you are going to hash-brown them later, reduce a 4-minute potato to 3½ minutes.

In microwave potato cooking, it all starts with baking the potato, then, using your browning skillet and following directions that came with it, you can parlay that baked potato into many easy dishes, cottage, country or steak fried, scalloped, hashed brown, hot potato salad and even creamed potatoes. Just remember when adapting recipes from conventional cooking into microwave, the time difference is sharply different. A rule of thumb is that the microwave oven cooks in one-fourth the time. But add one word to that rule, "generally." With baked potatoes (and some other vegetables) it is much faster, as we have mentioned. However, when you do bake that potato then cube it for creaming, that one-fourth time comes into play. But caution again: Follow the directions that came with the browning skillet as to preheating and cooking, and remember to always allow for carry-over cooking time which, in microwave cookery, is accentuated. We have found no advantage in using the microwave oven for boiling or steaming potatoes.

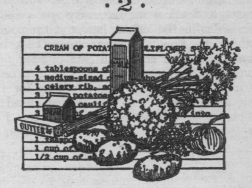

Soups

It is difficult with the potato not to serve up superlatives with every recipe, but that restraint is not needed regarding potatoes and soup. Soup and potatoes, potatoes and soup—a natural combination with the potato acting as an enhancer, an emulsifier, a blender of flavors. But such is the magic of the potato that its own personality is never lost, no matter what it is mated with.

For example, clam chowder would not be the tasty and robust soup that it is without potatoes, and the French *Garbure* would be sort of a messy medley without the potato to bind it together. And can you imagine a potato and leek soup without the potato?

Potatoes can produce the velvety classic soup, vichyssoise, or a simple but very tasty mashed potato soup. Even their skins alone can make a soup, but we'll forgo that one.

When we think of potato skin soup, we recall a

story about 18th-century Paris when the poor's mainstay was potato soup. Someone had invented a giant soup syringe. Soup bowls or basins were nailed to wooden tables in the restaurants, and the soup was squirted into the bowls. If payment wasn't immediate, the soup was quickly suctioned back into the syringe.

Historic, that's potato soup.

Alsatian Potato Soup

4 ounces of salt pork
2 cups of shredded cabbage
3 cups of diced potatoes
2 small onions, coarsely chopped

1 teaspoon of salt
½ teaspoon of pepper
⅛ teaspoon of allspice
2 quarts of chicken broth
3 tablespoons of chopped parsley

Blanch the salt pork in boiling water for 5 minutes, drain and cut into ½-inch cubes. In a large pot, cook the pork cubes until brown and crisp. Stir in the cabbage, cover and cook for 10 minutes. Add the potatoes, onion, salt, pepper, allspice and chicken broth. Bring to a boil, cover and simmer for 35 minutes. Remove the cover and cook for 15 minutes. Taste for seasoning. Serve in bowls, sprinkle with parsley.

SERVES 6 TO 8.

Potato and Bacon Soup

8 slices of bacon, cut crosswise into ¼-inch pieces
2 medium-sized onions, coarsely chopped
4 large potatoes, peeled and diced

5 cups of chicken broth
½ teaspoon of salt
Pinch of cayenne
1 cup of sour cream
2 tablespoons of chopped fresh dill or 2 teaspoons of dillweed

In a large pot, sauté the bacon until the pieces are crisp and golden. Pour off all but 3 tablespoons of fat.

Remove the bacon, drain and reserve. Add the onion, potatoes, broth and salt to the pot and simmer for 20 minutes, or until the potatoes can be mashed against the side of the pan. Stir in the cayenne. Transfer to a blender container or food processor to puree. Return the puree to the pan, then stir in the sour cream and half of the cooked bacon. Heat just to a simmer. Taste for seasoning. Serve with the remaining bacon pieces and dill sprinkled on top.

SERVES 6.

Potato-Ball Soup

3 medium-sized potatoes	Salt and pepper to taste
½ cup of flour	Pinch of nutmeg
2 egg yolks	2 tablespoons of butter
3 tablespoons of grated cheese (your choice)	2 tablespoons of olive oil
2 tablespoons of soft butter	2 quarts of hot beef broth
	2 tablespoons of chopped parsley

Boil the potatoes until tender, peel and put through a ricer.

In a bowl, combine the potatoes, flour, egg yolks, cheese, soft butter, salt and pepper and nutmeg. Turn the mixture out on a floured board and flatten to a ½-inch thickness. Cut into ½- by ¾-inch pieces and roll these into balls (lightly oiling the hands will make the balls easier to roll). In a frypan, heat half of the butter and oil and sauté the balls until golden, adding more butter and oil as needed. Drain on paper towels. Pour the hot broth into soup bowls. Sprinkle the parsley on the broth, then float the potato balls on top.

SERVES 6.

Surfer's California Clam Chowder

4 slices of bacon, diced
1 large onion, chopped
1 large celery rib,
  scraped and chopped
1 medium-sized carrot,
  scraped and chopped
4 cups of peeled, diced
  potatoes
1 (8-ounce) bottle of
  clam juice

2 (8-ounce) cans of minced
  clams, drained (reserve
  the liquid)
2 cups of water
Salt and pepper to taste
Pinch of marjoram
1 (10-ounce) can of cream
  of tomato soup, undiluted
1½ cups of milk
2 tablespoons of chopped
  parsley

In a large saucepan, over low heat, cook the bacon until it is transparent. Pour off all but 2 tablespoons of fat. Add the onion, celery and carrot and sauté, stirring, until the vegetables are coated with the fat. Add the potatoes, clam juice, reserved clam liquid, water, salt, pepper and marjoram. Simmer for 20 minutes. Add the tomato soup. Stir well to mix and simmer for 10 minutes, or until the potatoes are cooked (do not overcook as the potatoes should hold their shape). Add the minced clams and milk. Simmer, stirring occasionally, until just heated through. Sprinkle with parsley.

SERVES 6.

Central American Potato Soup
with Chicken and Pumpkin

3 tablespoons of butter	4 cups of chicken broth
1 medium-sized onion, chopped	2 cups of cubed, fresh pumpkin (½-inch cubes)
1 garlic clove, minced	3 large potatoes, peeled and cut into ½-inch cubes
1 teaspoon of salt	Pinch of hot red pepper flakes
½ teaspoon *each* of ground coriander and allspice	2 cups of cubed cooked chicken (½-inch cubes)
1 bay leaf	

2 tablespoons of fresh chopped coriander or parsley

In a large pot, melt the butter. Add the onion and garlic and cook for 2 minutes. Stir in the salt, coriander, allspice and bay leaf. Add the chicken broth, pumpkin, potatoes and the red pepper flakes. Bring to a boil then simmer for 15 minutes, or until the potatoes and pumpkin are tender but still firm. Taste for seasoning. Add the chicken and simmer until heated through. Remove the bay leaf. Sprinkle coriander or parsley on top of individual servings.

SERVES 6 TO 8.

Potato and Cheese Soup

3 tablespoons of butter	2 cups of medium cream
1 medium-sized white onion, diced	2 cups of milk
1 garlic clove, minced	2 cups of grated Gruyère cheese
2 medium-sized leeks (white part only), diced	Salt to taste
4 medium-sized potatoes, peeled and diced	2 tablespoons of chopped fresh basil
2 cups of chicken broth	½ cup of peeled, seeded, finely chopped, well drained, ripe tomato

In a large pot, melt the butter and sauté the onion, garlic and leeks, stirring, for 5 minutes. Add the potatoes and broth and cook 20 minutes, or until the potatoes can be mashed against the side of the pot. Cool slightly and pour into a blender container or food processor to puree. Return the soup to the pot, add the cream and milk. Heat to a simmer, then add the cheese, and over low heat, cook, stirring, until the cheese has melted. Taste for seasoning, then, if necessary, add salt. Serve with the basil and fresh tomato sprinkled on top.

SERVES 6 TO 8.

Chilled Potato-Beet Soup

2 cups of mashed potatoes
2 cups of cooked, coarsely chopped beets
4 scallions (white part only), coarsely chopped
1 teaspoon of salt
½ teaspoon of pepper
3 tablespoons of lemon juice
1½ cups of chicken broth
1 cup of crushed ice
½ cup of sour cream
2 tablespoons of minced fresh dill

In the container of an electric blender, combine the potatoes, beets, scallions, salt, pepper and lemon juice. Cover and blend at high speed. With the motor running, add the chicken broth and ice. Taste for seasoning. Serve chilled with a large dollop of sour cream sprinkled with dill on top of each serving.

SERVES 4 TO 6.

Chilled Bombay Curried Potato Soup

2 tablespoons of butter
2 medium-sized onions, chopped
1 garlic clove, minced
2 teaspoons of curry powder

4 large potatoes, peeled and cubed
4 cups of chicken broth
1 teaspoon of celery salt
1¼ cups of medium cream
2 tablespoons of minced fresh chives

In a large pot, melt the butter. Add the onion and garlic and cook for 2 minutes. Stir in the curry powder. Add the potatoes, broth and celery salt. Simmer until the potatoes can be mashed against the side of the pot. Taste for seasoning. Cool slightly and blend in an electric blender or push all contents through a strainer. Refrigerate and when ready to serve mix in the cream. Sprinkle the chives on top. Soup should not be served icy cold but just chilled.

This is also good served hot but once the cream has been added, do not boil but just heat through.

SERVES 6.

Potato-Corn Chowder

4 ounces of fatback (pork for beans), cut into ¼-inch cubes
1 medium-sized onion, finely chopped
1 large celery rib (with the leaves), scraped and finely chopped

3 medium-sized potatoes, cut into ½-inch cubes
2 cups of water
2 cups of corn kernels (fresh or frozen)
Salt and pepper to taste
4 cups of milk
3 tablespoons of butter

In a large pot, over medium heat, cook the fatback until crisp and golden. Remove with a slotted spoon, leaving the fat in the pot and reserving the fatback. Add the onion and celery and cook until the onion is transparent. Add the potatoes and water and cook, covered, for 15 minutes, or until the potatoes are almost tender. Add the corn, salt, pepper and milk and simmer, uncovered, for 10 minutes, or until the potatoes and corn are just tender. Taste for seasoning. Just before serving stir in the butter. Serve with the crisp fatback sprinkled atop and some hearty crackers on the side.

SERVES 6.

Cream of Potato-Cauliflower Soup

4 tablespoons of butter
1 medium-sized onion, chopped
1 celery rib, scraped and chopped
3 large potatoes, peeled and diced
1 medium-sized cauliflower, broken into florets
3 cups of chicken broth

2 cups of milk
Salt to taste
1 teaspoon of Worcestershire sauce
1 cup of medium cream
½ cup of small diced croutons, fried in butter until golden
3 tablespoons of chopped chervil or parsley

In a large pot, over medium heat, melt the butter. Add the onion and celery and cook for 3 minutes. Stir in the potatoes and cauliflower; cook for 2 minutes. Pour in the chicken broth and milk, sprinkle in salt and simmer covered, for 15 minutes. Remove the cover and simmer 15 minutes longer, or until the vegetables can just be mashed against the side of the pot. Slightly cool then pour the contents of the pot into a blender container or food processor to puree. Return to the pot, stir in the Worcestershire sauce and cream and heat just to a simmer. Taste for seasoning. If the soup seems too thick for your taste, stir in a small amount of milk or broth. Serve with the croutons floating on top with a sprinkling of chervil or parsley.

SERVES 6 TO 8.

Cream of Potato-Carrot Soup

3 tablespoons of butter

1 large onion, thinly sliced

3 medium-sized potatoes, peeled and thinly sliced

3 carrots, scraped and thinly sliced

8 cups of chicken broth

Salt and pepper to taste

1 cup of light cream

1 teaspoon of dillweed

½ teaspoon of Tabasco sauce

1 cup of sour cream

1 small carrot, grated

In a large pot, over medium heat, melt the butter. Add the onion, potatoes, sliced carrots and cook, stirring, for 5 minutes. Add the broth, salt and pepper. Bring to a boil, lower heat and simmer for 20 minutes, or until the vegetables can just be mashed against the side of the pot. Slightly cool and pour the soup into a blender container or food processor to puree. Stir in the light cream, dillweed and Tabasco sauce. Just before serving stir in the sour cream and heat to a simmer. Cook the grated carrot in boiling water for 1 minute and drain. Serve with the grated carrot sprinkled on top.

SERVES 6.

Cream of Potato and Watercress Soup

6 tablespoons of butter

2 medium-sized white onions, chopped

2 bunches of watercress, washed well, stems removed and discarded, and one-third shredded and set aside for later use

5 medium-sized potatoes, peeled and each cut into several pieces

6 cups of chicken broth

1½ teaspoons of salt

½ teaspoon of pepper

1 cup of heavy cream

In a soup pot, melt 3 tablespoons of the butter and cook the onion until soft. Add the watercress (reserving the one-third you shredded), potatoes and chicken broth. Bring to a boil, then simmer until the potatoes are cooked. Place in a blender and puree. Return to the pot, season with salt and pepper and stir in the cream. Bring to a boil, then stir in the remaining 3 tablespoons of butter and shredded watercress, stirring until the butter has melted.

SERVES 6 TO 8.

Potato-Cucumber Soup

7 medium-sized potatoes, peeled and sliced

2 medium-sized white onions, peeled and sliced

4 tablespoons of butter

1 tablespoon of salt

2½ cups of water

2 medium-sized cucumbers, peeled, seeded and coarsely grated

2 cups of half-and-half, scalded

½ cup of heavy cream, scalded

1½ teaspoons of chervil

Pepper

In a pot, combine the potatoes, onions, butter, salt and water. Bring to a boil, reduce to a simmer, cover and cook for 30 minutes, or until the potatoes are tender. Puree in a blender. Return the puree to the pot. Stir in the cucumber, half-and-half, cream and chervil, blending well. Bring to a simmer and cook for 10 minutes. Taste for seasoning, adding pepper and more salt, if needed.

SERVES 6.

French Cold Green Potato Soup

3 tablespoons of butter
4 scallions, thinly sliced
3 medium-sized leeks, thinly sliced
1 celery rib, scraped and thinly sliced
2 cups of shelled peas or 1 package of frozen, defrosted

2 large potatoes (about 7 ounces each), cut into ¼-inch slices
4 cups of rich chicken broth
Salt and pepper to taste
About 1 cup of medium cream

Heat the butter in a large saucepan. Add the scallions, leeks, celery and cook for 5 minutes. Add the peas and potatoes and stir until they are well coated with butter. Pour in the broth and simmer for 20 minutes, or until the potatoes are tender. Season with salt and pepper. Put through a food mill or puree in a blender. Cool and refrigerate until ready to serve. Just before serving, stir in 2 tablespoons of cream for each cup of soup.

SERVES 6.

Note: Do not serve icy cold but just chilled.

Garbure

This has as many versions as there are provinces in France. But one ingredient is certain: potatoes. So is another: a ham bone. This is the perfect way to use the rest of that ham that has been sliced into a memory.

1 cup of navy beans, soaked in cold water for 4 hours and drained

5 medium-sized potatoes, peeled and cubed

1 small white turnip, peeled and cut into cubes smaller than the potato cubes

1 medium-sized onion, chopped

2 medium-sized carrots, scraped and chopped

2 medium-sized leeks (white part only), sliced

1 small cabbage, shredded

2 ripe tomatoes, peeled, seeded and chopped

⅛ teaspoon of dried thyme

1 ham bone (with some meat)

½ pound of fatback (pork for beans), diced and sautéed until crisp; pour off half of the fat

Salt and pepper to taste

Water to cover

In a large pot, place all ingredients (including the fat from the fatback) and cover with water. Bring to a boil, then reduce to a simmer and cook, partially covered (prop the pot cover open with a wooden spoon handle), for 1½ to 2 hours. Taste for seasoning, and pour the soup over toasted, garlic-buttered slices of French bread. Remove any meat from the ham bone, cut it up and sprinkle it over each serving.

SERVES 6.

Green Swirl Soup

This should be made with new potatoes, fresh from the ground, and with fresh parsley, chives and watercress.

4 tablespoons of butter

6 medium-sized potatoes, peeled and thinly sliced

3 medium-sized white onions, minced

3 celery ribs, scraped and minced

4 cups of chicken broth

1½ teaspoons of salt

½ teaspoon of pepper

1 cup of heavy cream

3 tablespoons of chopped broadleaf parsley

3 tablespoons of chopped chives

1 cup of chopped watercress

In a large pot, melt the butter and stir in the potatoes and onion, sautéing for 5 minutes. Add the celery, broth and salt and pepper. Cover, bring to a boil, lower to a simmer and cook for 20 minutes, or just until the vegetables can be mashed against the side of the pot. With a slotted spoon remove 1 cup of the vegetables, drain well (allowing the liquid to drain back into the soup pot) and reserve. Pour the soup from the pot into a blender jar (the jar might not accommodate it all so blend in stages) and puree. Transfer to a bowl and stir in all but 3 tablespoons of the cream. Combine the reserved vegetables, parsley, chives and watercress in the blender jar with the 3 tablespoons of the cream and puree. Transfer to a bowl. Refrigerate both bowls. When ready to serve, ladle the white puree into soup bowls and swirl in some of the green puree.

SERVES 6.

Vernon Jarratt's Golden Soup

Vernon Jarratt is the owner of George's, one of Rome's most famous restaurants.

6 tablespoons of butter
1 medium-sized onion, peeled and chopped
2 large potatoes, peeled and diced
1 pound of tomatoes, put through a food mill
1 quart of a good beef or chicken stock
Salt and pepper to taste
4 tablespoons of grated Parmesan cheese
Croutons

In a large pot, melt 3 tablespoons of the butter and sauté the onion until slightly golden. Add the potatoes and cook, stirring, for 3 minutes. Stir in the tomatoes and cook for 10 minutes. Pour in the stock, bring to a boil, lower to a simmer, cover and cook for 25 minutes. Season with salt and pepper. Stir in the remaining 3 tablespoons of butter and half of the cheese. Ladle into hot soup bowls, sprinkle on the remaining cheese and float the croutons.

SERVES 4.

Italian Potato Soup

6 medium-sized potatoes
2 tablespoons of butter
1 tablespoon of olive oil
1 medium-sized onion, finely chopped
1 carrot, scraped and cut into ¼-inch cubes
1 garlic clove, minced

½ cup of tomato puree
5 cups of chicken broth
½ cup of finely chopped celery leaves
Salt and pepper to taste
½ cup of grated Asiago or Parmesan cheese

Boil the potatoes until tender, drain and mash. In a large saucepan, over medium heat, heat the butter and oil and cook the onion, carrot and garlic, stirring, for 3 minutes, or until the vegetables are well coated. Add the tomato puree, chicken broth, celery leaves, mashed potatoes, salt and pepper. Simmer for 15 minutes, or until the carrot cubes are just tender. Serve with the cheese sprinkled over individual servings.

SERVES 6 TO 8.

Judy's Fast Potato Soup

7 medium-sized potatoes, peeled and cubed
6 tablespoons of butter
6 cups of light cream or half-and-half
⅛ teaspoon of cayenne
¾ teaspoon of celery salt
Salt and pepper to taste
3 whole scallions, trimmed and chopped

Boil the potatoes, covered, in a very small amount of salted water until tender but firm, being careful not to overcook or the cubes fall apart. Drain well, then add the butter, cream, cayenne, celery salt, salt and pepper. Heat to the boiling point; sprinkle the top with black pepper then the scallions. Serve immediately.

SERVES 6 TO 8.

La Chaudrée

This is France's contribution to the art of making chowder; in fact we got the English word from this dish.

6 large onions, cut in
thick slices

1 large celery rib,
scraped and sliced

3 garlic cloves, peeled
and halved

Bouquet garni (2 sprigs
of parsley, a pinch of
thyme, 1 bay leaf and
2 whole cloves tied in
cheesecloth)

10 crushed peppercorns

5 medium-sized potatoes,
peeled and cut into
½-inch slices

5 tablespoons of butter

3 pounds of fish fillets (cod
and haddock are good),
cut into 2-inch chunks

Salt and pepper

3 cups of dry white wine

3 cups of water

In a large pot, layer the bottom with the onion, celery, garlic, bouquet garni and the peppercorns. Arrange the potato slices on this, overlapping if necessary to make one layer. Cut up the butter and dot it over the potatoes. Arrange the fish chunks on the potatoes and season with salt and pepper. Pour in the wine and water, cover and bring to a boil. Reduce to a simmer and cook for 25 minutes, or until the potatoes are tender. Taste for seasoning, remove the bouquet garni and serve with hot, crusty bread and some of the dry white wine that went into the chowder.

SERVES 6.

Lisbon Mashed Potato and Cabbage Soup

It is amazing the flavor water has after potatoes are boiled in it. That water is the base of a famous Portuguese soup.

5 medium-sized potatoes
½ small cabbage (cut out and discard the coarse veins), very finely shredded
2 tablespoons of olive oil
1 tablespoon of butter
½ teaspoon of pepper

Peel the potatoes and cook until tender in 6 cups of water with 1½ teaspoons of salt. Remove the potatoes from the water (reserve the water) and mash them. Return the mashed potatoes to the pot with the reserved water. Stir in the cabbage, olive oil, butter and pepper, mixing well. Bring to a boil then simmer for 15 minutes, or until the cabbage is tender.

SERVES 4 TO 6.

Mashed Potato Soup

As often as we have accomplished innovative meals with the magic of potatoes, we stood with mouths open when a friend whipped up this luncheon in no time. The secret was that she had four cups of mashed potatoes left over from dinner the night before.

8 tablespoons (1 stick) of butter
6 medium-sized white onions, chopped
4 cups of mashed potatoes
2 quarts of half-and-half
Salt and pepper to taste
Pinch of mace
2 tablespoons of chopped parsley

In a large saucepan, melt the butter and sauté the onion until soft. Blend in the mashed potatoes. Stir in the half-and-half, add the salt, pepper and mace. Mix well. Bring to a boil, stirring constantly. Sprinkle with the parsley.

SERVES 8 TO 10.

Mediterranean Fish Soup with Garlic Sauce

This is an excellent soup even without the unusual garlic sauce. But the sauce gives it character (as Pesto, page 61, and Skordalia, page 98 do other dishes) and a remarkable flavor. In fact, it makes fish soup a conversation piece.

5 medium-sized potatoes, peeled and thinly sliced

8 medium-sized ripe tomatoes, peeled and coarsely chopped

3 medium-sized onions, coarsely chopped

3 garlic cloves, chopped

3 pounds of white-meated fish (cod, haddock, etc.), cut into thick slices

3 strips of lemon rind

2 tablespoons of chopped broadleaf parsley

¼ teaspoon of dried thyme

Salt and pepper to taste

1 small bay leaf

3 cups of dry white wine

3 cups of water

In a large pot, place the potatoes, tomatoes, onion and garlic. Arrange the fish on top, then the lemon rind on top of the fish. Sprinkle with parsley and thyme, and lightly with salt and pepper. Add the bay leaf and pour in the wine and water. Cover, bring to a boil, reduce to a simmer and cook for 15 or 20 minutes, or until the fish and potatoes are just tender, still somewhat firm. Remove the fish and the potatoes (a slotted spoon and spatula are good for this). Strain the liquid in the cooking pot into a hot bowl. Stir in half of the garlic sauce (see below) and save the rest to pass at the table. Taste for seasoning. In deep hot soup bowls, place the potatoes, top with serving portions of fish, pour in the soup, and serve with warm, crusty bread.

SERVES 6.

Garlic Sauce

Slightly less than 2 cups:

This famous French sauce, called *aioli*, is used with more than soup. For example, it is often served with cold sliced lamb or beef, surrounded with hot boiled potatoes, or with a very large platter of poached fish, also circled with hot boiled potatoes. Some sauce is dribbled over the potatoes and the fish or meat, and the rest passed at the table. It is also used just with tiny new potatoes that have been boiled in their skins.

4 garlic cloves, put through a garlic press
2 egg yolks
¾ teaspoon of salt
½ teaspoon of pepper
1½ cups of olive oil
1 teaspoon of strained fresh lemon juice

In a bowl, place the garlic, egg yolks, salt and pepper. Beat until well blended with a wire whisk, rotary or electric beater or blender. Add the olive oil gradually, lightly dribbling it in, beating constantly, adding it faster as the sauce thickens. When it is thick and smooth, beat in the lemon juice. This is always served cold, as it is, in effect, mayonnaise.

New England Clam Chowder

One main reason for the success of this soup is adding the clams last so that they do not become overcooked and rubbery, one of the consistent complaints of clam chowder lovers. (This is not the case, however, with Red Welles' chowder as he makes certain his clams are tender, using canned baby clams, see page 34.)

½ pound of fatback (pork for beans) streaked with lean, cut into small cubes
7 large potatoes, peeled and diced
2 medium-sized onions, chopped
2 dozen fresh clams, shells well scrubbed to remove all sand; save and strain the liquor and chop the clams
1 quart of milk, scalded
Salt and pepper to taste
2 tablespoons of butter
1 tablespoon of chopped parsley

In a large pot, fry the fatback until crisp. Stir in the potatoes, onion and one-half of the liquor from the clams. Cover tightly and simmer, stirring occasionally, until the potatoes are just tender, about 10 minutes. Stir in the clams and cook for exactly 2 minutes. Remove from the heat for 5 minutes. Pour in the scalded milk, the remaining clam liquor; season with salt and pepper. Heat to a simmer, then remove from the heat and stir in the butter and parsley. Serve.

SERVES 6.

Soup Parmentier

This is a considerably heartier version of the classic Soup Parmentier.

3 or 4 leeks (about 1-inch in diameter)

3 tablespoons of butter

1 large carrot, scraped and cut into ¼-inch cubes

1 large celery rib, scraped and cut into ¼-inch cubes

6 cups of chicken broth or any white stock

5 medium-sized potatoes, peeled and cut into ½-inch cubes

1 cup of chopped celery leaves

Salt and pepper to taste

1 small zucchini (unpeeled), cut into ½-inch cubes

½ cup of heavy cream

2 tablespoons of chopped fresh chives

Thoroughly wash the white and the light green part of the leeks. Slice them lengthwise and cut into ½- to 1-inch pieces. Melt the butter in a large pot over medium heat. Add the leeks, carrot and celery and simmer for 5 minutes, stirring to coat the vegetables with the butter. Pour in the broth and simmer, covered, for 15 minutes. Add the potatoes and celery leaves. Season with salt and pepper and simmer, uncovered, for 10 minutes. Add the zucchini and cook for 5 minutes, or until the potatoes and zucchini are tender but not mushy. Taste for seasoning. Just before serving, stir in the cream. Sprinkle the chives over each serving.

SERVES 6 TO 8.

Red (Francis) Welles' Famous Clam Chowder

Red Welles is well known in Washington Depot, Connecticut, for a number of accomplishments: his leadership in the New Milford Hospital fund drive, his golf, his friendliness and his expertise as the local postmaster. But for his clam chowder, he is famous. Red promises that he hasn't withheld any secrets. He always makes a big batch because it freezes so well.

½ pound of butter
2 cups of diced onion
2 cups of diced celery
2 cups of diced green pepper
2 cups of diced carrots
2 cups of diced leeks (white part only)
24 tablespoons of flour
1 gallon of milk, scalded
2 cups of medium cream, scalded
2 teaspoons of Worcestershire sauce

2 teaspoons of monosodium glutamate
2 teaspoons of salt
1 teaspoon of dried thyme
10 drops of Tabasco sauce
½ teaspoon of white pepper
4 cups of diced potatoes
2 tablespoons of chopped parsley
4 (10-ounce) cans of baby whole clams and their juice

In a large pot, melt the butter, and add all of the vegetables, except the potatoes and parsley. Simmer, uncovered, for 8 to 12 minutes, stirring occasionally until the vegetables are only slightly tender. Gradually stir in the flour, blending well with the vegetables. Simmer for 5 minutes. Blend in the milk and cream. Stir in the Worcestershire sauce, monosodium glutamate, salt, thyme, Tabasco and pepper. Add the potatoes, parsley, clams and their juice and cook over moderate heat, stirring occasionally for 30 minutes, or until the potatoes are no longer crisp. Taste for seasoning.

SERVES 25.

Potato-Rice Soup

3 slices of lean bacon, coarsely chopped

1 garlic clove, minced

½ cup of rice

1 (1-pound) can of tomatoes including the liquid, chopped

4 cups of chicken broth

Salt and pepper to taste

Generous pinch of marjoram

6 medium-sized potatoes, peeled and cut into bite-sized pieces

2 tablespoons of chopped parsley

½ cup of grated Asiago or Parmesan cheese

In a large saucepan, over medium heat, cook the bacon until golden. Add the garlic and rice and cook for 1 minute, stirring. Add the tomatoes, broth, salt, pepper and marjoram and bring to a boil. Add the potatoes, lower heat and simmer for 15 minutes, or until the potatoes and rice are tender. Sprinkle with the parsley and serve the cheese at the table.

SERVES 6 TO 8.

Potato-Spaetzle Soup

4 tablespoons of butter

4 medium-sized potatoes, peeled and cut into ½-inch cubes

1 medium-sized onion, chopped

1 celery rib, scraped and chopped

Salt and pepper to taste

6 cups of beef broth

½ cup of spaetzle, cooked according to package directions

2 cups of any cooked diced meat or fowl (½-inch cubes)

In a large pot, over medium heat, melt the butter and add the potatoes, onion, celery, salt and pepper. Cook, stirring, until all are well-coated with butter. Pour in the broth and simmer for 30 minutes, or until the potatoes are tender. Stir in the spaetzle and meat. Taste for seasoning. Simmer until heated through.

SERVES 6 TO 8.

Spanish Potato-Fish Chowder

3 tablespoons of olive oil

2 medium-sized onions, chopped

2 garlic cloves, minced

2 small carrots, scraped and thinly sliced

3 large, ripe tomatoes, peeled, seeded and chopped or 1 (1-pound) can of tomatoes (with liquid), chopped

1 cup of clam broth

½ cup of dry white wine

¼ cup of Madeira

1 small bay leaf

A light pinch *each* of cinnamon, saffron and red pepper flakes

Salt and pepper to taste

4 small potatoes (about 1 pound), peeled and cut into ¼-inch slices

2 pounds of salmon, snapper (or other fish of your choice), filleted and cut into 2-inch pieces

½ teaspoon of grated lemon rind

3 tablespoons of chopped parsley

In a large saucepan, heat the oil. Add the onion, garlic and carrots and cook for 5 minutes, stirring, or until the vegetables are coated. Add the tomatoes, clam broth, the wines, bay leaf, cinnamon, saffron and red pepper flakes, salt and pepper. Simmer, covered for 10 minutes. Add the potatoes and simmer for 15 minutes. Add the fish and simmer, uncovered, for 15 minutes, or until the potatoes are tender and the fish can be easily pierced with a fork. Stir in the lemon rind. Remove the bay leaf. Taste for seasoning. Sprinkle parsley on top and serve.

Serves 6.

Soupe au Pistou

2 quarts of chicken broth
4 medium-sized potatoes, peeled and cut into 1-inch cubes
½ pound of fresh green beans, cut into 1-inch pieces
2 carrots, scraped and sliced
1 medium-sized onion, chopped
2 teaspoons of salt

½ teaspoon of pepper
1 small, unpeeled zucchini, cut into ¼-inch slices
1 (16-ounce) can of kidney or navy beans, drained
4 garlic cloves, put through a garlic press
¼ cup of tomato puree
1 tablespoon of dried basil
½ cup grated Parmesan cheese
½ cup of chopped parsley

¼ cup of olive oil

In a large pot, combine the chicken broth, potatoes, green beans, carrots, onion, salt and pepper. Bring to a boil and simmer, covered, for 10 minutes. Add the zucchini and simmer for 10 minutes longer, or until all the vegetables are tender. Stir in the canned beans.

Meanwhile, prepare the sauce. Combine the garlic, tomato puree, basil, cheese and parsley. Using a wire whip, gradually beat in the oil, a teaspoon at a time, until you have a thick sauce. Just before serving, stir the sauce into the hot soup. Taste for seasoning. Serve with buttered, warm, crusty bread and cold beer.

SERVES 6 TO 8.

Potato and Spinach Soup

2 tablespoons of butter
1 large onion, coarsely chopped
4 medium-sized potatoes, peeled and each cut into 8 pieces
2 cups of chicken broth
1 (10-ounce) package of fresh spinach, coarsely chopped, or 1 (10-ounce) package of frozen chopped spinach, defrosted

½ teaspoon of Lawry's seasoned salt
½ teaspoon of celery salt
Pinch of mace
Pepper to taste
1 cup of milk
1 cup of medium cream
3 tablespoons of dry sherry
½ cup of chopped mushrooms

In a large saucepan, melt the butter. Add the onion and cook for 2 minutes. Add the potatoes and broth and cook, covered, for 10 minutes. Add the spinach, salts, mace and pepper. Simmer for 10 minutes longer, or until the potatoes can be mashed against the side of the pot. Cool slightly, then put into a blender or food processor to puree. Return to the saucepan, add the milk and cream and heat to a simmer. Taste for seasoning. Stir in the sherry just before serving. Sprinkle the mushrooms on top of each serving.

If the soup seems too thick, add a small amount of hot broth.

SERVES 6.

Vichyssoise

2 tablespoons of butter	4 medium-sized potatoes, peeled and thinly sliced
4 medium-sized leeks (white part only), washed well and chopped	4 cups of chicken broth
	¼ teaspoon of nutmeg
2 medium-sized white onions, chopped	1½ teaspoons of salt
	1½ cups of medium cream

2 tablespoons of chopped watercress

In a large pot, over medium heat, melt the butter and sauté the leeks and onion for 5 minutes. Add the potatoes and chicken broth. Cook, covered, for 15 minutes, or until the potatoes can be mashed against the side of the pot. Cool slightly, pour into a blender container and blend for a few seconds until you have a velvety smooth mixture. Add the nutmeg and salt and blend for 2 or 3 seconds. Taste for seasoning. Chill. Just before serving stir in the cream. Serve chilled (not icy cold), garnished with the watercress.

This may also be served hot, but the classic version is cold.

SERVES 6 TO 8.

· 3 ·

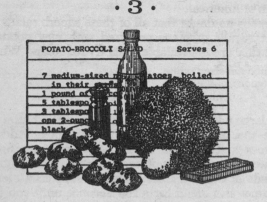

POTATO-BROCCOLI SALAD   Serves 6

7 medium-sized new potatoes, boiled
    in their ~~skins~~
1 pound of ~~broccoli~~
5 tablespoons ~~oil~~
3 tablespoons ~~vinegar~~
one 2-ounce ~~can~~
black

Salads

What is that great American relaxer and outdoor feast, the picnic, planned around? People. Sure. But let's not be prosaic. It has to be the potato salad. It is the culinary masterpiece around which all other picnic foods revolve. Hot dogs and potato salad, hamburgers and potato salad, cold sliced ham—and potato salad. You name the picnic food and the potato salad makes it perfect fare.

And that potato salad is as varied and innovative as the imagination of the person who prepares it. Ingredients that mate with the sliced or cubed potato glistening with mayonnaise or other dressing run from sliced hard-cooked egg and olives to lima beans, cucumber, tuna, shrimp and mushrooms. One of the pleasures of a picnic is the anticipation of sampling a new and different potato salad.

But the potato salad in itself is full of surprises. Most countries have their own versions, the hot Ger-

man with bacon bits, the warm Italian with black
pepper, olive oil and white wine, the salad-stuffed
tomato of America.

There is no doubt that all of these superb salads are
even tastier if they are prepared with new potatoes.
But if they are unavailable, then try for Round Whites
or Round Reds.

Asia Minor Potato Salad

7 medium-sized new potatoes
Salad Dressing (see page 42)
2 garlic cloves, minced
6 scallions (white part only), coarsely chopped
2 cups of small cubes of cooked lamb tongue
6 small gherkins, coarsely chopped
2 tablespoons of chopped broadleaf parsley

Boil the potatoes in their skins until tender, then
drain and dry in the pan over heat. While the potatoes
are still warm, peel and cut them into ¼-inch slices.
Pour on half of the salad dressing, blending well but
gently. Mix in the garlic, scallions, tongue and gherkins. Taste, then add more dressing, if desired. Chill
before serving and garnish with the parsley. Pass
Mideastern flat bread that has been split, buttered
and toasted.

SERVES 6.

Salad Dressing

About 1 cup.
 ¼ cup of dry white wine
 3 tablespoons of lemon juice
 ⅔ cup of olive oil
 ¼ teaspoon of sugar
 ¼ teaspoon of paprika
 1 teaspoon of salt
 ½ teaspoon of ground cumin

Blend all of the above ingredients 3 hours before
serving.

Austrian Salad

4 medium-sized new
 potatoes
1¼ cups of Vinaigrette
 Sauce (see Niçoise
 Salad, page 58)
2 cups of canned
 cannellini (white)
 beans, drained
6 leeks cooked in water
 until tender (see
 page 43), cut into
 1-inch pieces
Crisp Boston lettuce
 leaves

1 (10-ounce) package of
 fresh spinach, cooked as
 directed (next page) and
 coarsely chopped, or 1
 (10-ounce) package of
 frozen, whole leaf spin-
 ach, cooked and coarsely
 chopped
3 hard-cooked eggs,
 quartered
¼ pound of Westphalian
 ham (or a good boiled
 ham), thinly sliced and
 cut into strips

2 tablespoons of chopped broadleaf parsley

Boil the potatoes in their skins until tender. Then
peel and dice them while still warm. Marinate the
warm potatoes in ½ cup of the sauce. Marinate
separately the white beans, the leeks and the spinach,
each in ¼ cup of sauce. Place them in the refrigerator
for 1 hour. Line a serving dish with the lettuce and
arrange the marinated vegetables, separately, on the
leaves. Garnish with the eggs and ham. Sprinkle the
parsley.

To cook the spinach: Bring to a boil 4 quarts of water. Add the spinach and push it down into the water with a fork. When the water returns to a boil, cook 1 minute then remove the spinach with a fork and drain. Cool and chop.

To cook the leeks: Trim the leeks, removing the outside leaves and the green part and cut in half lengthwise to (not through) the root end. Wash well. Tie the leeks together in several places and simmer in water for about 15 minutes, or until just tender. Cool and cut.

SERVES 4 TO 6.

Potato, Baby Limas, Fresh Mushroom Salad

This is excellent with assorted cold meats and a "spritzer"—white wine over ice mixed with soda.

5 medium-sized new potatoes
1 cup of baby lima beans, cooked and drained
4 scallions (white part only), chopped
4 medium-sized fresh mushrooms, thinly sliced

¼ cup of lemon juice ⎫
6 tablespoons of olive oil ⎬ BLENDED INTO A SAUCE
Salt and pepper to taste ⎭

1 tablespoon *each* of chopped fresh broadleaf parsley, tarragon and chervil or 1 teaspoon of dried

Boil the potatoes in their skins until tender, then drain and dry over heat. Peel the potatoes and cube them. In a bowl, combine the potatoes, lima beans, scallions and mushrooms. Add the lemon juice–oil sauce (amount depending upon your taste) and the herbs. Toss well, but gently. Serve at room temperature.

SERVES 4.

Potato and Baby String Bean Salad

It is important to get small, firm new potatoes, and young, tender string beans.

1½ pounds of very small new potatoes
1 pound of young string beans

½ cup of olive oil
2 tablespoons of dry white vermouth
2 small white onions, minced
2 tablespoons of minced watercress   BLENDED
1 tablespoon of fresh minced chives
Salt and pepper to taste

Crisp Boston lettuce leaves
1 tablespoon of minced broadleaf parsley

Boil the potatoes in their skins until just tender. Then peel and cut lengthwise into ¼-inch strips. Cook the beans in boiling water for 5 minutes (do not overcook, they should be crunchy). Chill the beans in cold water and drain. In a large bowl, combine the potatoes and beans. In stages, pour in the blended dressing, tossing gently each time. Vegetables should not be swimming in the dressing, but they should be well mixed. Arrange the lettuce in a salad bowl, then the potatoes and beans. Sprinkle with the parsley.

SERVES 4.

Belgian Potato Salad

4 medium-sized new potatoes
½ cup of pitted black olives
6 cooked artichoke hearts, quartered
¾ cup of Anchovy Sauce (see below)
¼ pound of fatback (pork for beans)
6 medium-sized Belgian endive, washed, trimmed and
   cut into 1-inch pieces (separate the leaves)
2 ripe tomatoes, peeled, sliced and drained for ½ hour
1 tablespoon of capers, rinsed in cold water and drained

Boil the potatoes in their skins until tender. Peel and
slice while still warm. In a large bowl, mix the warm
potatoes, olives and artichoke hearts with one-third of
the Anchovy Sauce and refrigerate for 1 hour. Blanch
the fatback in hot water for 10 minutes. Cut into
½-inch cubes and sauté until crisp and golden. Drain
on paper towels. Place the endive in a salad bowl,
mix with one-third of the sauce and spoon the potato–
olive–artichoke hearts mixture onto it. Taste and add
more sauce, if necessary. Arrange the tomato slices
on top and sprinkle them with the crisp fatback and
capers.

SERVES 6.

Anchovy Sauce

About 1 cup.
   2 hard-cooked eggs, coarsely chopped
   8 anchovy fillets
   ¾ cup of olive oil
   2 tablespoons of wine vinegar
   Black pepper to taste

Place the eggs and anchovy in a blender container.
Blend for 5 seconds. Gradually add the oil, blending
for 2 or 3 seconds after each addition. Blend in the
vinegar and pepper.

Potato-Broccoli Salad

7 medium-sized new potatoes
1 pound of broccoli
5 tablespoons of olive oil
3 tablespoons of lemon juice
1 (2-ounce) can of anchovy fillets, drained
Black pepper to taste
Salt (optional)

Boil the potatoes in their skins until tender (do not overcook), then peel them. Peel the broccoli stems (if stems are very thick, divide by cutting from the floret end to bottom of stem to make several ½-inch stems). Cook in boiling water until tender but still crunchy (better underdone than overdone). In a saucepan, over medium heat, heat the oil, lemon juice and anchovies. Cut the potatoes and broccoli into bite-sized cubes. Place in a bowl, pour over the hot olive oil–lemon juice–anchovy sauce. Sprinkle with pepper. Mix carefully but well. Taste, then salt, if necessary. Serve either hot or cold.

To serve cold, marinate in the sauce in the refrigerator. Remove from the refrigerator an hour before serving. It should not be icy cold.

SERVES 6.

Chilled Mashed Potato Salad

Here's a unique potato salad no guest will have tasted and all will relish. This is an excellent and different summer salad. We like it with juicy steaks or hamburgers from the charcoal grill.

6 medium-sized potatoes
Salt and pepper to taste
3 tablespoons of soft butter
3 tablespoons of light cream
3 hard-cooked eggs

⅓ cup of minced scallions (white part only)
½ cup of minced celery, including some of the leaves
1 cup of cooked tiny peas
Salad Dressing (see page 48)

12 large stuffed green olives, halved

Boil the potatoes in their skins until tender, drain and dry in a pan over heat. Peel the potatoes and put through a potato ricer into a bowl. Season with salt and pepper, add the butter and cream and blend well. Cool to room temperature. Chop 1½ cooked eggs and stir them, the scallions, celery and peas into the potatoes. Stir just enough of the salad dressing into the potatoes so that they are well-blended, but avoid making them too moist; stir in small amounts of the dressing at a time, tasting until you have achieved a taste combination that pleases. Garnish with the remaining eggs, sliced, and the olives. Chill before serving.

SERVES 4.

Salad Dressing

Makes about 1 cup.

    2 teaspoons of sugar
    1½ teaspoons of flour
    1 teaspoon of dry mustard
    ½ teaspoon of salt
    1 egg, beaten
    ⅓ cup of cider vinegar
    ½ cup of sour cream

In the top of a double boiler, blend all of the dry ingredients. Add the egg and mix well. Add the vinegar, a little at a time, then the sour cream, beating well so the mixture is smooth. Cook over boiling water, stirring, until the dressing is thick and smooth. Refrigerate. This cold dressing is also excellent on crisp lettuce salads and on cold vegetables.

Potato-Cucumber Salad with Sour Cream and Dill Sauce

    7 medium-sized new potatoes
    1 to 1½ cups of Sour Cream and Dill Sauce (see page 49)
    2 medium-sized cucumbers, peeled, cut in half lengthwise, seeds removed and cut into ¼-inch slices
    Tender, center leaves of romaine or other tender lettuce
    ¼ cup of chopped fresh dill

Cook the potatoes in their skins until tender, then peel and slice while still warm. In a large bowl, mix the warm potatoes with ½ cup of the sauce. Refrigerate for 1 hour. Add the cucumbers and ½ cup of the remaining sauce. Taste, add more sauce if necessary. Line a salad dish with the lettuce, spoon in the potato-cucumber mixture and sprinkle with the dill. Serve chilled but not icy cold.

SERVES 6.

Sour Cream and Dill Sauce

Makes slightly less than 2 cups.
1½ cups of sour cream
¼ cup of chopped fresh dill
1 teaspoon of minced onion
⅛ teaspoon of sugar
¼ teaspoon of cumin powder
Salt to taste

Combine all ingredients and blend.

Curried Potato Salad

5 medium-sized new
  potatoes
2 tablespoons of butter
1 tablespoon of olive oil
4 large scallions (white
  part only), chopped
2 teaspoons of curry
  powder
½ teaspoon of allspice
¼ teaspoon of red
  pepper flakes

1 tablespoon of chopped
  broadleaf parsley

BLENDED:
1 cup of sour cream
¼ cup of chopped
  white raisins
1 teaspoon of salt

Boil the potatoes in their skins until tender, drain and
dry over heat. Peel and dice them. In a large frypan,
heat the butter and oil and sauté the scallions for 1
minute. Stir in the curry powder, allspice and potatoes, tossing well, but gently. Add the red pepper
flakes and parsley, toss. Place the potato-scallion mixture in a serving bowl, pour over and stir in the sour-
cream blend. Chill slightly. Toss again before serving.

SERVES 4.

Danish Fisherman's Potato Salad with Piquant Mayonnaise

6 medium-sized new potatoes
1½ cups of dry white wine
1 pound of bay or sea scallops (if sea scallops are used, quarter them)
½ cup of water
Piquant Mayonnaise (see below)
Salt and pepper to taste
Boston lettuce to line salad bowl
1 teaspoon of capers

Boil the potatoes in their skins until tender, drain and dry in a pan over heat. While the potatoes are still warm, peel and cut them into ½-inch cubes. Sprinkle them with ½ cup of the wine. Poach the scallops in the remaining 1 cup of wine and the water for about 6 minutes, or until they are firm but tender (do not overcook). Drain and cool slightly. Drain any excess wine from the potatoes. Mix the potatoes and scallops with half of the mayonnaise. Taste, then add more mayonnaise, salt and pepper, if desired. Line a salad bowl with the lettuce and arrange the salad in the bowl. Garnish with the capers. Serve warm or chill.

SERVES 6.

Piquant Mayonnaise

Makes about 1¼ cups.

1 cup of mayonnaise
2 tablespoons of lemon juice
3 shallots, finely chopped
2 teaspoons of capers

Combine all the ingredients and blend well.

Dijon Potato Salad with Walnut Oil

With its different, delicate flavor walnut oil is wor
its somewhat expensive price. It is available in
gourmet and specialty shops.

3 tablespoons of walnut oil	¼ teaspoon of sugar
7 medium-sized new potatoes	2 tablespoons of tarragon vinegar
2 garlic cloves, crushed	1 tablespoon of chopped chives
1½ teaspoons of salt	1 tablespoon of chopped chervil
½ teaspoon of pepper	

1 bunch of watercress

Cook the potatoes in their skins, drain, then dry over
heat. Peel the potatoes, or rub the skins off and slice.
In a large bowl, mix all of the ingredients except the
potatoes and watercress. Add the potatoes and with
a wooden spoon and fork gently toss without breaking the potatoes. Arrange the watercress on a serving
dish. Spoon the potatoes onto the bed of watercress
and serve at room temperature.

SERVES 6.

Potato-Dill Salad with Old-Fashioned Boiled Dressing

This is a good one for that barbecue when you serve hot dogs and hamburgers. It's a piquant salad with character.

The Dressing

Makes about 1⅓ cups.

2 eggs	**BLENDED:**
½ cup of cider vinegar	½ teaspoon of dry mustard
½ cup of heavy cream	½ teaspoon of salt
2 tablespoons of butter	2 tablespoons of flour
⅛ teaspoon of cayenne	½ cup of sugar

In the top of a double boiler, whip the eggs until they are a light lemon color. Thoroughly mix in the blended dry ingredients. Cook the egg mixture over the boiling water (it must not touch the water) and gradually add the vinegar, stirring vigorously, until the dressing thickens. Remove from the heat, cool slightly and gradually add the cream, taking care that the sauce doesn't curdle as you stir it in. Stir in the butter and cayenne and cool. Taste for seasoning.

The Salad

6 medium-sized new potatoes
⅓ bunch of fresh dill, shredded
3 scallions (white part only), chopped
1 large dill pickle, chopped
About 1 cup of boiled dressing
Watercress

Boil the potatoes in their skins until tender, then drain and dry over heat. While still warm, peel and cube them. In a bowl combine the warm potatoes, dill, scallions and pickle. Spoon in the dressing (amount depends on your taste) and blend gently but well.

SERVES 4.

French Potato Salad

from Barbara M. Valbona

1½ pounds of new potatoes
1 teaspoon of coarse salt
3 grinds of black pepper
1½ tablespoons of tarragon vinegar
4 tablespoons of olive oil
½ teaspoon of dry mustard
1 tablespoon of chopped parsley
1 teaspoon of chopped chives

Boil the potatoes in their skins until they can be pierced. Cool and slip off skins. Slice thinly into a glass bowl. Combine remaining ingredients except parsley and chives. Toss with the potatoes until well coated. Put to one side, covered with a plate, and cool to room temperature. Fold in the herbs and serve. This should always be served at room temperature.

SERVES 6.

Genovese Hot Potato Salad

6 medium-sized potatoes (about 2 pounds)
¼ cup of olive oil
3 tablespoons of dry white wine
1½ teaspoons of salt
½ teaspoon of black pepper
1 garlic clove, finely minced
⅛ teaspoon of dried oregano
4 tablespoons of chopped broadleaf parsley

Boil the potatoes in their skins until tender, drain and dry in a pan over heat. Peel the potatoes while still hot. (Having the potatoes hot improves the flavor when blended with the dressing.) Cut the potatoes into ¼-inch slices and place in a bowl. In another bowl thoroughly blend the oil, wine, salt, pepper, garlic, oregano and parsley. Gently blend with the sliced potatoes. Taste for seasoning and serve while still warm.

SERVES 4.

German Potato Salad

8 medium-sized new
    potatoes
6 scallions (use some of
    the green part),
    chopped
½ cup of chicken broth
2 tablespoons of olive oil

1 tablespoon of wine vinegar
½ teaspoon of dry mustard
¼ teaspoon of celery seeds
Salt and pepper to taste
½ cup of sour cream
2 tablespoons of minced
    fresh dill

Boil the potatoes in their skins until tender, drain and dry over heat. While still warm, peel and cut into ¼-inch slices. Set aside and keep warm. In a saucepan, combine the scallions, broth, olive oil, vinegar, mustard, celery seeds, salt and pepper and simmer for 2 minutes. Cool slightly and stir in the sour cream, mixing well. Pour over the warm potatoes and mix gently but well. Sprinkle the dill on top and serve at room temperature.

SERVES 6.

Hot German Potato Salad with Bacon

This has become a classic and is so tasty that the Germans serve it with one of their many sausages as a meal. We like it with that mild veal sausage Weisswürste.

    8 medium-sized new potatoes
    8 slices of lean bacon, cut into small dice
    1 medium-sized onion, finely chopped
    2 tablespoons of white vinegar
    ½ cup of chicken broth
    Salt and pepper to taste
    ½ teaspoon of caraway seeds
    2 tablespoons of chopped parsley

Boil the potatoes in their skins until tender, drain and dry over heat in a pan. Peel and cut into ¼-inch slices. In a frypan, over medium heat, cook the bacon until golden. Pour off all but 3 tablespoons of fat. Add the onion and cook until transparent. Add the vinegar, broth, salt, pepper and caraway seeds. Simmer, stirring, for 1 minute. Pour over the hot potatoes, mixing well but carefully. Taste for seasoning. Sprinkle the parsley just before serving.

SERVES 6.

Potato Salad à la Lisbon

7 medium-sized new
potatoes
¼ cup of Madeira
2 tablespoons of dry
white wine
1 sweet Bermuda onion,
sliced and separated
into rings
½ cup of Gruyère cheese
slivers

3 small, tender celery
hearts, finely sliced
1 tablespoon of chopped
fresh oregano or 1
teaspoon of dried
¼ cup of chopped fresh
mushrooms
1 cup of vinaigrette sauce
(see Potatoes Vinaigrette,
page 69)

Boil the potatoes in their skins and drain and dry over
heat in a pan. While still hot, peel and cut into ¼-inch
slices. Put the potatoes in a bowl and sprinkle with the
Madeira and the white wine, tossing gently. Marinate
for ½ hour. Pour off any excess wine in the bottom
of the bowl. Add the onion rings, cheese, celery,
oregano and mushrooms. Toss carefully but well with
the vinaigrette sauce (amount depends upon your
taste).

SERVES 6.

Potato-Lobster Salad

There is this about the potato: You can match it with the most expensive and elegant of foods and it not only will hold its own but add dimension and character. We know epicures who will only eat Iranian caviar ($$$$$$ a pound) on fluffy baked potatoes; others who demand fresh poached salmon mated with tiny steamed new potatoes covered with warm, freshly-made hollandaise sauce. For us, lobster becomes even more palatable paired with potatoes.

    6 medium-sized new potatoes
    1½ cups of fresh baby soy beans
    Boston lettuce leaves to line a salad bowl
    2 boiled 1½-pound lobsters, cooled, meat removed; cube all of the meat but the claws and reserve the upper half of the shells
    1 tablespoon of chopped canned red pimiento
    1½ cups of mayonnaise mixed with 3 tablespoons of lemon juice

Boil the potatoes in their skins until tender, drain and dry over heat in a pan. Peel and cube them and set aside to cool. Cook the soy beans in lightly salted water until tender but still firm. Line a salad bowl with lettuce leaves. In another bowl, combine the potatoes, three-fourths of the lobster meat, soy beans, pimiento and half of the mayonnaise mixture. Toss well but carefully. Taste and add more mayonnaise, if needed. Mound the salad on the lettuce in the bowl. Rim with remaining lobster meat, garnish with dabs of mayonnaise, and the lobster claws. Upend, pyramid fashion, the upper halves of the lobster shells in the center of the salad.

    SERVES 4.

Niçoise Salad

5 medium-sized new
potatoes

½ to 1 cup of Vinaigrette
Sauce (see below)

½ pound of cooked
young green beans, cut
into 1-inch pieces

½ cup of plump, black
Italian olives

3 scallions with tops,
trimmed and chopped

1 (7½-ounce) can of
"solid" white tuna

Crisp Boston lettuce leaves

12 anchovy fillets, drained

2 ripe tomatoes, skinned,
each cut into 6 wedges,
then allowed to drain for
½ hour

2 tablespoons of chopped
fresh basil

Boil the potatoes in their skins until tender, peel and
while still warm, cut into ¼-inch slices. Mix the warm
potatoes with ¼ cup of the Vinaigrette Sauce and
marinate in the refrigerator for 1 hour. Add the green
beans, olives, scallions and tuna, plus another ¼ cup
of the sauce. Mix well but gently. Taste and add more
sauce, if necessary.

Line a salad bowl with the lettuce leaves and spoon
in the salad. Arrange the anchovy fillets like the spokes
of a wheel on top of the salad with the tomato wedges
between them. Sprinkle the tomatoes with basil. Do
not serve the salad too cold.

SERVES 6.

Vinaigrette Sauce

Makes about 1 cup.

2 tablespoons of lemon juice
2 tablespoons of wine vinegar
¾ cup of olive oil
1 garlic clove, minced
¼ teaspoon of Dijon mustard
⅛ teaspoon of sugar
¾ teaspoon of salt
½ teaspoon of freshly ground pepper

Combine all the ingredients and mix well.

Pasquale's Potato Salad

This was our father's and father-in-law's specialty. The potatoes should be mixed into the dressing while still warm and served at room temperature. This is a simple salad, but with surprising authority. Pasquale liked it with cold roast veal or lamb sprinkled with lemon juice.

5 medium-sized new potatoes
1 teaspoon of salt
Freshly ground black pepper
4 tablespoons of a good quality olive oil
Plump Italian black olives

Boil the potatoes in their skins until tender, drain and dry over heat in a pan. While still warm, peel and cube them. In a bowl, combine the warm potatoes, salt and a liberal grinding of black pepper (it is important that it be peppercorns from the pepper mill). Add the olive oil, tossing all together well but gently so the potato cubes remain intact. Garnish with the olives.

SERVES 4.

Persian Red Potato Salad

12 small new Red potatoes

6 small, tender carrots, scraped and shredded

1 small red onion, coarsely chopped

1 cup of cooked small lima beans or fava beans

Tender, crisp romaine lettuce leaves

1 ripe, firm avocado

2 tablespoons of fresh lemon juice

Several large radishes, sliced

BLENDED INTO A
SALAD DRESSING:

1/4 cup of olive oil

2 tablespoons of yogurt

2 tablespoons of tarragon vinegar

Pinch of turmeric

Salt and pepper to taste

Boil the potatoes in their skins until tender, drain and dry over heat in a pan. Peel the potatoes and cut into bite-sized pieces, cool slightly and mix with the carrots, onion, beans and the oil-yogurt mixture. Taste for seasoning. Line a salad bowl with the lettuce leaves and spoon in the salad. Just before serving cut the avocado into slices lengthwise, mix with lemon juice and drain. Garnish the salad with the avocado and radish slices.

SERVES 6.

Portuguese Potato and Sardine Salad

6 medium-sized new potatoes

2 (3¾-ounce) cans of Portuguese boneless and skinless sardines, drained

¼ cup of sour cream

¼ cup of mayonnaise

2 tablespoons of lemon juice

½ teaspoon of Dijon mustard

2 celery ribs, scraped and chopped

Salt and pepper to taste

Crisp tender romaine lettuce leaves

1 large red onion, thinly sliced

2 tablespoons of chopped broadleaf parsley

Boil the potatoes in their skins until tender, drain and dry over heat in a pan. Peel and cube them. Mash 1 can of the sardines in a bowl. Add the sour cream, mayonnaise, lemon juice, mustard and blend well. In a large bowl combine the potatoes and celery. Add the sardine salad dressing, salt and pepper and mix gently but well. Line a salad bowl with the lettuce leaves and spoon in the salad. Garnish the top with the remaining sardines making spokes in a wheel and rim with the onion slices, overlapping if necessary. Sprinkle on the parsley.

SERVES 4 TO 6.

Potato Pesto Pork Salad

This is a salad that must be served in the summer when basil and broadleaf parsley grow fresh in the garden. It cannot be prepared with substitutes. It is a dramatically-dressed dish that will have guests agape.

Pesto Sauce

The food processor has made this once complicated sauce unbelievably simple.

Makes about 2 cups.

2 cups of fresh basil leaves, washed and dried

1 cup of fresh broadleaf parsley, washed and dried

⅓ cup of grated Parmesan cheese

½ cup of grated Romano cheese

1 tablespoon of pignolia (pine nuts)

1 garlic clove

3 tablespoons of butter

½ cup of olive oil

BLANCHED QUICKLY TO REMOVE SKINS:

12 almonds

12 walnut halves

Place all ingredients in a food processor with cutting blade (or in a blender container; but the blender will take longer as you will have to stop frequently to scrape sides of the container) and blend until you have a smooth green sauce, the consistency of very heavy cream.

6 medium-sized new potatoes

3 cups of cold cooked pork (preferably the loin poached in a white stock and white wine), cut julienne

Crisp leaves of Boston lettuce

Large plump black Italian olives

Boil the potatoes in their skins until tender, drain and dry over heat in a pan. Peel and cut into large dice. In a bowl, place the potatoes and pork, adding enough Pesto Sauce to lightly coat the ingredients when gently tossed. Don't overdo the Pesto Sauce; the salad shouldn't be swimming in it.

Line a salad bowl with the lettuce leaves, arrange the diced potatoes and pork and garnish with halved black olives. Don't serve this refrigerator cold; the flavor is improved if served at room temperature.

If you have Pesto left over, freeze it to toss later with pasta, or to add to soup to give it zing.

SERVES 4 TO 6.

Standby Picnic Potato Salad

If this is to be served at a summer picnic, it is wise not to mix it with a dressing that contains eggs such as mayonnaise. It could be dangerous if it sets around on a hot day. If you are going to keep it in a refrigerated bag, then go ahead and use the mayonnaise, mixed with a tablespoon of fresh lemon juice.

7 medium-sized new potatoes
4 hard-cooked eggs, coarsely chopped
3 celery ribs, scraped and sliced
1 tablespoon of chopped broadleaf parsley
12 stuffed green olives, coarsely chopped
1 cup of Vinaigrette Sauce (see Potatoes Vinaigrette, page 69)
1 canned pimiento, cut into strips
1 (3¾-ounce) can of sardines, drained and sprinkled with lemon juice

Boil the potatoes in their skins until tender, drain and dry over heat in a pot. While still hot, peel and cube them. In a bowl, combine the potatoes, eggs, celery, parsley and olives. Pour in the sauce (amount depending on your taste) and mix well but gently. Garnish with the pimiento strips and the sardines.

Then pass the hamburgers and the beer!

SERVES 6.

Racquet Club Potato Salad

5 medium-sized new potatoes
2 cups of cooked chicken, cut julienne
¼ cup of finely chopped celery
Piquant Vinaigrette Sauce (see below)
6 hard-cooked eggs, halved
Crisp Boston lettuce leaves
2 tablespoons of chopped parsley

Boil the potatoes in their skins (be careful not to over-cook). While still warm, peel and dice. In large bowl, combine the hot potatoes, chicken and celery. Pour in ¾ cup of Piquant Vinaigrette Sauce. Toss. Refrigerate to chill and marinate. Remove the yolks from the eggs. Mash them and add enough of the remaining Vinaigrette Sauce to moisten. Stuff the egg whites with the yolks. Line a salad bowl with the lettuce leaves. Spoon in the chilled (not icy cold) potato salad. Garnish with the stuffed eggs and the parsley. The eggs will taste better if served at room temperature.

SERVES 6.

Piquant Vinaigrette Sauce

Makes about 1½ cups.

¾ cup of olive oil
¼ cup of wine vinegar
¼ cup of water
2 tablespoons of prepared mustard
3 scallions, chopped

1 tablespoon of capers, rinsed and dried
2 tablespoons of bacon-flavored bits
1½ teaspoons of seasoning salt

4 drops of Tabasco sauce

Combine all the ingredients and mix well. Refrigerate.

Potato-Shrimp–Sour Cream Salad

This is an elegant salad to serve on a hot summer's day with a cold white wine and hot Potato Rolls (page 96).

5 medium-sized new potatoes

¼ cup of mayonnaise
½ cup of sour cream
1 tablespoon of chopped fresh chives   } BLENDED INTO A SAUCE
½ teaspoon of salt
½ teaspoon of pepper
½ teaspoon of celery seeds

½ pound of cooked, shelled, small shrimp (about 32 to a pound)
Boston lettuce leaves

Boil the potatoes in their skins until tender, drain and dry over heat in a pan. Peel and cube them. In a bowl, toss the potatoes with the sauce. Add shrimp and mix carefully but well. Serve on the lettuce leaves, chilled.

SERVES 4.

Potato-Sausage Salad

6 medium-sized new potatoes
4 hot Italian sausages
¼ cup of dry red wine
1 cup of plain yogurt
¼ cup of minced Bermuda onion
1 tablespoon of garlic-wine vinegar
1 tablespoon of crushed dillweed
Salt and pepper to taste
Crisp, tender Boston lettuce leaves
4 hard-cooked eggs, quartered
2 ripe tomatoes, peeled, sliced and drained

Boil the potatoes in their skins until tender, drain and dry over heat in a pan. Peel and cut into medium-thick slices. Prick the sausages in several places (to prevent the casings from bursting) and poach them in a saucepan in the red wine, covered, over medium heat, for about 10 minutes, turning at least once. Remove the cover and brown the sausages. Drain, cool, remove casings and cut into medium-thick slices.

In a bowl blend the yogurt, onion, vinegar, dillweed, salt and pepper. Add the potato slices and toss gently. Line a salad bowl with the lettuce leaves, then arrange the potato and sausage slices on them. Garnish with the eggs and the tomato slices.

SERVES 4 TO 6.

Potato-Stuffed Tomatoes

This is a different and refreshing summer salad.

6 large, ripe tomatoes
Salt and pepper to taste
4 medium-sized new
  potatoes
2 small scallions (white
  part only), minced
1 cup of diced fontina
  cheese (½-inch cubes)

WELL BLENDED:
¼ cup of mayonnaise
Pinch of cayenne
¼ teaspoon of grated
  lemon rind
½ tablespoon of chopped
  fresh basil
Bunch of watercress

Cut a slice from the stem end of the tomatoes. Remove the seeds and the center pulp (leaving the pulp around the sides and bottom). Sprinkle the insides lightly with salt and pepper and invert to drain for 1 hour. Boil the potatoes in their skins until tender, drain and dry over heat in a pan. Peel and dice them. In a bowl, combine and blend well the potatoes, scallions, cheese and mayonnaise. Taste for seasoning. Fill the tomatoes with the potato mixture and dot with the basil. Serve on a bed of watercress.

SERVES 6.

Potato Summer Salad

3 medium-sized new
 potatoes
½ of a medium-sized
 head of cauliflower,
 broken into florets
8 uniform, fresh
 asparagus, stems
 peeled
½ cup of tender, shelled
 small peas (do not
 cook)

2 tablespoons of fresh
 chopped parsley
Crisp Boston lettuce leaves
8 cherry tomatoes, halved

BLENDED INTO A
SALAD DRESSING:
½ cup of wine-herb
 vinegar
¼ cup of olive oil
Salt and pepper to taste

Boil the potatoes in their skins until tender, drain and
dry over heat in pan. While they are still warm, peel
the potatoes and cut into thick slices or wedges and
mix with one-half the salad dressing. Refrigerate to
chill and marinate. Steam the cauliflower and asparagus separately until just tender-crisp. Refrigerate to
chill. To serve, toss the potatoes, cauliflower, peas and
parsley with half of the remaining dressing. Mix the
asparagus with the other half. Line a salad bowl with
the lettuce, spoon in the potato salad and garnish
with the asparagus and tomatoes. Do not serve too
cold as the flavor is improved if served at nearly room
temperature.

SERVES 6.

Potato-Tomato Salad

6 medium-sized new potatoes
6 large romaine lettuce leaves
4 dead-ripe, but firm, medium-sized tomatoes, peeled
    and thickly sliced
½ pound of celeriac (celery root), sliced, cooked until
    tender in lightly salted boiling water and drained
4 hard-cooked eggs, sliced
1 large red Italian onion, thinly sliced and separated
    into rings
1 cup of Vinaigrette Sauce (see Potatoes Vinaigrette,
    page 69)

Boil the potatoes in their skins, drain and dry over
heat in a pan. Peel and cut into ¼-inch slices. Arrange on the lettuce leaves the potatoes, tomatoes,
celeriac, eggs and onion (in that order) and dribble
the sauce over all.

SERVES 6.

Potato-Tuna Salad

This is a light but delicious meal in itself for a hot
day when the kitchen is off limits.

5 medium-sized new potatoes
1 (7-ounce) can of fancy, solid-white tuna, drained and
    broken up into small, bite-sized pieces
2 celery ribs, scraped and diced
1 tablespoon of lemon juice
1 garlic clove, pushed through a garlic press ⎱ BLENDED
¾ cup of mayonnaise
Salt and pepper to taste
4 hard-cooked eggs, halved crosswise

Boil the potatoes in their skins, drain and dry over
heat in a pan. Peel and cube them. In a bowl, place
the potatoes, tuna and celery, tossing gently. Add the

garlic mayonnaise (amount depends on your taste), salt and pepper and toss gently, but blending well. Chill and serve garnished with the eggs.

SERVES 4.

Potato Salad Turkish Style

7 medium-sized new potatoes
¼ cup of garlic-wine vinegar

3 tablespoons of lemon juice
¼ cup of olive oil
½ teaspoon of dry mustard
½ teaspoon of ground cumin
2 tablespoons of chopped broadleaf parsley
2 tablespoons of chopped fresh mint leaves
Salt and pepper to taste

} BLENDED INTO A SAUCE

12 black olives
4 large radishes, sliced
2 scallions, trimmed and coarsely chopped

Boil the potatoes in their skins, drain and dry over heat in a pan. Peel and cube them. Place the potatoes in a bowl with the vinegar, toss well but gently. Marinate for ½ hour and pour off any excess vinegar in the bottom of the bowl. Add the sauce and the olives, mix well but carefully. Garnish with radishes and sprinkle the scallions on top. Serve with cold chicken that has been broiled with lemon juice.

SERVES 6.

Potatoes Vinaigrette

2 pounds of small, firm new potatoes

3 tablespoons of wine vinegar

¾ cup of olive oil

¼ teaspoon of Dijon mustard

½ cup of chopped parsley

1 garlic clove, minced

Salt and pepper to taste

1 tablespoon of minced chives

6 crisp leaves of Boston lettuce

1 (2-ounce) can of flat anchovy fillets, drained

Boil the potatoes in their skins until tender, drain and dry in a pan over heat (be careful not to burn them). In a bowl, combine the vinegar, olive oil, mustard, parsley, garlic, salt, pepper and chives. Blend thoroughly. Peel the potatoes and cut them into ¼-inch slices. Arrange the potato slices on the lettuce leaves on individual plates, garnish with the anchovy fillets. Just before serving spoon on the desired amount of vinaigrette sauce.

SERVES 6.

4

Specialties

Special: "Surpassing what is common or usual, exceptional." That dictionary definition for this chapter could be the wrap-up description for the potato itself. But these are indeed very special recipes. Ranging from poultry stuffing to unique dumplings and croquettes, this could be the chapter to turn to when you need to add a new dimension to your dining.

For example, if you can get a nice fresh ocean fish to broil or cook in your own fashion, convert it into a culinary creation and guest-surprise with the Greek potato sauce for seafood, *skordalia*. Or treat your guests—and yourself—with delicacy and delight by serving a light and delicious potato soufflé, or add taste intrigue and mystery by blending sauerkraut with creamy mashed potatoes, as the Dutch do, or with applesauce, as the Germans do when offering potatoes with pork.

And don't fret if you find you've salted or spiced your soups, stews or main dishes to death. Add cut-up potatoes to absorb some excess flavor. Tame the game bird, too, by adding cut-up potato, alone or in combination with onion, apple or celery to its cavity, to absorb some of the "wild" flavor.

Potato skins from baked potatoes cut into one-inch strips can make unique hors d'oeuvres. Arrange the strips on a cookie sheet, then brush with butter, sprinkle with salt and pepper, grated Parmesan cheese or mixed herbs. Bake to crisp goodness at 475° F. in just about 8 minutes.

Add a bay leaf or favorite herb to the water in which you boil potatoes, then use it in soups, gravies and sauces, also as the liquid, instead of milk, in mashed potatoes. Flavored or not, potato water can also be used as part of the liquid ingredient when making cakes, quick breads and other baked goods.

The point to be made here is that the potato is indeed very special, from its skin, to the trail it leaves in the water in which it cooks, it is the original "waste not, want not" vegetable.

Amsterdam Mashed Potatoes and Sauerkraut

This is a favorite dish all over Holland, but, we are told, originated in Amsterdam. It seems an unusual pairing; but when you try it as an accompaniment with roast pork you'll realize it is an innovative culinary accomplishment.

6 medium-sized potatoes (about 2 pounds), peeled
  and halved
1½ teaspoons of salt
5 tablespoons of butter
About ½ cup heavy cream
1 medium-sized onion, minced
1 (1-pound) can of sauerkraut, well drained
1 cup of water
Salt and pepper to taste

Boil the potatoes in water with the salt added until tender. Drain well, return to heat and dry well, being careful not to burn them. Put the potatoes through a potato ricer into a bowl. Beat in 3 tablespoons of the butter and enough of the cream to make the potatoes creamy-fluffy. In a saucepan, melt the remaining 2 tablespoons butter and sauté the onion until soft. Blend in the sauerkraut and water. Cover and simmer for 35 minutes, stirring occasionally so sauerkraut doesn't burn, adding small amounts of additional water if necessary. When all water has cooked off and sauerkraut is tender, blend it well with the mashed potatoes. Season to taste and serve the potato-kraut very hot.

SERVES 6.

Apple-Shaped Potato Croquettes

¼ cup of flour
1 recipe of Duchess Potatoes (page 230)
2 eggs, beaten
½ cup of fine bread crumbs
Vegetable oil for deep frying
Parsley with stems

Sprinkle a large piece of wax paper with the flour.
Cool the potatoes so they can be shaped. Then, on
the floured paper, form them into the shape of small
apples. Carefully dip the "apples" in the beaten egg,
then dredge in the bread crumbs. Refrigerate for 30
minutes, then deep-fry until golden brown, a few at
a time, draining them on paper towels. Keep them
warm in a 200° F. oven. Before serving, put a "stem"
in each, a short parsley stem with a leaf or 2 on it.

SERVES 4 TO 6.

Potato-Apple Stuffing

This is a unique and appreciated stuffing for about
any bird, but especially good for duck or goose.

Grated rind of a small orange
1 large apple with skin on, finely chopped
2 cups of freshly mashed potatoes
4 tablespoons of orange juice
2 medium-sized white onions, minced
1½ teaspoons of salt
½ teaspoon of pepper

In a bowl, blend the orange rind, apple and potatoes.
In a saucepan, bring the orange juice to a boil, reduce
the heat to a simmer and cook the onions in it until
soft. Drain the onions, but save the liquid to make a
sauce for the bird, if you like. (It can be blended in
the roasting pan, mostly drained of its fat, with 2

tablespoons of vinegar, heavy cream and orange liqueur. This is great with duck or goose; orange somehow has an affinity with these birds.) Whip the onions and salt and pepper into the potato stuffing. When you stuff the bird, remove the fat from the cavity, season with salt and pepper, stuff, sew the opening shut and truss the bird. If a duck or goose, cook on a rack, breast up, and prick the legs, thighs and lower breast to enable excess fat to escape.

MAKES APPROXIMATELY 3 CUPS.

Athenian Potato Soufflé

4 large potatoes
  (2 pounds)
4 tablespoons of butter
2 tablespoons of yogurt
2 tablespoons of heavy
  cream
½ cup of finely crumbled
  feta cheese
Salt and pepper to taste
1 medium-sized white
  onion, minced
3 tablespoons of minced
  broadleaf parsley

3 large egg yolks, beaten
½ teaspoon of paprika
½ teaspoon of cumin
3 egg whites, stiffly beaten
3 medium-sized ripe
  tomatoes, skinned, seeded
  and cut into ½-inch
  slices (allow the slices to
  drain in a large strainer
  for a few minutes)

Boil the potatoes in their skins until tender, drain and dry over heat in a pan. Peel the potatoes and put them through a potato ricer into a bowl. Beat in the butter, yogurt, cream, cheese, salt, pepper, onion, parsley, egg yolks, paprika and cumin. Fold in the egg whites. Spoon the mixture into a buttered soufflé or baking dish. Arrange the tomato slices in a border around the edge of the dish on top of the potato soufflé, overlapping if necessary, sprinkle with salt and pepper. Bake, uncovered, in a preheated 350° F. oven for 40 minutes, or until well-puffed and set in the center.

SERVES 6.

Bavarian Potato Dumplings

The Bavarians like these with sauerbraten.

7 medium-sized potatoes
1½ tablespoons of flour
1½ tablespoons of farina
2 eggs, lightly beaten
1½ teaspoons of salt
¼ teaspoon of nutmeg
½ teaspoon of sugar
½ cup of bread crumbs, fried brown in butter

Boil the potatoes, drain and dry over heat in a pan. Peel and mash. In a bowl, place the potatoes and beat in the flour, farina, eggs, salt, nutmeg and sugar. Shape the potato mixture into little dumplings the size of ping-pong balls. Bring a pot of salted water to the boil; carefully lower the dumplings in on a slotted spoon. Lower the heat to a simmer and cook for 20 minutes. Remove and sprinkle the bread crumbs over them. Serve immediately with stew-type dishes.

SERVES 6.

Potato "Brioche"

3 cups of mashed potatoes, seasoned with salt and
    pepper
2 large eggs, beaten
Pinch of cayenne
Pinch of nutmeg
¼ pound of Gruyère cheese, cut into ½-inch cubes
Fine dried bread crumbs

In a bowl, mix the mashed potatoes with the eggs, cayenne and nutmeg. Shape into balls that will not quite fill the cup of a muffin tin. Butter the muffin tins and place a ball in each. Make a depression in the top of each and drop in a cube of cheese. Sprinkle the top with bread crumbs and bake in a preheated 400° F. oven for 15 minutes, or until the top is crisp and golden.

MAKES ABOUT 12.

Bruno Valbona's Pizza Gnocchi

1 recipe of Gnocchi (page 237)
1 cup of vegetable oil
1½ cups of Putanesca Sauce (see below)
½ pound of mozzarella cheese, thinly sliced

Roll out dough to a ½-inch thickness. Using a 3-inch, round cookie cutter, cut out rounds from the dough. In a frypan, heat sufficient oil to fry a few rounds at a time, frying until golden on both sides. Place on a cookie sheet. Spoon a tablespoon of sauce on each round and top with a slice of mozzarella. Place under a broiler until the cheese bubbles.

SERVES 6.

Putanesca Sauce

Makes about 4 cups.

2 garlic cloves, minced
2 tablespoons of olive oil
8 anchovies, finely chopped
1 (2-pound, 3-ounce) can of Italian plum tomatoes, pushed through a food mill

8 stuffed green olives, finely chopped
8 pitted black olives, finely chopped
1 teaspoon of chopped capers
1 teaspoon of dried sweet basil

¼ teaspoon of dried red pepper flakes

In a deep saucepan, sauté the garlic in the olive oil until soft (do not brown). Add the anchovies and tomatoes and simmer for 10 minutes. Blend in the olives, capers, basil and red pepper flakes. Simmer, uncovered, for 20 minutes, or until sauce has thickened. If any is left over, freeze it and use it on vermicelli or any string pasta.

Caramelized Potatoes

Most of us associate caramelizing potatoes with sweet potatoes (which aren't potatoes at all), coating them in a marmalade or sugared fruit sauce. Yet, real potatoes caramelized are one of the delicacies of the table, excellent with all kinds of roast meats, especially so with *gigot*, the tender leg of spring lamb, cooked the French fashion so that it slices pink. We like to surround the leg of lamb with these shiny golden beauties.

8 small potatoes (not too small, but not so large as medium)
1 cup of rich beef broth
¼ cup of dark brown sugar, loosely packed

Boil the potatoes in their skins until tender, drain and dry over heat in a pan, then peel. Into a saucepan, pour the beef broth and bring it to a boil. Quickly reduce to a simmer and add the sugar, stirring until it is dissolved. Cook, stirring, until the liquid becomes thick and syrupy. Add the potatoes, turning them until they are evenly coated. Serve them whole and hot from the saucepan with roasted meat.

SERVES 4.

Potato-Carrot Popovers

6 cups of grated potatoes, well drained and squeezed
   dry in a kitchen towel
3 egg yolks, beaten
½ cup of grated raw carrot
5 tablespoons of melted butter
1½ teaspoons of salt
1 teaspoon of baking powder
1 cup of sifted all-purpose flour
3 egg whites, stiffly beaten

In a bowl, place the potatoes, and with a wire whisk,
beat in the egg yolks, carrot, butter, salt, baking
powder and flour. Gently fold in the egg whites.
Lightly butter muffin tins and fill two-thirds full. Bake
in a preheated 425° F. oven for 18 minutes, or until
a toothpick can be run into a muffin and withdrawn
clean.

MAKES ABOUT 2 DOZEN.

Potato-Carrot Pudding

4 medium-sized carrots,
   scraped and grated
1 cup of milk
4 large potatoes, peeled
   and grated
⅓ cup of fine cracker
   crumbs
1½ teaspoons of salt
Pinch of cayenne
5 tablespoons of soft butter
3 egg yolks, beaten
3 egg whites, stiffly beaten

Simmer the carrots in the milk for 10 minutes. Mix
together the carrots, the milk they cooked in, the
potatoes, cracker crumbs, salt, cayenne and butter.
Stir in the egg yolks. Fold in the egg whites. Pour
into a buttered 1½-quart baking dish and bake in a
preheated 375° F. oven for 45 minutes, or until set
and the top is golden.

SERVES 6.

Charlie's Corn 'Taters

This was the dish of a farmer-neighbor when we lived on our farm, "Bluff's End" in Roxbury, Connecticut. It was always made when the corn could be picked fresh from the fields. Charlie used to serve these with his farm-raised tender pork chops and apple cider (a little on the hard side). Ah, memories!

4 medium-sized potatoes, peeled and grated into cold water
3 young, tender ears of fresh corn, shucked and kernels cut from the cob
5 tablespoons of flour
2 eggs, beaten
3 tablespoons of heavy cream
1½ teaspoons of salt
½ teaspoon of pepper
Vegetable oil

Drain the potatoes and place them in a cloth, squeezing very dry. In a bowl, combine the potatoes, corn, flour, eggs, cream, salt and pepper and blend well. In a frypan, heat ½ inch of oil until it sizzles. Scoop the batter out with a tablespoon and fry, 4 corn 'taters at a time, until golden brown on both sides.

SERVES 4.

Potato-Cheese Puff

5 medium-sized potatoes
4 tablespoons of soft butter
2 egg yolks
½ cup of cottage cheese
Salt and pepper to taste
2 egg whites, stiffly beaten

Boil the potatoes in their skins until tender, drain and dry over heat in a pan. Peel and put through a potato ricer. In a bowl, mix the potatoes with the butter, egg yolks, cheese, salt and pepper. When well mixed, fold in the egg whites. Spoon into a buttered 2-quart casserole. Bake in a preheated 400° F. oven for 25 minutes, or until the potatoes are puffed and golden.

SERVES 6.

Potato Croquettes con Guacamole Sauce

5 medium-sized potatoes
1 cup of cornmeal (cook according to directions on box and use this just after being cooked while it is still soft)
6 tablespoons of soft butter
½ cup of grated sharp cheese
Salt and pepper to taste
1 tablespoon of cooking oil
4 tablespoons of butter
2 cups of chopped, cooked chicken or pork, seasoned with ½ teaspoon of cumin, ½ teaspoon of salt and mixed with ½ cup of Guacamole Sauce (see page 81)

Boil the potatoes in their skins until tender, drain and dry over heat in a pan. Peel and mash them. Combine the potatoes, cornmeal, soft butter, cheese, salt and pepper. Mix well until smooth and shape into flat croquettes. Heat the oil and butter in a large frypan and brown the croquettes. Add more butter and oil, if needed. Spoon equal amounts of the chopped meat on the croquettes and top with the Guacamole Sauce.

SERVES 4 TO 6.

Guacamole Sauce

Makes approximately 1½ cups.

2 ripe avocados
3 tablespoons of lime juice
2 scallions, trimmed and minced
1 large ripe tomato, peeled, seeded and finely chopped
1 hot green chili, minced, or a good pinch of hot red
  pepper flakes
1 tablespoon of chopped fresh coriander or ½ teaspoon
  of ground coriander
Salt to taste
3 slices of bacon, fried crisp, drained on a paper towel
  and crumbled

Peel, pit and mash the avocados. Add the remaining
ingredients, with the exception of the bacon, and
blend until smooth. Stir in the bacon just before
serving.

Empanada

from Barbara M. Valbona

5 tablespoons of butter
2 tablespoons of oil
1 cup of chopped onion
3 links of sweet Italian
  sausage
2 cups of peeled, thinly
  sliced potatoes

1 loaf frozen bread dough
  (or an equal amount of
  homemade dough)
Garlic powder
Salt and pepper to taste
Red pepper seeds (optional)
Melted butter

In a skillet, heat 3 tablespoons of the butter and the
oil and sauté the onion until golden. Remove from
the skillet and set aside. Brown the sausage and leave
slightly undercooked. Remove, cool and slice thin. To
the sausage drippings add the remaining 2 tablespoons
butter and brown the potatoes until golden, but firm.
  Roll the dough into an oblong.
  Mix the onion, sausage and potato. Season with

garlic powder, salt, pepper and red pepper seeds. Spoon the mixture onto one side of the dough. Fold the other half of the dough over the stuffing and pinch securely on all open sides.

Bake in a preheated 350° F. oven for 30 minutes, or until golden. Brush the top with melted butter.

SERVES 6.

Potato-Fish Balls with Cucumber Sauce

 2 cups of finely chopped, cooked fish (your choice)
 4 cups of finely chopped, boiled potatoes
 2 eggs, beaten
 2 tablespoons of cream
 1 tablespoon of fresh minced dill or 1 teaspoon of
  dillweed
 1 teaspoon of salt
 ½ teaspoon of pepper
 Fat for deep frying

In a bowl, combine all the ingredients (except the fat) and mix well. Shape into balls about 2 inches in diameter, then roll between your palms, making them slightly longer than wide. Cook in the hot deep fat until golden. Serve with Cucumber Sauce.

SERVES 4 TO 6.

Cucumber Sauce

Makes slightly more than 2 cups.
 1 cucumber
 3 tablespoons of butter
 3 tablespoons of flour
 1 cup of milk
 1 cup of medium cream
 Salt and pepper to taste

Peel the cucumber and cut into quarters lengthwise. Cut out the seeds and discard them. Coarsely chop the cucumber and place in a sieve to drain. In a fry-pan over medium heat, melt the butter. Stir in the flour and cook, stirring constantly, until you have a smooth paste. Gradually stir in the milk, then the cream, and cook, stirring, until you have a medium-thick smooth sauce. Season with salt and pepper, add cucumber and serve.

French Potato Pie

This is spectacular served with perfectly cooked pink fillets of beef.

Dough for a double-crust 10-inch pie

7 medium-sized potatoes, peeled and sliced paper-thin

2 medium-sized white onions, chopped

4 garlic cloves, minced

1½ teaspoons of salt

½ teaspoon of pepper

¼ teaspoon of mace

4 tablespoons of butter

⅔ cup of heavy cream

1 small egg, lightly beaten

1 teaspoon of chopped broadleaf parsley

1 teaspoon of chopped chives

Divide the pastry dough into two parts, one slightly larger than the other. Roll out the larger part and line a 10-inch pie plate with it. Arrange a layer of potato slices on the pastry; sprinkle with some of the onion, garlic, salt, pepper and mace. Dot with butter. Repeat until potatoes are used. Pour half the cream over the potatoes. Roll out the remaining dough and cover the pie. With wet fingers, seal the edges and then cut a slit in the center of the pastry. Blend the egg with the remaining cream and lightly brush the top of the pie with the mixture. Bake in a preheated 400° F. oven for 25 minutes or until golden brown. Blend the parsley and chives with the remaining egg-cream mixture. Using a small funnel inserted into the center slit, pour in the herb-cream mixture. Bake for another 10 minutes.

SERVES 6.

Potato Fritters Duchess

This is a unique potato offering to serve a crowd with a big juicy roast of beef.

1 recipe of Duchess potatoes (page 230)
1 recipe of *chou* paste (see Potatoes Dauphine, page 227)
Salt and pepper to taste
Vegetable oil for deep frying

In a large bowl, blend the Duchess potatoes with the *chou* paste seasoning with salt and pepper. Using a pastry bag with a plain tube, form small rings, or doughnuts, onto a sheet of foil. Heat the oil in a deep-fryer and carefully slide the fritters off the sheet of foil into the deep fat. Fry only a few at a time so as not to crowd them. Cook for 2 minutes, turn them and cook for another minute, or until they puff and are golden brown. Drain and serve immediately.

MAKES ABOUT 25.

George's Grate Fennel Potato Pudding

3 eggs, beaten
1 teaspoon of baking powder
¼ cup of potato starch
8 tablespoons (1 stick) of butter, melted
6 medium-sized baking potatoes, peeled, grated and squeezed dry in a kitchen towel

1 medium-sized onion, grated
1½ teaspoons of salt
½ teaspoon of pepper
1 teaspoon of crushed fennel

In a bowl, combine the eggs, baking powder, potato starch and 4 tablespoons of the butter and mix thoroughly. Add the potatoes, blending well. Stir in the onion, salt, pepper and fennel. Lightly butter a baking dish, spoon in the potato mixture and smooth the top without pressing down too much. Sprinkle with the remaining 4 tablespoons butter. Bake, covered, in a preheated 350° F. oven for 40 minutes. Uncover and bake for 15 minutes at 400° F. until potatoes are cooked and the top is golden.

SERVES 4 TO 6.

German Mashed Potatoes with Applesauce

It is important that the mashed potatoes themselves be well dried out as other liquids will be added. After they are mashed, set the pan over low heat, stirring so they won't scorch. Do not add any liquid until all the water has evaporated.

5 medium-sized potatoes
About ½ cup of hot milk
2 tablespoons of soft butter
1 teaspoon of salt
⅛ teaspoon of nutmeg
3 tablespoons of warm applesauce
1 tablespoon of white vinegar
2 teaspoons of sugar

Boil the potatoes in their skins until tender, drain and dry over heat in a pot. Peel the potatoes and rice them. Dry thoroughly. Place them in a bowl with milk, butter, salt and nutmeg and whip well. Beat in the warm applesauce, vinegar and sugar. The effect should be slightly sweet-sour.

SERVES 4.

German Potato Noodles

This works best if the potatoes are boiled a day in advance and refrigerated.

    5 large baking potatoes
    1 tablespoon of soft butter
    1 large egg
    1 large egg yolk
    2 teaspoons of salt
    2 to 3 cups of flour

Boil the potatoes in their skins until tender, drain and dry over heat in a pot. Peel the potatoes and rice them. In a bowl, place the riced potatoes and butter and thoroughly mix with the egg, egg yolk and salt. Gradually, work in 2 cups of flour. Turn out onto a floured pastry board and knead in small amounts of additional flour until you have a smooth dough. Roll out the dough as thinly as possible, and cut into strips of the width and length desired. These can be sautéed in butter, and browned on both sides, or they can be cooked in simmering salted water, drained and served like other noodles.

SERVES 4 TO 6.

Hungarian Potato Noodles

    4 medium-sized baking potatoes
    ½ to 1 cup of flour
    1½ teaspoons of salt
    2 eggs
    5 tablespoons of butter

Boil the potatoes in their skins until tender, drain and dry over heat in a pot. While still hot, peel and rice them. In a bowl, place the hot potatoes and blend in the flour, salt and eggs. Turn out onto a floured pastry board and knead in just enough additional flour to make a mixture that can be rolled out. Roll out as thinly as possible. Cut into desired size noodles; ¼ inch wide and 4 inches long is usual. Dry on a cloth for 20 minutes. Lightly butter a baking dish and carefully crisscross the noodles in it. Dot liberally with the butter and bake, uncovered, in a preheated 375° F. oven for 25 minutes, or until the top is browned.

SERVES 4.

Potato and Ham Croquettes

4 tablespoons of butter
3 scallions (white part only), minced
2 cups of unseasoned mashed potatoes
1½ cups of minced cooked ham
¼ teaspoon of dry mustard
Black pepper and salt to taste
Flour for dredging
1 tablespoon of olive oil

In a frypan, heat 1 tablespoon of the butter and sauté the scallions for 1 minute. In a bowl, combine the potatoes, ham, scallions, mustard and pepper. Blend well. Taste for seasoning and add salt if necessary. Make 3- by 2- by ½-inch croquettes. Heat the remaining 3 tablespoons of the butter and the oil and brown on both sides. Add more butter and oil, if needed. This is superb for breakfast with a poached or fried egg on top.

SERVES 4.

Potato Knishes

Since this is a Jewish dish, chicken fat is used, but if you don't have it, use butter.

4 tablespoons of rendered chicken fat
3 shallots, minced
9 medium-sized mushrooms, finely chopped
2 cups of freshly cooked potatoes, riced and cooled
½ cup of potato flour or all-purpose flour
1 egg, beaten
1 teaspoon of salt
½ teaspoon of pepper

In a saucepan, heat the fat and cook the shallots over medium heat for 3 minutes, or until soft. Add the mushrooms and cook over high heat, stirring, until most of the moisture cooks off. Set aside. In a bowl combine the potatoes, flour, egg, salt and pepper and blend well. Mix into a smooth dough. Divide into 12 parts, each about 2 inches in diameter. Flatten, place a heaping teaspoon of mushrooms in the center, pulling the dough around the mushrooms, completely encasing them. Lightly butter a cookie sheet and arrange the knishes, not touching. Bake in a preheated 375° F. oven for 25 minutes, or until golden.

MAKES ABOUT 12.

Lucania Potato-Salami Croquettes

Made into small balls, these are excellent served with cocktails.

6 medium-sized potatoes
⅓ pound of sliced Genoa salami, skin removed and chopped
¼ cup of grated Parmesan cheese
2 eggs, beaten
¼ pound of mozzarella cheese, in small dice
1 tablespoon of minced broadleaf parsley
½ teaspoon of pepper
Salt to taste
1 egg, beaten (for dipping croquettes)
1 cup of bread crumbs
Vegetable oil for frying

Boil the potatoes in their skins until tender, drain and dry over heat in a pot. Peel the potatoes and rice them. Put the potatoes in a bowl and with a wire whisk beat in the salami, Parmesan cheese, eggs, mozzarella, parsley and pepper. Taste and add salt if necessary. Cool, then spoon out the mixture, and with oiled, or floured hands, roll into croquettes the size and shape desired. The Italians form cylinders. Dip the croquettes into the beaten egg, then dredge in the bread crumbs. Spread on wax paper. Pour an inch of oil in a deep frypan, heat to 380° F. and fry the croquettes until golden. Drain on paper towels and serve hot.

SERVES 6.

Mashed Potato Dumplings

1½ cups of flour
1 teaspoon of salt
2 teaspoons of baking powder
1 tablespoon of minced parsley
½ cup of mashed potatoes
3 tablespoons of vegetable shortening
2 tablespoons of milk } BEATEN
1 large egg } TOGETHER

In a bowl, combine the flour, salt, baking powder and
parsley, blending well. Add the potatoes and shortening and using a pastry blender, work until the mixture
looks like coarse bread crumbs. Stir in the milk-egg
mixture, making a soft dough. Divide into 12 balls.
These dumplings can be cooked on top of any stew-
type dish. Cook at a simmer, uncovered, for 10 minutes, and then covered, for 10 minutes longer.

SERVES 4 TO 6.

Mock Potato Scrapple

2 tablespoons of butter
1 tablespoon of olive oil
⅓ cup of diced, lean-
streaked fatback (pork
for beans)
5 medium-sized potatoes,
peeled and cut into
small cubes

4 large scallions (white part
only), chopped
1 small sweet red pepper,
cored, seeded and
chopped
1½ teaspoons of salt
½ teaspoon of pepper
⅛ teaspoon of savory

5 eggs, separated

In a large frypan, over medium heat, heat the butter
and oil and sauté the fatback for 5 minutes, or until
golden. Stir in the potatoes, scallions, red pepper, salt,
pepper and savory. Cook, stirring occasionally, for 15
minutes. Beat the egg yolks until light lemon color;
beat the whites until stiff. Cool the potato mixture,

then stir in the egg yolks and fold in the egg whites. Spoon into a lightly buttered 2-quart casserole and bake, covered, in a preheated 375° F. oven for 20 minutes, or until the eggs are cooked and the potatoes are tender and the top is golden brown.

SERVES 6.

Potatoes Moussaka

This dish, a Greek specialty, also rates as a potato specialty, and is usually prepared with ground lamb. But such is the magic of potatoes that they are often substituted. We prefer our moussaka this way, served with 2-inch-thick, juicy, medium-rare loin lamb chops.

4 tablespoons of olive oil
6 large potatoes, peeled and cut into ¼-inch slices
2 garlic cloves, minced
2 medium-sized white onions, chopped
5 large, ripe tomatoes, peeled, seeded and chopped

3 tablespoons of lemon juice
1½ teaspoons of salt
½ teaspoon of pepper
⅓ cup of pignolia (pine nuts)
1 tablespoon of chopped fresh mint
1½ cups of finely crumbled feta cheese

In a deep saucepan, heat 2 tablespoons of the oil and brown the potato slices, one layer at a time, quickly on both sides, adding more oil as needed. Drain on paper towels. In the same pan, sauté the garlic and onion until soft. Add the tomatoes, lemon juice, salt, pepper, pignolia and mint. Blend, cover, and simmer for 8 minutes. Stir in half of the cheese and cook, uncovered, for 10 minutes, stirring until the sauce is smooth and thick. Butter a large baking dish or casserole and arrange a layer of potato slices on the bottom, spoon over some of the sauce. Repeat the layers ending with a layer of sauce on top. Sprinkle with the remaining feta cheese. Bake, covered, in a preheated

375° F. oven for 20 minutes. Uncover and cook for 10 minutes, or until the potatoes are tender.

SERVES 6.

Neapolitan Pissaladière

4 medium-sized, ripe, but firm tomatoes, peeled

1 recipe of Potato Piecrust (page 94)

Olive oil

1 cup of cubed fontina cheese (cubes should be very small)

½ teaspoon of dried oregano

½ teaspoon of dried basil

Salt and pepper

½ cup of grated Asiago or Parmesan cheese

12 pitted black olives, halved lengthwise

12 anchovy fillets

Slice the tomatoes and drain in a large strainer for 1 hour. Roll the dough into a 12-inch circle or into the shape of the pan you'll use (it should be a very shallow pan). Lightly oil the pan, place the pastry into it and bake in a preheated 350° F. oven for 15 minutes, or until the edges are golden. If the pastry puffs during the cooking, prick it in several places with a fork. Brush the top with olive oil. Arrange the tomato slices on the pastry. Sprinkle on the fontina cheese. Sprinkle with oregano and basil, and lightly with olive oil, salt and pepper. Sprinkle on the grated cheese. Arrange the olives and anchovies on top and bake in a preheated 400° F. oven for 25 minutes, or until the cheese is bubbling and golden.

SERVES 6.

New Potatoes Poached in Herbs

Here is a specialty from our mentor, the great French chef Antoino Cilly, who loves new potatoes, fresh from the ground.

3 garlic cloves, crushed
1 medium-sized yellow
   onion, sliced
2 teaspoons of salt
16 small, but not tiny,
   new potatoes, large
   enough for 4 to a
   serving (do not peel)
2 tablespoons of fine
   olive oil, warm
Freshly ground black
   pepper

WRAPPED IN DOUBLE THICK-
NESS OF CHEESECLOTH AND
TIED INTO A PACKET:
1 celery rib
1 sprig of broadleaf
   parsley
1 bay leaf
½ teaspoon of oregano
½ teaspoon of marjoram
½ teaspoon of thyme

In a large pot, place the garlic, onions, salt and the wrapped herbs. Cover with warm water, bring to a boil, cover the pot and simmer 30 minutes. Remove the cover, add the potatoes and simmer for 20 minutes, or until the potatoes are tender. Drain well, discard the packet of herbs and dry the potatoes in the pot over low heat. Serve very hot lightly rolled in the olive oil and with pepper milled over them.

SERVES 4.

Potato Piecrust

Makes two 8-inch pastry shells or a top crust for an 8- by 12-inch meat, fowl or vegetable pie, or a 12-inch-in-diameter pizza.

  1½ cups of all-purpose flour
  1 teaspoon of salt
  ½ teaspoon of sugar
  ½ cup of cold, unseasoned mashed potatoes
  ¼ cup of butter
  ¼ cup of Crisco
  1 tablespoon of water

Mix together the flour, salt and sugar. Add the mashed potatoes and mix well. Cut in the butter and Crisco with a pastry cutter until rice-sized particles are formed. Add the water and mix well with a fork. Press the mixture into a ball, wrap in plastic wrap and chill for 1 hour. Roll out between sheets of lightly floured wax paper into the desired thinness and size.

Pommes de Terre Amandine
(Potatoes and Almonds)

  5 medium-sized potatoes
  3 eggs
  3 tablespoons of butter
  ¼ teaspoon of nutmeg
  Salt and pepper to taste
  Flour for dredging
  1 cup of fine bread crumbs mixed with 1 cup of finely
    chopped almonds
  Oil for deep frying

Boil the peeled potatoes until tender, drain and dry over heat in a pot, then mash. Combine the potatoes with 1 whole egg and 1 egg yolk (save the white), butter, nutmeg, salt and pepper. Shape the mixture into croquettes (size depending on your preference). Refrigerate for 2 hours.

In a shallow bowl, beat the remaining egg with the egg white. Dredge the croquettes with the flour. Dip them into the beaten egg, then dredge with the bread crumbs–almond mixture. Deep fry about 5 minutes, or until golden brown. Do not crowd while frying. Fry 3 or 4 at a time, draining them on paper towels and keep warm in a 250° F. oven.

SERVES 1.

Potato Pudding for Roast Beef

Serve this pudding with juicy roast beef and tell your guests this is the way it is offered in Yorkshire.

7 medium-sized Idaho potatoes	¼ teaspoon of thyme
⅓ cup of hot cream	1½ teaspoons of salt
4 tablespoons of the pan drippings from the roast beef	½ teaspoon of pepper
2 tablespoons of melted butter	2 eggs, beaten (reserve 2 tablespoons)
	Cayenne

Boil the potatoes in their skins until tender, drain and dry over heat in a pot. Peel and mash them. Put the potatoes in a bowl and with a wire whisk beat in the cream, pan drippings, butter, thyme, salt and pepper. Add the eggs (reserving the 2 tablespoons) and whip them in. Lightly butter a cake pan of sufficient size. Spoon in the potatoes, smoothing the surface, cake-fashion. Brush on the 2 tablespoons of beaten egg and lightly sprinkle with cayenne. Cook, uncovered, in a preheated 425° F. oven for 15 minutes or until browned.

SERVES 6.

Potato Rolls

¼ cup of lukewarm
water

1 package of granulated
yeast

3 tablespoons of sugar

1 cup of hot milk

2 teaspoons of salt

4 to 6 cups of flour

1 cup of mashed potatoes,
well dried out over heat,
mixed with 1 stick of
soft butter

2 eggs, beaten

½ teaspoon of baking
powder

Melted butter to brush tops
of rolls

Pour the lukewarm water into a 1-cup measuring cup.
Sprinkle in the yeast and 1 teaspoon of the sugar and
stir. Allow to sit in a draft-free place for 8 minutes,
or until it rises and doubles in volume.

In a large bowl combine the milk, remaining sugar
and salt. Stir in the yeast mixture and 2 cups of flour,
½ cup at a time. Add the potatoes; mix well, then
beat in the eggs, the baking powder and 2 more cups
of flour, ½ cup at a time.

Turn out onto a lightly floured board and knead for
about 10 minutes, adding small amounts of flour until
you have a smooth and elastic ball of dough. Place
in a warm, buttered bowl and turn it once bringing
the buttered side up. Cover with a towel and set in a
warm, draft-free place to rise. When it doubles in
bulk (about 1 hour) punch it down, then let it rise
again. Butter the muffin tins. When the dough has
doubled in bulk the second time, break off pieces to
make small balls that will fill the tins two-thirds full.
Place in a draft-free place to rise to fill the tins. Brush
the tops with melted butter and bake in a preheated
425° F. oven from 12 to 15 minutes, or until golden.

MAKES ABOUT 2½ DOZEN ROLLS.

Potato Rice Ring

from Barbara M. Valbona

½ cup of chopped onion, sautéed in butter until golden
4 medium-sized potatoes, cooked and mashed
1½ cups of uncooked rice (undercook slightly until firm)
3 eggs, beaten
½ cup of cream
½ cup of chopped fresh parsley
½ cup of chopped pimiento
Salt and pepper to taste

Blend all ingredients thoroughly and press into a buttered ring mold. Set into a pan of water. Bake in a preheated 350° F. oven for 30 minutes. Cool slightly before unmolding.

The ring may be filled with creamed spinach, broccoli and cheese sauce, crabmeat au gratin or any of your own favorites.

This mixture can be formed into patties and browned in butter or rolled into small balls and deep fried for hors d'oeuvres.

SERVES 8.

Potato Salad Dressing

from Diana Hunter

1 medium-sized potato
1 medium-sized onion, finely chopped
½ cup of beef broth
½ cup of olive oil
2 tablespoons of sherry or red-wine vinegar
Salt and pepper to taste

Boil the potato in its skin until tender, drain and dry over heat in a pot. Peel and put through a potato ricer. When cool combine with the remaining ingredients and blend well. Use on a green salad, a tomato-and-cucumber salad or any salad of your choice.

MAKES ABOUT 1½ CUPS.

Potato Seafood Sauce
(Skordalia)

Called *skordalia,* we discovered this unique sauce
served over a whole fish, a *singagrida,* an Aegean fish
tasting like a lake trout, in the famed restaurant of
Athanasios Vassileanas in Piraeus, a harbor settle-
ment not far from Athens.

4 small baking potatoes

3 garlic cloves, minced } BLENDED INTO A PASTE
2 teaspoons of salt

2 small egg yolks
⅓ cup of olive oil
4 tablespoons of lemon juice
Pepper to taste
1 tablespoon of pignolia (pine nuts)

Boil the potatoes in their skins until tender. Peel and
put through a ricer. Stir into a very smooth puree. In
a bowl, thoroughly blend the potatoes with the garlic-
salt paste. With a hand beater or a whisk, beat in the
egg yolks, then the oil, a small amount at a time,
beating until each portion has been absorbed. Beat
in the lemon juice and pepper. Taste for seasoning
(it should be highly seasoned), then stir in the nuts.
The sauce should have the consistency of mayonnaise.
If it seems too thick, beat in a small amount of lemon
juice diluted with a little warm water.

MAKES ABOUT 2 CUPS.

Note: See Eggplant Appetizer (page 99). These
eggplant sticks are excellent with this sauce.

Eggplant Appetizer

Here are some eggplant sticks to dip in the *skordalia*, Potato Seafood Sauce, to serve at cocktail time, further proving the versatility of this sauce and the potato.

1 medium-sized eggplant, peeled and cut lengthwise
    into strips ¼ inch thick, ½ inch wide, 3 inches long
1 tablespoon of salt
½ cup of flour blended with 1 teaspoon of salt
Vegetable oil

Liberally sprinkle the eggplant strips with salt; place on a drain board or in a colander; weigh them down for 1½ hours (placing a flat dish with a flatiron on it will do the job) to press the bitter juices out. Dredge the strips with the seasoned flour. Evenly brown the strips in about ½ inch of oil over medium heat. They should be golden and crisp. Drain on paper towels.

SERVES 4.

Sesame Potato Bread

8 tablespoons (1 stick)   2 packages of active dry
    of butter   yeast
1½ cups of sieved hot   ⅓ cup of warm water
    cooked potatoes   5½ cups of flour
2 tablespoons of sugar   1 egg white, slightly beaten
2 teaspoons of salt   with 1 tablespoon of
1 cup of milk, scalded   water
                    Sesame seeds

In a large mixing bowl, combine the butter and potatoes, stirring until the butter is melted. Add the sugar, salt and milk. Stir until the mixture is smooth and cooled to lukewarm. Dissolve the yeast in the water and stir into the potato mixture. Add 3 cups of the flour, beating until smooth. Gradually stir in enough of the remaining flour to make a moderately stiff dough which does not stick to the sides of the bowl. Turn out on a lightly floured board and knead until smooth and elastic (about 10 minutes), working in only as much additional flour as necessary to prevent the dough from sticking (about 1 cup). Place the dough in a buttered bowl, turning to butter all sides. Cover and let rise in a warm place until doubled in bulk, about 1 hour.

Punch the dough down and divide into four parts. Roll each between buttered palms to form a strand about 15 inches long. Spiral-wrap two strands together to form a twist-loaf, tucking ends under. Lift into buttered loaf pan (9 by 5 inches). Repeat with the remaining strands. Cover and let rise in a warm place until almost doubled in bulk, about 20 to 30 minutes. Gently brush tops of loaves with egg-white mixture. Sprinkle generously with sesame seeds. Bake in a preheated 400° F. oven for 10 minutes. Reduce heat to 350° F. and bake 35 minutes longer, or until golden brown. Turn loaves out of pans onto wire racks to cool.

MAKES 2 LOAVES OF BREAD.

Sour Milk Potato Rolls

All ingredients should be at room temperature unless otherwise stated.

2 cups of buttermilk, heated but not boiling
1 teaspoon of salt
2 tablespoons of sugar
1 yeast cake, crumbled

1 cup of cooked riced potatoes } BLENDED WHILE
½ cup of butter } POTATOES ARE STILL HOT

2 eggs, beaten
7 cups of sifted all-purpose flour

1 egg yolk } BEATEN TOGETHER INTO
2 tablespoons of milk } AN "EGG WASH"

Into ½ cup of buttermilk, mix the salt, sugar and yeast cake. Let set for 15 minutes. Pour into a large bowl and blend in the remaining buttermilk and the buttered potatoes, beating together well. Mix in the eggs and 6 cups of flour, blending well. Turn out onto a floured board and knead in the remaining flour making a smooth, elastic ball of dough. Butter a bowl and drop the dough into it, rotating until the whole ball is lightly buttered. Wet a cloth, wring it out well, cover the bowl and let the dough rise until it doubles in bulk. Punch down. Grease enough muffin tins to accommodate the rolls and fill each one-third full. Glaze the tops by lightly brushing them with the "egg wash." Bake in a preheated 425° F. oven for 15 minutes, or until golden.

MAKES ABOUT 40 ROLLS.

South American Potato Croquettes con Peanut Sauce

Peanut Sauce

2 tablespoons of olive oil
1 medium-sized onion, finely chopped
1 garlic clove, minced
4 medium-sized ripe tomatoes, peeled, seeded and
    chopped or 1 (1-pound) can of tomatoes, with their
    liquid, chopped
½ teaspoon of turmeric
½ cup of peanut butter or finely ground unsalted
    peanuts
Salt to taste

In a frypan, over medium heat, heat the oil and cook the onion and garlic for 5 minutes, or until the onion is just soft. Add the tomatoes and turmeric and cook for 15 minutes, or until the sauce is smooth and some of the watery content of the tomato has evaporated. Stir in the peanut butter and simmer for 3 minutes, or until it has blended with the sauce.

1 recipe for Parisian Potato Balls (page 226). Do
    not make balls of the mixture but 12 uniform-sized,
    oval-shaped croquettes
2 tablespoons of butter
1 tablespoon of olive oil

In a frypan, heat the butter and oil and cook the potato croquettes until golden on both sides. Do not crowd them in the pan. Add more butter and oil, if necessary. Drain on paper towels. Serve with the peanut sauce spooned over.

SERVES 4 TO 6.

Stuffed Clams #1

12 large clams, scrubbed
and steamed

2 tablespoons of butter

½ cup of minced celery
(scrape before mincing)

2 tablespoons of chopped
shallots

Pinch of thyme

1½ cups of mashed
potatoes

1 egg, beaten

½ teaspoon of Worcester-
shire sauce

2 tablespoons of cream

Salt and pepper to taste

Melted butter

Paprika

Remove the clams from their shells, reserving the
liquid and the shells. Chop the clams. In a frypan,
over medium heat, melt the butter. Add the celery
and shallots and cook for about 1 minute. Off the
heat stir in the thyme, potatoes, chopped clams, egg,
Worcestershire sauce, cream, salt and pepper and
enough of the clam liquid to slightly moisten the
mixture. Butter 12 of the largest shells and evenly
spoon in the stuffing. Sprinkle the top with the melted
butter and paprika. Place on a baking sheet and bake
in a preheated 375° F. oven for 15 to 20 minutes, or
until the top is golden.

MAKES STUFFING FOR 12 LARGE CLAM SHELLS.

Stuffed Clams #2

1 medium-sized ripe
tomato, peeled, seeded,
chopped and put into
a sieve to drain

½ cup of chopped
broadleaf parsley

2 garlic cloves, put
through a garlic press

2 tablespoons of olive oil

1 teaspoon of oregano

3 (8-ounce) cans of minced
clams, drained

1½ cups of mashed
potatoes

¾ cup of bread crumbs

Salt and pepper to taste

½ cup of grated Asiago
or Parmesan cheese

In a bowl, combine the tomato, parsley, garlic, oil,
oregano, clams, potatoes, ¼ cup of bread crumbs,

salt and pepper. Mix well. Lightly oil the shells or ramekins. Spoon in equal amounts of the mixture. Sprinkle the tops first with some of the remaining bread crumbs, then the cheese. Place on a baking sheet and bake in a preheated 375° F. oven for 15 to 20 minutes, or until the tops are golden.

MAKES STUFFING FOR 8 LARGE CLAM SHELLS OR 4 SMALL RAMEKINS.

Potato Stuffing

To stuff a 9- or 10-pound turkey or goose.
This is an old-fashioned American recipe often used with a Christmas bird. Substituting it for your regular bread stuffing will offer a taste treat.

> 2½ cups of hot mashed potatoes (do not add milk or cream when mashing but do add 2 tablespoons of butter)
> 1½ cups of bread crumbs
> 2 white onions, minced
> 2 celery ribs with leaves, minced
> 2 eggs, beaten
> 1½ teaspoons of Bell's Seasoning (a unique commercial mixture of herbs and spices)
> 1½ teaspoons of salt

In a bowl, blend all ingredients into a smooth mixture. Stuff the bird, trussing well. We like this best with goose, which we cook on a rack, uncovered, in a preheated 350° F. oven for 20 minutes per pound.

Swedish (Potatiskorv) Potato Sausage

We discovered this superb potato sausage in a Stockholm restaurant. After three sausage-munching visits, we managed to persuade the chef to give us the recipe.

3 large potatoes (1½ pounds), peeled and cut into small chunks
1 pound of pork shoulder or butt
1 pound of beef chuck
1 pound of veal
2 medium-sized onions

½ cup of cold water
5 teaspoons of salt
½ teaspoon of sugar
2 teaspoons of allspice
¼ teaspoon *each* of white pepper and black pepper
½ pound of sausage casings

Put the potatoes, pork, beef, veal and onion through a grinder once. Transfer to a bowl. Add the water, salt, sugar, allspice and the peppers. Mix well; use your hands, and mix and remix. It is important that the blending is thorough. Make a small, flat patty of the mixture and cook in butter to taste. Add more salt and pepper to the mixture if needed. Cut the casings in desired lengths and stuff. To cook, place the sausages in a saucepan and cover with boiling water. Bring to a simmer, cover and simmer for 45 minutes. Drain. Serve hot, cut into 2-inch lengths.

MAKES ABOUT 5 POUNDS.

Watercress Potato Soufflé

Watercress gives a delicate, yet peppery, authority to this dish, which we like to serve with a lemony broiled chicken.

2½ cups of mashed potatoes
½ cup of yogurt
1 cup of grated Asiago or Parmesan cheese
¼ cup of chopped watercress
1½ teaspoons of salt
3 egg yolks, beaten
3 egg whites, stiffly beaten

In a bowl, blend the potatoes, yogurt, cheese, watercress, salt and egg yolks. Whip into a smooth, light mixture. Fold in the egg whites. Turn into a lightly buttered 1½-quart casserole. Bake, uncovered, in a preheated 375° F. oven for 40 minutes, or until puffed and golden.

SERVES 4.

5

Main Provider

The potato is haute cuisine, in plain language, the best of the best. Historians point this out by recording that potatoes were the favorite vegetable of Madame de Pompadour, mistress of France's King Louis XV. In an attempt to prove she could match the talents of the most famous male chef of the day, she concocted Potatoes Pompadour, an elegant crown of mashed potatoes filled with rich creamed fish. This dish added Madame de Pompadour's name to the long list of haute cuisine potato dishes created in France.

The profit in the potato thus lies not only in this versatility, and in its vitamin and mineral content, but in its almost magical personality that permits it to perfectly pair with other ingredients to provide a complete meal. You can create your own "Pompadour" with bits of leftover beef, chicken; any meat that remains in the refrigerator can be paired with the potato in a main-dish casserole. Great hashes can be concocted with canned meats, for example, corned beef; pies can be prepared with mashed potatoes and leftover lamb or beef (or with meat cooked especially for this superb dish); puffy, magnificent soufflés can be filled with sauced meat; omelets stuffed with potatoes; sliced potatoes can be layered with ham and cream and scalloped.

But without the potato all of this meal magic is hardly inspired or even palatable. For instance, ever try a hash without potato? Or a potato-less scalloped dish? Or Shepherd's Pie without mashed potatoes?

Literally, with mere pennies spent for the potatoes, dinner, supper or lunch, can be easy, inexpensive, and even inspired. With one proviso: You must read this chapter. It's the Main Provider.

Potatoes Abruzzese

For this hearty dish that we discovered in Italy's Abruzzi, where the best cooks are, you need a large frypan—and a large appetite.

4 sweet Italian sausages
4 hot Italian sausages
Olive oil (optional)
2 medium-sized green peppers, cored and sliced
4 medium-sized potatoes, peeled and cut into ¼-inch slices
3 medium-sized yellow onions, thinly sliced

Pierce the sausages in several places so the casings won't burst while cooking. In a large frypan, cook the sausages over medium heat, browning evenly. (You may need a little olive oil to keep them from sticking to the pan, but chances are good that there will be enough fat in the sausages without adding more.) If the sausages are fatty, discard all but 3 tablespoons of the fat. If not, add olive oil to make up this amount. Add the peppers and potatoes to the frypan. Cover and cook over medium heat for 10 minutes, or until the peppers and potatoes are almost tender. Add the onion, cover and cook for 15 minutes, or until the onions are soft. Serve with warm, buttered, crusty Italian bread and cold beer.

SERVES 4.

Potatoes Baked with Haddock

5 medium-sized Idaho potatoes, peeled and cut into
⅛-inch slices
2 garlic cloves, chopped
4 tablespoons of chopped broadleaf parsley
1 teaspoon of dillweed
½ cup of olive oil
Salt and pepper to taste
4 haddock steaks, each large enough for an individual
serving (about ⅓ pound)
¼ cup of dry bread crumbs

In a bowl, combine the potatoes, half each of the garlic, parsley, dillweed, olive oil. Add salt and pepper and blend well. Evenly line the bottom of a casserole large enough to hold the fish in one neat layer with the potato slices. Bake, uncovered, in a preheated 450° F. oven for 15 minutes. Remove from the oven. Place the haddock steaks on the potatoes. In the same bowl you mixed the potatoes, combine the remaining garlic, parsley, dillweed and oil, blending. Pour over the fish. Lightly season with salt and pepper. Sprinkle with bread crumbs and bake, uncovered, in a 400° F. oven for 12 minutes. Baste the potatoes and fish well with the oil mixture in the casserole and bake another 6 minutes.

SERVES 4.

Potatoes Baked with Steak

Believe it or not, this is an economy meal. When you buy a piece of bottom round for pot roast, cut off 4 steaks about ½ inch thick. Pound them well with a mallet, or with the edge of a plate.

BLENDED:
1 cup of flour
1 teaspoon of salt
½ teaspoon of pepper
4 (½-inch-thick, about 6 ounces each) slices of bottom round, well pounded

2 tablespoons of butter
1 tablespoon of olive oil
2 cups of beef broth
4 medium-sized potatoes, peeled and cut into ¼-inch slices
Salt and pepper to taste
3 medium-sized onions, thinly sliced

Place the seasoned flour on a piece of wax paper and dredge the steaks evenly. In a frypan, heat the butter and oil, and over medium heat, brown the steaks on both sides. Remove. Pour the beef broth into the frypan and stir, scraping the bottom of the pan to loosen the browned particles. Simmer for 5 minutes. In a shallow casserole arrange the potatoes in one layer, overlapping, sprinkle lightly with salt and pepper and cover with a layer of onions. Place the browned steaks on the onions and pour the beef broth over the steaks. Cover and bake in a preheated 375° F. oven for 45 minutes, or until the steaks are tender. Serve with pan juices spooned over steaks and potatoes. Pass warm, buttered crusty bread and cold beer.

SERVES 4.

Potato and Beef Soufflé

6 medium-sized potatoes (about 2 pounds)
8 tablespoons (1 stick) of soft butter
½ cup of warm milk
Salt and pepper to taste
¼ teaspoon of nutmeg
½ cup grated Gruyère cheese

5 egg yolks, well beaten
5 egg whites, stiffly beaten
4 cups boiled, braised or roast beef, cut into ½-inch cubes and mixed with enough Brown Sauce to coat them
Brown Sauce (see below)

Boil the potatoes in their skins until tender, drain and dry over heat in a pan. Peel the potatoes and put them through a potato ricer into a bowl. Combine the potatoes with the butter, milk, salt, pepper, nutmeg and cheese and beat with an electric beater to mix well. When slightly cooled, beat in the egg yolks, blending well. Fold in the egg whites. Place one-third of the potato mixture in the bottom of a deep, buttered 9-inch baking dish. Make a ½-inch-thick lining for the sides of the dish with the potatoes. Spoon the beef cubes over the layer of potatoes. Cover with an even layer of the remaining potatoes and bake, uncovered, in a preheated 375° F. oven for 1 hour, or until the top is golden. Serve with the Brown Sauce.

Brown Sauce

Makes about 2 cups.

3 tablespoons of butter
1 small onion, chopped
1 small garlic clove, minced
Pinch of thyme
Salt and pepper to taste
3 tablespoons of flour
2½ cups of warm beef broth } BLENDED
¼ cup of tomato puree

In a saucepan, over medium heat, melt the butter and cook the onion and garlic until the onion is soft. Add the thyme, salt and pepper. Stir in the flour, blending well. Stir in the beef broth–tomato puree mixture, a small amount at a time, blending into a smooth, medium-thick sauce. Taste for seasoning.

SERVES 6.

Potato-Broccoli Puree with Scrambled Eggs

6 medium-sized potatoes, cooked, mashed and kept hot
1 (10-ounce) package of frozen chopped broccoli, cooked according to package directions, drained well and pureed in a blender
1 tablespoon of chopped broadleaf parsley
Salt and pepper to taste
9 large eggs, scrambled and seasoned to your taste
Watercress

In a bowl, place the hot mashed potatoes, hot pureed broccoli and the parsley, blending well, and seasoning to taste. Place the puree in a large warm serving platter and top with the scrambled eggs. Garnish with watercress. We like this for lunch with hot, buttered Sour Milk Potato Rolls (see page 101) and cold glasses of Canadian ale.

SERVES 6.

Potato-Cabbage Casserole, Hungarian Style

6 medium-sized potatoes
1 medium-sized savoy cabbage, trimmed (center core removed and shredded)
1 tablespoon of cider vinegar
4 slices of lean bacon, coarsely chopped
Salt and pepper to taste
1 cup of heavy cream
¼ cup of bread crumbs
3 tablespoons of butter

Boil the potatoes in their skins until almost tender, drain and dry over heat in a pot. Peel and cut into slices slightly more than ¼ inch thick. Cook the cabbage in very little salted water with the vinegar, covered, until tender-crisp. Drain. Butter a deep baking dish. Alternate layers of potatoes and cabbage, sprinkling each layer with bacon and salt and pepper. The last layer should be cabbage. Pour the cream over the top layer. Sprinkle on the bread crumbs, dot with butter and bake in a preheated 375° F. oven for 30 minutes, or until heated through and the top is golden.

SERVES 6.

Chips and Fish

In every other cookbook the fish would come first. Not here!

5 medium-sized Idahoes, peeled, cut into strips ⅜ inch by ⅜ inch or whatever size you prefer
Vegetable oil, enough to fill a fryer or frypan to a 4-inch depth

A frying thermometer helps with this dish. The oil should be at 375° F. The potatoes must be very dry. Don't try to cook too many at a time and don't salt them. That is done by the guest at the table. The cooking will be fast; don't overcook; the potatoes should be golden and crisp. Try a few first as a test, then proceed. Drain on paper towels and keep warm in a 250° F. oven. The fish can be fried in the same oil. But after the chips and fish dinner, discard the oil.

Batter for Fish

1 egg yolk
2 tablespoons of butter, melted and cooled
1 cup of flour
6 tablespoons of buttermilk
½ teaspoon of salt
1 egg white, stiffly beaten

In a large bowl, place the egg yolk, butter, flour, buttermilk and salt, and with a wire whisk gently whip into a smooth batter. Fold in the egg white. There are about as many types of batter as there are fish to dip it in.

Frying the Fish

2 pounds of boned cod or haddock, cut into 2- by 4-inch pieces, fish must be very dry to absorb the batter

Drop the pieces of fish, a few pieces at a time, into the batter, coating them well. Using a slotted spoon, place them, no more than 3 pieces at a time, into the fat preheated to 375° F. Four minutes frying time should do it. Fish should be golden on the outside but still moist inside. Drain on paper towels and place in the oven with the chips. Arrange the chips and fish on a large hot serving platter and pass the platter, salt and beer to guests.

SERVES 4.

Colcannon

Often the Irish, "the potato pilgrims," use potatoes and cabbage that have been cooked, making this leftover meal a Monday night specialty. We like the dish so much we prepare everything fresh.

    4 slices of bacon, diced
    4 medium-sized white onions, chopped
    2 cups of cooked, chopped cabbage
    5 medium-sized potatoes, freshly cooked and mashed
    Salt and pepper to taste
    4 to 6 eggs (depending upon number being served),
        poached

In a saucepan, cook the bacon until crisp; remove with a slotted spoon onto paper towel. Remove half of the bacon fat and reserve. In the remainder of the fat in the pan, sauté the onion until soft. In a bowl, place the onion, bacon, cabbage and mashed potatoes, seasoning to your taste. Blend well and shape into 4 to 6 thick patties. In a frypan, pour the remaining bacon fat and evenly brown the patties. Place a hot poached egg atop each and serve immediately. The dish is varied, sometimes served as one large cake; sometimes the bacon is omitted and leftover cold lamb mixed in, often it is sprinkled with cheese and browned in the oven. But we like it best in cakes—with eggs. Delicious!

SERVES 4 TO 6.

Curried Potatoes with Scallions and Eggs

8 tablespoons (1 stick) of butter
4 large potatoes, peeled and cut into ½-inch cubes
6 scallions (using some of the green part), chopped
1 teaspoon of salt
8 large eggs, lightly beaten with 4 tablespoons of cream,
   1 teaspoon of curry powder and 3 tablespoons of
   chopped parsley

In a large frypan, melt the butter. Add the potatoes and cook over low heat for 10 minutes, or until tender (but firm) and golden. Stir in the scallions, salt and cook for 5 minutes, or until the scallions are tender-crisp. Pour in the beaten egg mixture and cook, stirring, until the eggs have just set. Do not overcook the eggs; they should be creamy. Taste for seasoning, adding more salt, if needed.

SERVES 6.

Dublin Potato Stew

The Irish aren't known for subtle, or especially fine, cookery, but no one can better them in stews that use lamb for flavor and potatoes for bulk and personality. This is a dish we always have in Ireland, eaten with a good soda bread and a pint of excellent Irish beer.

6 medium-sized potatoes, peeled and cut into ½-inch slices
2 pounds of lamb shanks, boned and cut into ½-inch slices
Salt and pepper to taste
⅛ teaspoon of dried savory
⅛ teaspoon of dried oregano
⅛ teaspoon of dried thyme
2 cups of beef broth (the Irish often use just water, but beef broth makes the better stew)

In a casserole, make alternating layers of potatoes, meat and onions, seasoning each layer lightly with salt, pepper, savory, oregano and thyme. Pour in the beef broth, cover and bake in a preheated 325° F. oven for 2 hours, or until the meat and potatoes are tender.

SERVES 4.

Potatoes and Eggs Parma Style

3 medium-sized potatoes
¼ pound of fontina cheese
4 eggs
Salt and pepper to taste
4 tablespoons of grated Parmesan cheese
2 tablespoons of bread crumbs
1 tablespoon of butter

Boil the potatoes in their skins until tender but firm.
Peel and cut them into ¼-inch slices. Cut the cheese
into slices the same thickness as the potato slices.
Butter a large, shallow baking dish. Arrange the potatoes on the bottom in one layer, overlapping if
necessary. Top with the cheese slices. Break the eggs,
one at a time, into a saucer. Gently slide them onto
the cheese. Sprinkle with salt and pepper, the grated
cheese and bread crumbs. Dot with butter. Bake in a
preheated 400° F. oven for 15 minutes, or until the
eggs are set to your liking and the cheese has melted.

SERVES 4.

Potato Fish Balls

State of Mainers love this dish made with their famed mealy potatoes and cod from their cold coastal waters. We often make these into bite-sized balls and serve them with cocktails.

4 large potatoes (2 pounds)
1 pound salt cod, soaked in cold water overnight, drained and rinsed several times in cold water (see page 151)
3 tablespoons of soft butter
½ teaspoon of black pepper
1 large egg, beaten
Vegetable oil for deep frying

Boil the potatoes in their skins until tender, drain and dry over heat in a pan. Cook the cod in water until tender, drain well. Peel the potatoes. Mash them and the cod separately; place both in a bowl, add the butter, pepper and egg and beat into a smooth mixture. Refrigerate for 2 hours. Shape into balls, sized to your own preference and deep fry, without crowding, until crisp and golden. Drain on paper towels. Serve immediately or keep warm in a low oven.

SERVES 4.

Fish Flan

7 medium-sized baking potatoes
2½ cups of cooked haddock or cod, flaked
⅔ cup of medium cream
1 teaspoon of salt
½ teaspoon of pepper
⅛ teaspoon of mace
2 eggs, beaten (reserve 3 tablespoons)
⅓ cup of bread crumbs
1 tablespoon of butter
2 tablespoons of grated Parmesan cheese

Boil the potatoes in their skins until tender, drain and dry over heat in a pan. Peel and rice them. In a bowl, combine the potatoes, fish, cream, salt, pepper, mace and eggs. Whip into a smooth mixture with a wire whisk. Lightly butter a cake pan of sufficient size. Pour in the potato-fish mixture. Brush or spread the reserved beaten egg on top. Sprinkle with bread crumbs, then cheese. Bake, uncovered, in a preheated 400° F. oven for 25 minutes, or until thoroughly heated and the cheese has melted and the top is golden brown.

SERVES 6.

German Potato-Knockwurst Lunch

6 medium-sized potatoes	2 tablespoons of sugar
2 scallions, chopped	2 teaspoons of flour
6 knockwurst	1 teaspoon of salt
⅓ cup of white wine	¼ cup of vinegar
⅓ cup of water	½ cup of water
2 tablespoons of bacon drippings or salad oil	1 tablespoon of chopped parsley

Boil the potatoes in their skins, drain, peel and dice. In a large serving bowl, combine hot potatoes and scallions. Cover and keep warm. Poach the knockwurst in the wine and water for 10 minutes, drain and cut into ½-inch slices. In a large frypan over medium heat, brown the sliced knockwurst in bacon drippings. With a slotted spoon, remove the knockwurst, reserving drippings. Add the knockwurst to the potato bowl and keep warm. Into the hot drippings, stir the sugar, flour and salt until smooth and bubbly. Gradually stir in the vinegar and water. Cook, stirring constantly, until the sauce thickens and boils. Pour the sauce over the potatoes and knockwurst. Sprinkle with parsley.

SERVES 6.

Potatoes with Ground Meat, Turkish Style

8 medium-sized potatoes, peeled and cut into slices, slightly less than ½-inch thick

3 tablespoons of butter

2 tablespoons of olive oil

2 medium-sized onions, chopped

1 pound of ground lean lamb or beef

½ teaspoon of ground cumin

¼ teaspoon of cinnamon

2 tablespoons of chopped fresh mint or 1 teaspoon of dried

2 tablespoons of lemon juice

Salt and pepper to taste

3 ripe, firm tomatoes, peeled and cut into ½-inch slices

1 cup of beef broth

2 tablespoons of chopped fresh parsley

Dry the slices of potatoes. In a large frypan heat 1½ tablespoons of the butter and 1 tablespoon of the oil. Lightly sauté the potato slices, one layer at a time, on both sides, adding more butter and oil as needed. Remove the potatoes and arrange them in one layer in a casserole, overlapping if necessary. In the same frypan, sauté the onion until soft. Add the ground meat, cumin, cinnamon and mint and cook for about 10 minutes, or until the meat loses its pink color and most of the liquid has evaporated. Layer the beef-and-onion mixture on the potatoes. Sprinkle with lemon juice, salt and pepper. Arrange the slices of tomatoes on top, sprinkle with salt and pepper and pour the beef broth around the edges of the casserole. Cover and bake in a preheated 375° F. oven for 30 minutes. Remove cover and cook 15 minutes longer, or until the potatoes are tender. Sprinkle the parsley just before serving.

SERVES 6.

Potato-Ham-and-Egg Luncheon Pizza

6 large, ripe tomatoes or 6 cups of canned Italian tomatoes, chopped

1 garlic clove, thinly sliced

1 tablespoon of chopped fresh basil or 1 teaspoon of dried

1 tablespoon of olive oil

Salt and pepper to taste

8 small mushrooms, thinly sliced

4 cups of Gnocchi dough (page 237) into which has been mixed ½ cup of grated Asiago cheese

Olive oil to brown "pizzas"

6 poached eggs, well drained and trimmed, if necessary

9 thin slices of prosciutto ham (or any other good ham), cut julienne

¾ cup of grated provolone (or any sharp cheese of your choice) cheese

In a saucepan, over medium heat, cook the tomatoes, garlic, basil and oil, uncovered, for 10 minutes. Season with salt and pepper. Add the mushrooms and simmer until you have a smooth, thick sauce. While the sauce cooks, make the Gnocchi dough. Divide it into six parts and flatten into 5-inch rounds. Make a depression in the center of each. In a frypan, over medium heat, brown the potato "pizzas" in olive oil on both sides. Place on a baking sheet, side with the depression up. Place an egg in each depression, sprinkle the ham on and around it. Spoon some sauce over ham and egg, then sprinkle 2 tablespoons of the grated cheese over the sauce. Bake in a preheated 450° F. oven for 5 minutes, or until the cheese melts.

SERVES 6.

Old-Fashioned Hash #1

4 cups of cubed raw
  potatoes
3 cups of cooked meat
2 medium-sized white
  onions
1½ teaspoons of salt

½ teaspoon of pepper
⅛ teaspoon of thyme
2 tablespoons of butter
1 tablespoon of olive oil
6 large fried eggs

Put through the grinder or food processor, the potatoes, meat and onion. Blend and season with salt, pepper and thyme. In a frypan, heat the butter and oil over medium heat, and place the potato mixture in the pan, pressing it down into a cake with a spatula. Cook until a crust forms on the bottom (stir occasionally to make sure the hash cooks and browns evenly inside). Turn and cook until crusty-brown on the other side. Serve very hot on warm plates with the freshly cooked fried eggs.

SERVES 6.

Old-Fashioned Hash #2

6 medium-sized potatoes
2 tablespoons of butter
1 tablespoon of olive oil
3 medium-sized white
  onions, chopped
3 cups of diced cooked
  pork, beef, or chicken

6 medium-sized fresh
  mushrooms, sliced
1½ teaspoons of salt
½ teaspoon of pepper
⅛ teaspoon of savory
3 tablespoons of beef broth
6 large eggs, poached

Boil the potatoes in their skins, drain and dry over heat in a pot. Peel and dice them. In a frypan, heat the butter and oil and sauté the onion for 5 minutes. Stir in the potatoes and meat and cook for 10 minutes, or until browned. Add the mushrooms and cook for 3 minutes. Sprinkle with salt, pepper, savory and the beef broth, blending. Cook over medium heat until crusty brown underneath, turn and repeat. Scoop out with a spatula onto warm plates, topping each serving with a hot poached egg.

SERVES 6.

Hoppelpoppel

This is a popular German supper that we first sampled in Munich at the home of friends. It has become our favorite way to cook bacon and eggs, for that combination has always suffered when offered without potatoes.

4 medium-sized potatoes
2 cups of diced bacon
3 medium-sized white onions, chopped
8 eggs
2 tablespoons of medium cream
1 teaspoon of salt
½ teaspoon of pepper
1 tablespoon of minced fresh chives

Boil the potatoes in their skins until barely cooked, drain and dry over heat. Peel and cut into ¼-inch slices (slices should be firm, not overcooked). In a large frypan, sauté the bacon until crisp. Remove and drain on paper towels. Pour off all but 5 tablespoons of fat. Add the onion and cook for 5 minutes, or until soft. Add the potato slices, cooking over medium heat for 10 minutes, turning them to brown evenly (add more bacon fat, if needed). In a bowl, beat together the eggs, cream, salt, pepper and chives until well mixed. Sprinkle the bacon over the potatoes in the frypan. Pour in the egg mixture to cover evenly. Cook over low heat for 8 minutes, shaking the pan once the eggs begin to set to prevent sticking. Eggs should be well set, but still somewhat moist. Place a warm plate larger than the frypan over it; holding both together turn over onto the plate (brown side up) and serve, hot, in wedges.

SERVES 4.

Hungarian Potatoes and Sausage

6 medium-sized potatoes

3 large eggs, hard-cooked cut into ¼-inch slices

¾ pound of cooked kielbasa, cut into small cubes

¾ cup of fine bread crumbs

3 tablespoons of butter

WELL BLENDED:

1½ cups of sour cream

½ cup of light cream

1 teaspoon of salt

1 teaspoon of paprika

2 tablespoons of onion juice or minced onion

Boil the potatoes until tender but still firm, drain and dry over heat in a pan. When cool, cut into ¼-inch slices. In a buttered, 2-quart baking dish, arrange one-third of the potatoes in a layer, then a layer of one-half the egg slices, then one of half the sausage. Repeat, spooning one-half of the sour-cream mixture over the second layer of sausage. Arrange a third layer of potatoes on top. Spoon on the remaining sour-cream mixture. Sprinkle with the bread crumbs and dot with the butter. Bake, uncovered in a preheated 350° F. oven for 40 minutes, or until heated through and the top is golden.

SERVES 4.

Irish Breast of Veal with Lemon Potatoes

2 tablespoons of butter

1 medium-sized onion, chopped

½ pound of lean ground chuck

½ pound of mushrooms, chopped

1 (10-ounce) package of frozen chopped spinach, thawed and squeezed dry

1 egg, beaten

½ cup grated Jack cheese

½ teaspoon of basil

½ teaspoon of salt

⅛ teaspoon of pepper

1 breast of veal, boned

1 cup of beef broth (can be made with 1 bouillon cube)

2 onions, cut into chunks

6 medium-sized potatoes, unpeeled and cut into chunks

1 teaspoon of thyme

1 teaspoon of grated lemon rind

Paprika

Lemon slices

In a frypan over medium heat, melt the butter and sauté the chopped onion and chuck for 10 minutes, then transfer to a bowl. In the same pan, cook the mushrooms until moisture evaporates, add to the meat mixture. Repeat the same process for the spinach. Blend in the egg, cheese and seasonings. Taste for seasoning. Lay veal flat and spread stuffing on the center third of the area. Fold over both ends and tie with string. Place in a roasting pan, add the broth, cover pan with lid or foil and bake in a preheated 325° F. oven for 1½ hours. Sprinkle the onion and potato chunks with thyme, lemon rind and paprika. When the veal has baked 1½ hours, remove the foil and baste. Add the onion and potatoes to the roasting pan, stirring to coat with pan drippings. Bake for 45 minutes, or until the veal and potatoes are tender, stirring potatoes occasionally. Serve garnished with lemon slices.

SERVES 6.

Irish Potato Coddle

½ pound of thick-sliced bacon, cut into 2-inch pieces
½ pound of pork sausage links
2 large onions, sliced
4 large potatoes, peeled and sliced
Salt and pepper to taste
3 tablespoons of chopped parsley
2 cups of water

In a frypan, cook the bacon pieces until golden, then drain on paper towels. Prick the sausages in several places and brown evenly in the frypan in the bacon fat. Drain on paper towels and cut into ¼-inch-thick slices. In a casserole, alternate layers of the bacon, sausages, onions and potatoes, seasoning the onions and potatoes lightly with salt and pepper, and sprinkling all layers with parsley. Pour off all but two tablespoons of fat from the bacon-sausage frypan. Add the water and bring to a boil. Pour over the potato casserole, cover and bake in a preheated 350° F. oven for 45 minutes. Remove the cover and cook for 15 minutes, or until the top layer is browned and the potatoes are tender.

SERVES 6.

Jambota

from Barbara M. Valbona

This is an interesting way to dish up leftover meat, poultry, sausage or seafood.

2 tablespoons of butter
1 tablespoon of olive oil
3 garlic cloves, crushed
2 medium-sized white onions, thinly sliced
4 medium-sized potatoes, peeled and sliced medium thick

1 small red pepper, cored and sliced medium thick
1 small green pepper, cored and sliced medium thick
2 cups of chopped leftover meat and/or poultry, sausage, seafood
Salt and pepper to taste

In a frypan over medium heat, heat the butter and oil and sauté the garlic until golden. Discard the garlic. Sauté the onion until golden, then transfer to a bowl. Stir fry the potatoes until golden but still firm and add to the bowl. Stir fry the peppers lightly, place in the bowl. Blend in the leftover meat and/or whatever else you are using, season with salt and pepper. Butter a casserole, spoon in the *jambota* and bake, uncovered, in a preheated 350° F. oven for 15 minutes, or until the potatoes are done but the peppers are still firm.

SERVES 4.

Lancashire Hotpot

Accustomed to eating oysters raw or undercooked, when we first sampled this in the place of its birth we suspected that the oysters would be overdone and unpalatable. No doubt they are cooked; but the addition of the shellfish with the lamb and kidneys lends a surprisingly delicate flavor, lifting the entire dish into a culinary experience. Naturally, the base and the capping of glory are potatoes.

> 7 medium-sized Idaho potatoes, peeled and cut into
> ¼-inch slices
> 1½ pounds of ½-inch slices of lamb, cut from the leg,
> pieces not much larger than the potato slices
> Salt and pepper to taste
> 4 small white onions, thinly sliced
> 4 lamb kidneys, cored, soaked in salt water, rinsed well
> in cold water and thinly sliced
> 12 (or more) oysters
> 1½ cups of beef broth
> 1 tablespoon of melted butter

Butter a 2-quart casserole, layer it with one-half of the potatoes and all of the lamb. Sprinkle lightly with salt and pepper. Arrange a layer of one-half the onions, then the kidneys in one layer. Sprinkle salt and pepper. Layer the oysters, the remaining onions and end with a layer of potatoes, lightly seasoning with salt and pepper. Pour in the beef broth. Dribble the melted butter over the potatoes. Bake, covered, in a preheated 350° F. oven for 1½ hours. Remove the cover and bake for 30 minutes longer, or until the potatoes are crisply brown.

SERVES 6.

Maria Luisa's Timballo

6 medium-sized potatoes
1 cup of flour
1 teaspoon of salt
2 eggs, lightly beaten
4 tablespoons of olive oil
½ pound of mozzarella cheese, thinly sliced
3 tablespoons of butter

Salt and pepper to taste
¼ pound of prosciutto ham, cut julienne
3 tablespoons of grated Parmesan cheese
2 tablespoons of melted butter

Boil the potatoes until barely done, drain and dry over heat in a pot. Peel and cut into ¼-inch slices (slices should be firm). Combine the flour with the salt and place on wax paper. Put the eggs in a shallow bowl. Dredge the potato slices with the flour, then dip into the beaten eggs. In a frypan, heat the olive oil and evenly brown the potato slices, adding more oil as needed. Drain on paper towels. Lightly butter a casserole, and layer the potato slices, covering each layer with cheese, dotting with butter and seasoning with salt and pepper. The top layer should be cheese. Bake, uncovered, in a preheated 375° F. oven for 15 minutes, or until the potatoes are tender and the cheese has melted. Lattice the top with the ham strips, sprinkle with the grated cheese and melted butter. Slip under the broiler for 1 minute and serve immediately.

SERVES 6.

Mariners' "Scalloped" Potatoes

This is a favorite of some who live by or work on the sea. We first had it at the home of a fisherman, captain of his own craft, who did most of his fishing in the area near the Isles of Shoals, 10 miles straight out from the coast of Maine, in the Atlantic. The combination of mealy Maine potatoes and sweet bay scallops out of those cold waters has become an all-time favorite.

Step 1—The Potatoes

8 medium-sized potatoes
6 tablespoons of soft butter
2 large eggs, beaten
Salt and pepper to taste
½ cup of light cream
6 tablespoons of grated Gruyère cheese

Boil the potatoes in their skins until tender, drain and dry over heat in a pan. Peel and put through a potato ricer. (While the potatoes are cooking prepare Steps 2, 3 and 4.) Place the riced potatoes in a bowl. Add the butter, eggs, salt, pepper and cream, beating with an electric beater until smooth and fluffy. Set the potatoes and cheese aside until you are ready to assemble the dish.

Step 2—The Vegetable Mixture

2 tablespoons of butter
¼ cup of minced shallots
¼ cup of chopped celery
½ pound of small fresh mushrooms, thinly sliced
2 tablespoons of chopped parsley
Salt and pepper to taste

In a saucepan, melt the butter and sauté the shallots and celery until soft. Add the mushrooms and cook for 3 minutes. Stir in the parsley, salt and pepper. Set aside.

Step 3—Poaching Scallops

1½ pounds of bay or sea scallops (if sea are used, quarter them)
¾ cup of dry white wine or enough to just cover the scallops for poaching
Pinch of thyme

Place the scallops, wine and thyme in a saucepan and poach at a simmer for 4 minutes. Remove the scallops with a slotted spoon, set aside, reserving ½ cup of the poaching wine for the sauce below.

Step 4—The Sauce

4 tablespoons of butter
4 tablespoons of flour
½ cup of reserved scallop-poaching wine
2½ cups of medium cream
1 teaspoon of Worcestershire sauce
¼ cup of grated Gruyère cheese
Salt and pepper to taste

In a deep saucepan over medium heat, melt the butter, then gradually stir in the flour, stirring constantly until you have a thick, golden paste. Gradually stir in the poaching wine and the cream, continuing to stir until the sauce is medium-thick and smooth. Add the Worcestershire sauce, cheese, salt and pepper, stirring until the cheese has melted. To this sauce, add the poached scallops and the vegetable mixture, blending well. Divide among 6 individual ramekins. Evenly spread equal amounts of the beaten potatoes over the scallop mixture, sprinkling the top of each with 1 tablespoon of Gruyère cheese. Place the ramekins on a cookie sheet in a preheated 400° F. oven for 30 minutes, or until the sauce bubbles. Place under a broiler until the tops are crispy golden.

This may be assembled in one large baking dish but the individual ramekins are more interesting.

SERVES 6.

Potato Meat Loaf

The grated potato not only gives the meat loaf flavor, but makes it go farther, keeps it moist and helps prevent it from falling apart when cut.

2 medium-sized potatoes, grated, kept in cold water to prevent darkening, then well drained before being used

1½ pounds of ground chuck

1 egg, lightly beaten

1½ teaspoons of salt

½ teaspoon of pepper

2 tablespoons of tomato sauce

1 medium-sized onion, chopped and sautéed in butter until soft

1 tablespoon of chopped raisins

3 tablespoons of grated Romano cheese

In a bowl, place all ingredients, blending well. Butter a loaf pan, form the loaf with your hands, then place it in the pan, molding it. Bake, uncovered, in a preheated 375° F. oven for 50 minutes. Test frequently with a toothpick. If it withdraws clean the meat is ready. It is important not to overcook the meat loaf, moistness is part of its appeal.

SERVES 4.

New Zealand Potato-Lamb Pot

This one is simple, quick, inexpensive and tasty—the mark of a perfect meal anywhere.

2 tablespoons of butter
1 tablespoon of olive oil
1 pound of diced lamb shoulder
4 large potatoes (2 pounds), peeled and cut into ½-inch cubes
6 medium-sized white onions, quartered

6 small hard-cooked eggs, peeled and quartered
Salt and pepper to taste
1 (10½-ounce) can of condensed cream of mushroom soup blended with 1 cup of water
⅓ cup of dry bread crumbs

In a saucepan, heat the butter and oil. Brown the diced lamb evenly. Lightly butter a 2-quart casserole and place in it the lamb, potatoes, onions and eggs. Season with salt and pepper. Pour the soup-water blend over the potato-lamb mixture. Sprinkle with the bread crumbs and bake, uncovered, in a preheated 350° F. oven for 30 minutes, or until the top is crusty-brown and the potatoes and lamb are tender. (If the top gets brown before the potatoes and lamb are tender, cover the casserole loosely with foil.)

SERVES 4 TO 6.

No-Tomato, Potato-Shrimp Pizza

6 medium-sized potatoes
2 tablespoons of melted butter
2 tablespoons of butter
1 tablespoon of olive oil
2 medium-sized onions, thinly sliced
2 garlic cloves, thinly sliced
1 green pepper, seeded, cored and cut into ¼-inch strips
Pinch of hot red pepper flakes
Salt and pepper to taste
12 small pitted green olives, halved
1 tablespoon of capers, rinsed and drained
1 pound of medium-sized shrimp (about 32 to the pound), shelled and deveined

Boil the potatoes in their skins until tender, drain and dry in the pan over heat. Peel, mash into a smooth puree and season with salt and pepper. Generously butter a large, very shallow baking dish (one used for a chocolate roll is perfect). Spread the potatoes over the bottom in a ⅜-inch-thick layer (if the potatoes don't cover the entire bottom, don't worry), dribble the melted butter on top and bake in a preheated 425° F. oven for 40 minutes, or until the bottom is crispy and brown and the top golden.

Meanwhile, in a frypan, heat the remaining 2 tablespoons of butter and the oil and cook the onion, garlic and pepper until they are tender-crisp. Stir in the pepper flakes, salt, pepper, olives, capers and shrimp. Cook just until the shrimp turn pink and are firm (but not hard—do not overcook). Spoon the shrimp-vegetable mixture over the baked potato puree and serve.

SERVES 4.

Omelet Antoine-Auguste Parmentier

As lightly touched upon elsewhere, the potato became a favorite food in France through the efforts of one man, Antoine-Auguste Parmentier. He even boldly presented Marie Antoinette with a bouquet of sparkling white potato flowers, and then a eulogy upon the potato that changed France's eating habits. As with "Lyonnaise" being the key to the fact that a dish will be cooked with onions, "Parmentier" signals that potatoes play an important part in a recipe.

Everyone has a favorite way to cook omelets, so we will merely offer our own guideposts on the way to preparing a good omelet. Don't beat the eggs too long, never over 30 seconds; use a fork, not an egg-beater. If overbeaten, eggs become thin and tough when cooked. Don't heat the pan to the point where the butter browns instantly as the omelet probably will stick. Use a good tablespoon of butter and add ½ teaspoon of olive oil to help prevent sticking. For 6 eggs, the omelet pan should be at least 10 inches in diameter, and have sloping, rounded shoulders or edges, permitting the fluid eggs to spread evenly when the pan is tilted, also enabling the finished omelet to slide out easily.

    5 tablespoons of butter
    1 medium-sized potato
    1 tablespoon of chopped broadleaf parsley
    6 eggs
    Salt and pepper to taste
    ½ teaspoon of olive oil

Boil the potato in its skin until tender, drain and dry over heat. Peel and dice. In a saucepan, melt 1 tablespoon of the butter, brown the potatoes evenly, then stir in the parsley. Set aside. Keep warm. In a bowl, break the eggs and beat lightly with a table fork. Cut 3 tablespoons of the butter into small pieces.

Add to the beaten eggs, season with salt and pepper and blend well, without beating. In an omelet pan, over medium-high heat, melt the remaining tablespoon of butter and the olive oil. Pour in the beaten eggs. As the omelet cooks, with the side of a fork, carefully pull the partially cooked thickened edge of the omelet from the sides of the pan, permitting the fluid egg to pass underneath. At this point, spoon the potato-parsley mixture evenly onto the eggs. Cook until the potatoes are set in the eggs and the bottom of the omelet is also set, but the top still moist. Loosen the edges all around with the fork. Hold the omelet pan with both hands, shaking to flip over about one-third of the omelet. If this doesn't work, help the fold along by turning it over carefully with the fork. All the foregoing is done as the omelet cooks.

To serve: Holding the pan and the serving dish at an angle, slide the omelet (only half of it) onto the dish, flipping the remaining half atop. The omelet is now completely folded, classic French style.

SERVES 3.

Variations of Parmentier Omelets

1. Using above technique, add potatoes, in thin round slices, first browned in butter and lightly seasoned with salt, chervil and thyme. When the eggs are being beaten add bits of Emmentaler cheese.

2. To the potato, as it browns in butter, add 2 chopped scallions (all of the white part and some of the green). Stir into the beaten egg mixture in the mixing bowl.

3. To the potato, as it browns in butter, add 2 chopped shallots, cooking until soft. Stir this, plus 1 tablespoon of crumbled Roquefort cheese, into the beaten eggs in the mixing bowl.

These are classic combinations, but you can add anything your imagination dictates. Cook chopped ham with the potatoes or bits of bacon. Potatoes are the base and they meld with about anything, even cottage cheese.

Tip: Instead of placing the mixture onto the cooking omelet as many recipes suggest, we prefer to mix the cooked potato and other ingredients right into the beaten eggs. This can produce an omelet that will stick, so you will have to experiment. Adding butter to the beaten egg, and olive oil to the butter in the omelet pan helps prevent this.

Potato and Bacon Omelet

6 slices of bacon, cut into small pieces
4 medium-sized potatoes, peeled and cut into ¼-inch-thick slices
¼ cup of Swiss chard (do not use stems), cut julienne
8 eggs, *lightly* beaten
1½ teaspoons of salt
½ teaspoon of pepper

In a large frypan, cook the bacon for 4 minutes (pour off and reserve one-half of the bacon fat). Stir in the potatoes, cooking until the potatoes are golden and the bacon bits are crisp. Stir in the Swiss chard and cook for 3 minutes. Remove the bacon, potatoes and chard and set aside. Pour back into the frypan the bacon fat you took out, heat over medium heat until hot. Pour in the eggs, seasoning with salt and pepper. Evenly distribute the potato mixture over the eggs. Lower the heat and cook, without stirring, until the eggs are set on the bottom. Lift the edges so the uncooked part of the eggs flows underneath. When the eggs are set, flip into a fold with a fork and serve immediately while fluffy and hot.

SERVES 4.

Frittata

from Barbara M. Valbona

2 small new potatoes
2 tablespoons of butter
2 tablespoons of olive oil

SLICED IN A
FOOD PROCESSOR
1 small red onion
1 small green pepper
1 small red pepper
1 small zucchini

Salt and fresh ground black pepper
6 to 8 eggs
¼ pound of Parmesan cheese, grated
2 tablespoons of minced parsley
½ cup of minced prosciutto
½ teaspoon of oregano
Dash of Tabasco sauce

Boil the potatoes in their skins until tender but firm. Peel, and when cool, slice. In an ovenproof skillet heat the butter and oil and sauté the vegetables (not the potato) until cooked but not limp. Season with salt and pepper.

Beat the eggs in a bowl with a whisk until fluffy. Add 3 tablespoons of the cheese, parsley, prosciutto, oregano and Tabasco. Add the potatoes to the skillet with the other vegetables to heat. Pour the egg mixture over the vegetables and cook about 1 minute, or until the *frittata* has set. Sprinkle 3 tablespoons of Parmesan on top. Bake in a preheated 350° F. oven until the eggs have set and top is puffed.

SERVES 8.

Italian Mashed-Potato Omelet

2 large potatoes, peeled
and cut into small
pieces

2 cups of milk

1 teaspoon of salt

3 tablespoons of butter

Salt and pepper to taste

6 large eggs

1 medium-sized onion,
minced and cooked in
butter until soft

4 slices of cooked bacon,
drained and cut into
small pieces

3 tablespoons of olive oil

In a saucepan, cover the potatoes with the milk. Add the salt and simmer, covered, until tender. Drain and discard the milk. Place in a bowl, add the butter, salt and pepper, mash well, then whip into a puree. In another bowl, beat the eggs, then stir in the onions and bacon. Add to the potato bowl and blend well. In a large frypan, heat the oil over medium heat. Pour in the potato-egg mixture and cook 2 or 3 minutes, or until the bottom has set, shaking the pan from time to time (use a spatula) to keep the omelet from sticking. Place a large plate, inverted, over the pan. Firmly holding the plate over the pan, invert it, turning the omelet onto the plate, brown side up. Add more oil to the frypan, if necessary, and heat. Then slide the omelet back into the pan (brown side up) and cook until the other side is brown.

Instead of turning the omelet, you may, by using an ovenproof frypan, brown the top under a broiler.

SERVES 4.

Mexican Potato Omelet #1

3 tablespoons of olive oil

2 tablespoons of butter

3 medium-sized potatoes, peeled and cut into small cubes

1 large onion, minced

1 small hot chili pepper, chopped, or ¼ teaspoon of hot red pepper flakes

Salt and pepper to taste

6 eggs

2 tablespoons of cream

In a large frypan, heat the oil and butter. Add the potatoes, onion and chili pepper (or pepper flakes), salt and pepper. Cook over low heat, stirring so that they don't stick, for about 20 minutes, or until the potatoes are tender. Beat the eggs with the cream, salt and pepper and pour them over the potatoes, stirring until they begin to set. Shake the pan occasionally or loosen with a spatula to keep from sticking. Continue to cook about 2 minutes, or until the bottom of the omelet is brown. Lay a plate, larger than the pan, inverted on top of the pan. Firmly holding the plate over the pan, invert it, turning the omelet onto the plate, brown side up. Add more oil to pan, if necessary and heat. Slip the omelet back into the frypan (brown side up) and cook until the other side is brown. This omelet is also delicious served cold.

Instead of turning the omelet, you may, by using an ovenproof frypan, brown the top under a broiler.

SERVES 4.

Mexican Potato Omelet #2

4 tablespoons of olive oil

2 *chorizo* (or Italian) sausages, skinned and chopped

3 medium-sized potatoes, peeled and cut into small cubes

1 medium-sized onion, chopped

6 eggs, lightly beaten

Salt and pepper to taste

2 tablespoons of chopped coriander or parsley

1 teaspoon of chili powder

In a frypan, over medium heat, heat 1 tablespoon of the oil. Add the sausage and cook, stirring, for 5 minutes. Remove with a slotted spoon and set aside. Heat the remaining 3 tablespoons oil and sauté the potatoes and onion until the potatoes are tender. Return the sausage to the pan. Add the eggs, salt and pepper, coriander or parsley and chili powder. Cook, stirring, until the eggs begin to set. Cook about 3 minutes, or until the bottom is golden, shaking the pan or using a spatula to prevent sticking. Turn as for Mexican Potato Omelet #1 (page 141) or place under a broiler until the top is golden.

SERVES 4.

Pasquale's Potato Pie

7 medium-sized potatoes

1 teaspoon of salt

½ teaspoon of pepper

3 tablespoons of butter

4 tablespoons of grated Parmesan cheese

⅛ teaspoon of mace

About 1 cup of medium cream, warm

3 sweet Italian sausages, casings removed

3 hot Italian sausages, casings removed

Boil the potatoes in their skins until tender, drain and dry over heat in a pan. Peel and rice them. In a bowl, place the riced potatoes and with a wire whisk beat in the salt, pepper, butter, cheese and mace and enough cream to make a smooth and fluffy mixture. Taste for seasoning. Break up the sausages and cook in a frypan for 15 minutes. Drain well and mix into the potatoes, blending thoroughly. Lightly butter a deep casserole and fill with the potato mixture, smoothing the top cake-fashion. Bake, uncovered, in a preheated 375° F. oven for 15 minutes, or until the top is crusty brown. We like to serve this with fried zucchini.

SERVES 6.

Potato Pastitsio

The Greek classic of this name is made with pasta, but often potatoes are used. We've tried both; it's a standoff, but this is delicious.

7 medium-sized potatoes	Salt and pepper to taste
1 tablespoon of olive oil	2 eggs, lightly beaten
1 pound of ground chuck	4 tablespoons of finely crumbled feta cheese
2 medium-sized white onions, chopped	⅛ teaspoon of mace
2 tablespoons of tomato sauce	¼ cup of cream beaten with 1 egg
2 tablespoons of white wine	¼ cup of bread crumbs
	2 tablespoons of butter

Boil the potatoes in their skins until tender, drain and dry over heat in a pot. Peel and rice them. In a saucepan, heat the oil over medium heat and brown the meat and onion. Stir in the tomato sauce, wine, salt and pepper. Cover and simmer for 15 minutes. Remove the cover and simmer until all liquid has evaporated. In a bowl, combine the potatoes, eggs, 2 tablespoons of the cheese, mace, salt and pepper. Lightly butter a baking dish, layer it with half of the potatoes and cover with all of the meat. Top, smoothing it cake-fashion, with the remaining potatoes. Pour over the potatoes the cream-egg mixture. Sprinkle with bread crumbs, the remaining cheese and dot with butter. Bake, uncovered, in a preheated 350° F. oven for 25 minutes, or until the cheese is melted and the top brown.

SERVES 6.

Poached Potatoes Abruzzese

South of Rome, the province of Abruzzi is said to produce the best chefs in Italy. Contrary to common belief, Italians do not concentrate solely on pasta; they are also fond of potatoes and were among the first Europeans to use them and cook them imaginatively.

1 pound of dry lentils
3 (1-pound) *cotechino* sausages*
1 large carrot, scraped and chopped
1 large celery rib; scraped and chopped
2 garlic cloves, minced
Pinch of thyme
2 medium-sized onions, chopped

5 tablespoons of olive oil
Salt and pepper to taste
3 cups of chicken broth
4 large potatoes (2 pounds), peeled, cut and trimmed into the size and shape of walnuts
2 tablespoons of chopped broadleaf parsley
1 teaspoon of paprika

Rinse the lentils and soak in cold water for 4 hours, then drain. Simmer the sausages in hot water to cover for 2 hours. Place the lentils in a deep pot with the carrot, celery, garlic, thyme, half of the onions, 3 tablespoons of the olive oil, a good sprinkle of salt and pepper and the chicken broth. Bring to a boil, reduce to a simmer, cover and cook for 20 minutes. Add the potatoes, cover and simmer for 15 minutes, or until the potatoes are tender. Remove the skin from the sausages, cut them into ½-inch-thick slices and

* Large, flavorful (but mild) Italian sausage

add to the potato-lentil pot. In a saucepan, heat the remaining 2 tablespoons olive oil, then add the remaining onions and the parsley. Cook until the onions are soft. Stir in the paprika and blend into the potato-lentil-sausage pot. Simmer, uncovered, for 10 minutes. Taste for seasoning. Serve with plenty of warm, crusty, buttered bread and cold ale.

SERVES 6 TO 8.

Pork Pie with Potato-Cheese Crust

3 tablespoons of butter
2 medium-sized white onions, thinly sliced
5 medium-sized mushrooms, thinly sliced
2 tablespoons of flour
1½ teaspoons of salt
½ teaspoon of pepper
⅛ teaspoon of cayenne

1½ cups of beef broth
2 cups of diced, cooked lean pork

BLENDED WHILE POTATOES ARE HOT
3 cups of mashed potatoes
1½ cups of grated sharp Cheddar cheese

In a saucepan, melt the butter and cook the onion for 5 minutes; add the mushrooms and cook for 2 minutes. Stir in the flour, salt, pepper and cayenne, mixing well. Pour in the broth, a little at a time, stirring and simmering until thickened. Add the pork, blending well. Place in a buttered casserole. Spread and smooth the potato-cheese mixture atop and bake, uncovered, in a preheated 350° F. oven for 25 minutes, or until the top is slightly golden.

SERVES 4.

Quiche Barbara

from Barbara M. Valbona

½ cup of chopped onion
1 cup of thinly sliced
potato
2 tablespoons of butter
½ cup chopped
prosciutto

Salt and pepper to taste
9-inch pie shell (baked 10
minutes at 350° F.)
1 cup of shredded sharp
Cheddar cheese
3 eggs, slightly beaten

1⅓ cups of cream

In a skillet sauté the onion and potato in butter until golden. Add the prosciutto, salt and pepper. Spread the sautéed mixture on the bottom of the pie shell. Crumble the cheese over the above. Mix the eggs and cream and pour over the cheese. Bake in a preheated 375° F. oven for 30 to 35 minutes or until golden.

SERVES 6.

Note: The authors have tasted and cooked quiches with some of the best chefs. However, we nominate Barbara Valbona as Queen of the Quiche Makers. She has the best touch with this tricky dish we have ever encountered. The above is an excellent luncheon or quick supper dish.

Potato Ring

This is a dramatically unique way to serve potatoes and meat as a meal-in-one. Any of the creamed dishes —chicken, veal, dried beef with peas—or stew-type recipes are perfect to offer in the ring.

    5 large potatoes (2½ pounds)
    7 tablespoons of soft butter
    4 eggs, beaten
    ¼ pound of cooked ham, finely chopped
    1 tablespoon of minced parsley
    Salt and pepper to taste
    ½ teaspoon of Dijon mustard
    Bread crumbs (to dust inside of the mold)

Boil the potatoes in their skins until tender, drain and dry over heat in a pot. Peel the potatoes and put them through a potato ricer into a bowl. Beat in 5 tablespoons of the butter, eggs, ham, parsley, salt, pepper and mustard. Butter a 1½-quart ring mold, sprinkle the inside with bread crumbs and invert to remove excess. Evenly spoon in the potato mixture. Dot the top with remaining 2 tablespoons butter and bake, uncovered, in a preheated 350° F. oven for 25 minutes, or until set and golden on top. Invert onto a serving dish.

SERVES 6.

Potato and Rolled Chicken Breast Casserole

4 chicken breast halves,
skinned, boned and
flattened with a mallet
or rolling pin

2 slices of bacon, cut in
half

1 teaspoon of chopped
parsley

½ teaspoon of leaf sage

Salt and pepper

2 tablespoons of butter

2 medium-sized carrots,
scraped and coarsely
grated

1 scallion, trimmed and
chopped

1 pound of Swiss chard,
coarsely chopped (do
not use stems)

2 tablespoons of grated
Parmesan cheese

MIXED WELL WITH AN
ELECTRIC MIXER

3 medium-sized potatoes,
boiled until tender,
drained and dried

2 tablespoons of soft
butter

2 egg yolks

Salt and pepper to taste

Top each breast with a half slice of bacon and sprinkle with some parsley, sage, salt and pepper. Roll up each breast jelly-roll fashion and secure with string or toothpicks. In a heavy frypan, melt 2 tablespoons of butter. Evenly brown the chicken rolls (about 15 minutes). In a heavy saucepan with tight-fitting lid, in 1 inch of salted water, cook the carrots and scallion, covered, for 2 minutes. Add the chard and cook for 4 minutes, or until the vegetables are tender. Drain well and season with salt and pepper. In the bottom of a shallow, 2-quart casserole, arrange chard mixture and spread potato mixture evenly on top. Place chicken rolls on potatoes and sprinkle with Parmesan cheese. Bake, uncovered, in a preheated 375° F. oven 30 minutes, or until the chicken is tender.

SERVES 4.

Potato Roll Dinner

Here's that deliciously different meal-in-one dinner we're all looking for, a guest-grabber that will have you at the typewriter sending out recipes.

2 tablespoons of butter
2 medium-sized white onions, chopped
1 pound of ground lean chuck
½ pound of ground lean pork
2 tablespoons of grated Parmesan cheese
2 tablespoons of minced white raisins

½ teaspoon of oregano
1 teaspoon of salt
½ teaspoon of pepper
½ cup of bread crumbs
1 large egg, lightly beaten
2½ cups of mashed potatoes mixed with cream, butter, salt, pepper and 1 tablespoon of chopped fresh chives

In a saucepan, melt the butter and cook the onion for 5 minutes, or until soft. In a bowl, combine the onion and all of the remaining ingredients except the potatoes, mixing well. Spread out a large piece of wax paper and coat it with oil. Reserve ½ cup of the meat mixture for patching then spread out the remaining meat on the wax paper making a large rectangle about ½ inch thick. Press it into a solid cake. Layer the mashed potatoes on top, smoothing it flat, cake-fashion, with the flat of a knife. Lifting up the wax paper, and using your hands to help shape it, roll up the mixture as tightly as possible (like a chocolate roll), so the potatoes are completely encased. If there are any holes patch with the reserved meat. If not, pat it on the ends of the roll.

Carefully slide the roll off onto a shallow, lightly buttered baking pan, and bake, uncovered, in a preheated 350° F. oven for 1 hour, basting it three times during that period.

We find an electric knife, or a sharp serrated knife is helpful in slicing the roll for serving.

Adding a little flour and some beef broth to the baking pan, make a brown sauce to pass with the roll.

SERVES 6.

Potato-Salmon Custard

2 large potatoes (1 pound)
Salt and pepper to taste
1 (15½-ounce) can of red salmon, drained (reserve 2 tablespoons of the liquid)
3 tablespoons of butter.
1 celery rib, scraped and finely chopped

6 whole scallions, finely chopped
3 large eggs, beaten
2½ cups of light cream
½ teaspoon of dry mustard
1 tablespoon of chopped fresh dill of 1 teaspoon of dillweed

Boil the potatoes in their skins until tender, drain and dry in a pan over heat. Peel the potatoes and cut them into ¼-inch-thick slices. Butter a 1½-quart shallow baking dish and arrange the potato slices in a single layer, overlapping them if necessary. Sprinkle lightly with salt and pepper. Remove the skin and bones from the salmon, flake it with a fork and cover the potatoes with it. In a frypan heat the butter and sauté the celery and one-half of the scallions for 3 minutes, or until just soft. In a bowl, combine the eggs, cream, mustard, dill, salt, pepper, the reserved liquid from the salmon can and the cooked scallions and celery. Mix well. Carefully pour or spoon this mixture over the salmon and bake, uncovered, in a preheated 350° F. oven for 30 minutes, or until set. If the top gets too brown before it sets, cover loosely with foil. Sprinkle the remaining scallions around the edge of the dish and serve.

SERVES 4.

Potatoes with Salt Cod

This Italian dish is often served during the Christmas or Lenten season. Those dried, heavily salted fish you see stacked like cordwood inside, or outside, Italian markets are delicious—if treated properly. Cover the dry cod with cold water and soak overnight, changing the water at least once. Rinse well in fresh cold water and cut into 1-inch pieces. Barely cover with fresh water and poach 10 minutes. Drain.

6 medium-sized potatoes, peeled and thinly sliced
2 medium-sized yellow onions, thinly sliced
2 pounds of salt cod (treated as instructed above)
Pepper
½ cup of heavy cream
1 cup of bread crumbs
2 tablespoons of butter

Butter a casserole and arrange a layer of potatoes, then one of onion, then one of cod, lightly peppering (no salt!) each layer, and ending with a top layer of potatoes. Pour in the cream. Sprinkle with bread crumbs and dot with butter. Bake, uncovered, in a preheated 375° F. oven for 35 minutes, or until the potatoes are tender. There are many versions; some add olives and tomatoes; some soak and poach in milk.

SERVES 4 TO 6.

Sausages in Potato Blankets

This is an excellent supper or luncheon dish with a beet and endive salad.

8 standard-sized (about ¾ inches by 3 inches) breakfast sausages or 8 sausage patties shaped into cylinders the same size

1 small onion, finely minced

3 tablespoons of soft butter

Salt and pepper to taste

1 tablespoon of minced fresh parsley

5 cups of mashed potatoes

Flour for dredging

1 large egg beaten with 1 tablespoon of milk

1½ cups of fine bread crumbs mixed with 1 tablespoon of crushed celery seeds

Fat for deep frying

In a frypan, cook the sausages thoroughly. Drain on paper towels. Pour off all but 1 tablespoon of the fat and cook the onion in the same pan until soft. Combine the onion, butter, salt, pepper and parsley with the mashed potatoes. Cool. Divide the potato mixture into 8 equal parts. Use each part to completely encase one sausage. Dredge the "blankets" with flour. Dip into the egg-milk mixture. Dredge with the breadcrumb mixture and deep fry until golden. Drain on paper towels.

SERVES 4.

Scalloped Potatoes with Ham

This is a favorite American supper dish that pleases just about everyone.

4 tablespoons of butter
3 medium-sized white onions, chopped
4 tablespoons of flour
½ teaspoon of salt
1 teaspoon of celery salt
½ teaspoon of pepper
2 cups of half-and-half

1 cup of grated very sharp cheese (New York State Cheddar is usually used)
6 medium-sized potatoes, peeled and sliced ¼ inch thick
2 cups of diced (or sliced wafer thin) cooked ham

In a saucepan, melt the butter and cook the onion until soft. Stir in the flour, salt, celery salt and pepper, blending thoroughly. Reduce heat to low. Gradually stir in the half-and-half, stirring constantly until the sauce is smooth and thickish. Stir in the cheese, blending well and cook, stirring, until it has melted. Taste for seasoning. Butter a casserole and alternate layers of potatoes, ham and sauce, ending with potatoes covered with sauce. Bake, covered, in a preheated 375° F. oven for 45 minutes. Remove cover and bake for 20 minutes longer, or until the potatoes are tender and the top is golden brown.

SERVES 6.

Note: This can be varied, using leftover meat, chopped or sliced thinly, and with other vegetables such as sliced celery or chopped red or green sweet peppers. But the above is classic.

Shepherd's Pie #1

1 large white onion, minced

3 tablespoons of butter

2 tablespoons of flour

1½ cups of beef broth

4 cups of leftover lamb, beef or veal, cut into small cubes

Dash of Worcestershire sauce

2 tablespoons of minced parsley

Salt and pepper to taste

Pinch of mace

3 cups of mashed potatoes (mashed with cream and butter)

3 tablespoons of grated sharp Cheddar cheese

In a large saucepan, sauté the onion in 2 tablespoons of the butter until soft. Stir in the flour, then gradually add the beef broth. Mix in the meat cubes, Worcestershire sauce, parsley, salt, pepper and mace. Butter a 2-quart casserole. Spoon in the meat mixture, then cover with an even layer of the mashed potatoes. Dot with the remaining tablespoon of butter and sprinkle with the cheese. Bake, uncovered, in a preheated 400° F. oven for 30 minutes, or until heated through and the top is golden.

SERVES 6.

Shepherd's Pie #2

It is believed that the so-called "classic" shepherd's pie was created in Scotland, frugally built around leftover lamb and leftover mashed potatoes. But the French cook it, too. This is their version.

5 medium-sized potatoes
2 tablespoons of butter
3 medium-sized white onions, chopped

GROUND TOGETHER
1 pound of cold boiled beef
4 slices of bacon
1 tablespoon of chopped broadleaf parsley
Salt and pepper to taste

BLENDED INTO A PASTE
2 tablespoons of heavy cream
⅓ cup of bread crumbs
1 small egg, beaten
3 tablespoons of grated Swiss cheese

Boil the potatoes in their skins, drain and dry over heat. Peel and mash with butter and warm milk. Season to taste. In a saucepan, melt the butter and sauté the onion for 5 minutes, but do not let them brown. In a bowl, blend the ground meats and parsley and season with salt and pepper. Beat the bread crumbs–cream paste into the ground meat mixture. Stir it into the saucepan with the onion, mixing well, and simmer for 3 minutes. Remove, cool and blend in the egg. Lightly butter a deep casserole and layer the meat mixture in it. Cover with the mashed potatoes, smoothing the top cake-fashion. Sprinkle with the cheese, and bake, uncovered, in a preheated 400° F. oven for 20 minutes, or until thoroughly heated and golden brown.

SERVES 4.

Potato Stew with Chicken and Shallots

6 tablespoons of butter

1 tablespoon of cooking oil

5 medium-sized potatoes, peeled and cut into 1-inch cubes

12 shallots (or very small white onions), peeled and left whole

Salt and pepper to taste

4 half chicken breasts, boned

½ pound of small mushrooms, cut into halves

1 bay leaf

¼ cup of brandy

2 cups of chicken broth

2 tablespoons of minced parsley

In a frypan, over medium heat, heat 3 tablespoons of the butter and the oil. Add the potatoes and shallots, season with salt and pepper and, stirring, cook for 10 minutes, or until they are golden. Remove with a slotted spoon and arrange in the bottom of a casserole. To the same frypan, add the remaining 3 tablespoons butter, season and brown the chicken breasts on both sides. Remove from the pan and cut into bite-sized pieces. Arrange on top of the potatoes and shallots. Add the mushrooms (without cooking) and bay leaf to the casserole. Pour the brandy into the frypan and simmer to allow most of it to evaporate. Pour in the broth and simmer 1 minute. Add to the casserole. Bake, covered, in a preheated 350° F. oven for 20 minutes. Remove the cover and cook for 15 minutes, or until chicken and potatoes are tender. Sprinkle with the parsley just before serving.

SERVES 4.

Potatoes with Poached Duckling

The French often mate duckling with turnips, which seems an odd couple. But they also pair it with potatoes which seems perfect—and is.

1 (5-pound) duckling, cut into serving pieces

1 large peeled, quartered onion (one-quarter stuck with a whole clove)

3 cups of chicken broth

1 cup of dry white wine

1 teaspoon of salt

½ teaspoon of pepper

2 teaspoons of chopped fresh thyme leaves or ½ teaspoon of dried

4 large celery ribs, scraped and cut into 1-inch pieces

4 medium-sized carrots, scraped and cut into bite-sized pieces

5 medium-sized potatoes, peeled and quartered

Poach the duckling in water to cover, with the onion, for 20 minutes. Drain thoroughly and discard the onion. In a large pot, place the poached duckling and all remaining ingredients except the potatoes. Cover and simmer for 20 minutes. Skim off any surface fat. Add the potatoes, cover and simmer for 30 minutes, or until the duckling and vegetables are tender. Transfer them to a hot bowl and keep hot. Over high heat, reduce the liquid in the pot by two-thirds. Serve on a hot platter, the pieces of duckling centered, surrounded by the vegetables. Spoon the reduced pot liquid over all.

SERVES 4.

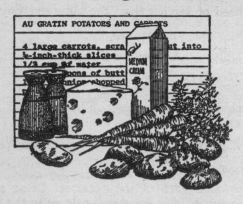

6

Accompaniments

Problem: You've decided to splurge, treat yourself well and have a nice fillet of beef for dinner, invite in a couple of special friends and forget about inflation, the shrinking dollar and the complicated world in general. Concentration is on what wine to serve with the fillet, what different vegetable, and, oh yes, what potato. For fillet and potato go together like bacon and eggs.

Nice mealy baked Idahoes would be O.K., so would hashed browns or steak fries. But that rarely served fillet deserves something a bit more special; so do you.

What about some Potatoes Parma, blended with egg and cheese, served crusty brown in cylindrical shapes? Why not forget about serving another vegetable and combine potatoes and carrots in an interesting way? Or whip up a Potato and Broccoli Puree?

Complicated? Require too much expertise?

Not at all. This chapter is designed to make life easy for people in a potato-rut, structured to assist those tired of serving them the same old way.

Accordion Potatoes

4 large, long baking potatoes, peeled
4 tablespoons of very soft butter mixed with 1
   tablespoon of cooking oil
Salt and pepper

Cut a thin slice from the bottom of the potatoes, lengthwise, so they'll sit up and not roll over. Run a metal skewer, a bit more than halfway down, lengthwise, through each of the potatoes. Using a sharp knife, every ⅛ inch, cut straight down to the skewer, so that you'll have about 20 to 30 deep gashes in each potato. Remove the skewers and rub the potatoes with the butter-oil mixture. Set in a shallow pan and bake in a preheated 375° F. oven for 40 minutes, or until the potatoes are golden and tender, at which time they will have opened like an accordion. Season with salt and pepper and serve immediately while still crisp.

SERVES 4.

Antoine Gilly's Grandmother's Potatoes

3 ounces of larding pork, diced
1 cup of sliced onion
1 garlic clove, peeled
½ cup of tomato sauce
6 tablespoons of dry white wine
Bouquet garni (2 sprigs of parsley, thyme and 1 bay leaf, tied together, if fresh, wrapped in cheesecloth, if dried)

1 teaspoon of salt
½ teaspoon of pepper
1½ pounds of early Rose potatoes, peeled and cut into 1-inch cubes
3 ounces of boiled ham, diced
1 tablespoon of chopped parsley

In a casserole, render the larding pork for 5 minutes to obtain sufficient fat. Add the onion and the garlic, sautéing until soft. Stir in the tomato sauce and wine, then add the *bouquet garni*, salt and pepper. Bring to a boil and stir in the potatoes and ham, keeping on the boil. Cover and cook in a preheated 350° F. oven for 35 minutes, or until the potatoes are tender. Remove the *bouquet garni* and check the seasoning. Sprinkle with the chopped parsley.

SERVES 4.

Potatoes with Anchovy Butter and Spinach

2 (10-ounce) packages of fresh spinach or 2 (10-ounce)
  packages of frozen leaf spinach (if frozen, precook
  only until leaves separate)
4 medium-sized potatoes
6 anchovy fillets, mashed, and mixed with 4 tablespoons
  of butter
Pepper to taste
1 cup of grated Gruyère cheese
3 tablespoons of fine dry bread crumbs
2 tablespoons of butter

If fresh spinach is used, cook each package separately.
Remove tough stems and spoiled parts. Bring 4 quarts
of water to a boil. Add to it 1 package of the spinach,
pushing the spinach down into the water with a large
fork. When the water comes to a boil again, cook the
spinach for 1 minute then remove with a fork and
drain. Using the same water, cook the remaining
package of spinach the same way and thoroughly
drain.

Boil the potatoes in their skins until tender, drain
and dry over heat in a pot. Peel and cut into ¼-inch
slices. Arrange half of the potato slices on the bottom
of a well-buttered shallow baking dish. Dot with half
of the anchovy butter. Sprinkle with pepper. Arrange
half of the spinach over the potatoes and sprinkle
with half of the cheese. Repeat, ending with cheese.
Sprinkle the bread crumbs over the top layer of cheese
and dot with the butter. Bake in a preheated 400° F.
oven for 15 minutes, or until heated through and the
top is golden brown.

SERVES 4 TO 6.

Note: The leafy part of Swiss chard may be substituted for the spinach, but it should be precooked a
few minutes longer.

Aunt Grace's Sticky Potatoes

Shirley Capp (represented elsewhere in this book) says that this is a favorite family recipe, handed down from her aunt, and high on the popularity list with her daughter and son-in-law, Lowell and Tom Judson. The Judsons, in turn, are famous for their farm in Wingdale, New York, and for the high quality potatoes they raise.

    4 medium-sized potatoes
    2 tablespoons of butter
    Salt and pepper to taste
    1½ tablespoons of flour
    1½ cups of milk, heated
    2 tablespoons of chopped broadleaf parsley

Boil the potatoes until tender, drain and dry over heat. Peel and cut into small cubes. In a deep saucepan, melt the butter, add the potatoes, stirring them into the butter. Season with salt and pepper. Sprinkle the flour over the potatoes, and, over low heat, gradually add the milk, stirring all the time, cooking until the milk has been absorbed and the potatoes are "sticky" moist. Taste for seasoning, stir in the parsley and serve very hot. This is excellent with your favorite chopped beef dish.

SERVES 4.

Au Gratin Potatoes and Carrots

4 large carrots, scraped and cut into ¼-inch slices

⅓ cup of water

4 tablespoons of butter

1 small onion, chopped

Pinch of thyme

½ teaspoon of sugar

7 medium-sized potatoes, peeled and cut into ⅛-inch slices

Salt and pepper to taste

1 cup of grated Swiss cheese (reserve ⅓ cup for the top)

2½ cups of medium cream, heated to a simmer

In a saucepan, combine the carrots, water, 2 tablespoons of the butter, onion, thyme and sugar. Simmer, covered, over medium heat for 10 minutes, or until the carrots are almost tender. If the liquid has not cooked off, remove the cover, raise the heat and quickly cook it off. Butter a shallow baking dish. Arrange a layer of potato slices in the bottom, sprinkle with salt and pepper and cheese. Top with a skimpy layer of carrots, and continue making layers until all of the potatoes, carrots and the ⅔ cup of cheese are used. Pour on the hot cream and sprinkle on the reserved ⅓ cup of cheese. Dot with the remaining 2 tablespoons of butter and bake in a preheated 325° F. oven for 30 minutes, or until the potatoes are cooked and the top is golden. If top begins to brown before potatoes are tender, cover loosely with foil.

SERVES 6 TO 8.

Austrian Paprika-Potatoes

6 medium-sized potatoes
(about 2½ pounds)
2 tablespoons of butter
1 tablespoon of olive oil
2 garlic cloves, minced
2 small green peppers,
seeded, cored and
chopped
1 tablespoon of
Hungarian paprika

2 small ripe tomatoes,
peeled, seeded and
chopped
1 teaspoon of salt
½ teaspoon of pepper
½ teaspoon of crushed
caraway seeds
1 cup of chicken broth

Boil the potatoes in their skins until tender, drain and
dry over heat in a pan, then peel. In a deep saucepan,
heat the butter and oil and sauté the garlic for 2 minutes, then add the peppers and cook for 4 minutes.
Stir in the paprika, blending well. Add the tomatoes,
salt, pepper, caraway seeds and chicken broth. Cover
and simmer for 10 minutes. Cut the potatoes into ¼-
inch-thick slices and place in the saucepan with the
sauce. Simmer, uncovered, for 5 minutes, or until the
potatoes are heated through, spooning the sauce over
them as they heat.

SERVES 6.

Potatoes Baked in Ale

3 medium-sized white onions, thinly sliced
Salt and pepper to taste
5 medium-sized potatoes, peeled and thinly sliced
1 cup of ale
3 tablespoons of butter
½ cup of heavy cream

Arrange a layer of onions in a buttered baking dish
and lightly season with salt and pepper. Cover with
a layer of potatoes, seasoning lightly. Repeat, ending
with a layer of potatoes. Pour the ale along the sides
and dot the top with butter. Bake, uncovered, in a

preheated 400° F. oven for 10 minutes. Reduce the heat to 350° F. and cook for 40 minutes longer. Pour the cream over the top and cook for another 10 minutes, or until potatoes are tender. We like these with a cold bottle—of ale, what else—and a hot bird.

SERVES 4.

Bacon-Flavored Roast Potatoes

This simple but delicious dish is a favorite in Maine.

    6 medium-sized potatoes, peeled, cut lengthwise into
        eighths, soaked for 1 hour in ice water, drained and
        dried well between paper towels
    1½ cups of melted bacon fat (butter can be used but
        bacon fat is better)
    Salt to taste

Dip the potatoes in the bacon fat, place in a shallow baking dish in one layer. Cook, uncovered, in a preheated 400° F. oven for 35 minutes, or until delicately browned. Turn them frequently for even browning. Sprinkle lightly with salt before serving.

SERVES 6.

Baked Potato Piroshki

Filling

    3 cups of mashed potatoes
    1 egg, beaten
    Salt and pepper to taste
    2 tablespoons of butter
    4 scallions (using some of the green ends), finely
        chopped
    2 hard-cooked eggs, chopped

In a bowl mix the potatoes with the beaten egg, salt and pepper. In a frypan melt the butter and sauté the scallions for 1 minute (mainly to soften them slightly). Add the scallions and the hard-cooked eggs to the potato mixture and blend well.

Pastry

2 cups of flour
1½ teaspoons of salt
⅓ cup of unsalted butter
⅓ cup of Crisco
½ cup of grated sharp Cheddar cheese
⅓ cup of cold water
1 egg yolk mixed with ¼ cup of milk

In a bowl, combine the flour, salt, butter, Crisco and cheese using a pastry mixer. Add the water and mix throughly with a fork. Divide and roll into 2 balls and wrap in wax paper. Refrigerate until ready to roll out, taking dough out of the refrigerator ½ hour before using.

Roll out as thinly as possible on a floured board. Cut into 3-inch circles. Place a tablespoonful of the filling just off center on each circle, moisten edge, fold over and press edges together with the tines of a fork or a pastry cutter. Brush with the egg yolk-milk mixture, place on a baking sheet and bake in a pre-heated 350° F oven for 20 minutes, or until browned. These make delicious hors d'oeuvres, or if cut larger, they are good served with meat dishes.

MAKES ABOUT 25.

Potato Balls with Curry Sauce

3 cups of plain, unseasoned mashed potatoes
4 scallions (with a small part of the green ends),
  minced
3 eggs, beaten
Salt to taste
¼ teaspoon of chili powder
Vegetable oil for deep frying

Combine all of the above ingredients (except the oil)
and mix well. Heat the oil in a deep fryer. Form balls
1 inch in diameter and drop a few at a time into the
hot oil. Cook until golden, remove with a slotted
spoon and drain on paper towels. Hold in a 250° F.
oven until all are cooked.

Sauce

1 tablespoon of butter
1 tablespoon of vegetable
  oil
1 medium-sized onion,
  chopped
2 teaspoons of curry
  powder
3 large, ripe tomatoes,
  peeled, seeded and
  chopped

1 cup of chicken broth
Salt to taste
¾ cup of yogurt
2 tablespoons of chopped
  fresh coriander or parsley

In a frypan, heat the butter and oil. Add the onion
and cook for 3 minutes, or until soft. Stir in the curry
powder and cook 2 minutes. Add the tomatoes, broth
and salt. Simmer for 15 minutes, or until the sauce
thickens. (This part of the sauce can be prepared
well in advance.) Just before serving, stir in the
yogurt, add the potato balls and heat through. Serve
with the coriander or parsley sprinkled on top.

SERVES 6.

Basil-Baked New Potatoes en Papillote

36 tiny new potatoes
1½ teaspoons of salt
4 tablespoons of butter
4 fresh basil leaves

Carefully scrape (don't peel) the skins off the potatoes. Place them on a large sheet of foil, sprinkle with salt and dot with butter. Bury the basil leaves among the potatoes. Wrap the foil tightly around the potatoes (with the seam on top), completely encasing them. Bake, in a preheated 400° F. oven for 30 minutes, or until the potatoes are tender. We like these potatoes, 6 to a serving, with broiled fresh fish.

SERVES 6.

Belgian Potatoes

5 tablespoons of butter
6 medium-sized potatoes, peeled and quartered
¼ cup of dry white wine
1 medium-sized onion, minced
Salt and pepper to taste
1 tablespoon of chopped fresh chives

In a heavy frypan, melt the butter. Add the potatoes, wine, onion, salt and pepper. Cover with a tight-fitting lid and cook over low heat for 45 minutes, or until the potatoes are tender. If the liquid should cook off before the potatoes are tender, add a few teaspoons of hot water. Sprinkle with the chives before serving.

SERVES 6.

Bogota Potatoes with Tomato-Cheese Sauce

6 medium-sized potatoes	Salt to taste
2 tablespoons of butter	¼ teaspoon of cayenne
1 medium-sized onion, minced	½ teaspoon of turmeric
3 large, ripe but firm tomatoes, peeled, seeded and finely chopped	½ teaspoon of ground cumin seed
	¼ cup of heavy cream
	1 cup of grated Edam or Gouda cheese

1 teaspoon of minced fresh coriander or parsley

Peel the potatoes and boil in salted water until tender. Drain and dry over heat in a pan. While the potatoes are cooking, prepare the sauce. In a large frypan, over medium heat, melt the butter. Add the onion and cook for 2 minutes until soft (do not brown). Stir in the tomatoes, salt, cayenne, turmeric and cumin, cooking until the sauce is smooth and thick. Stir in the cream and cheese and simmer, stirring, until the cheese has melted. Cut the hot potatoes into thick slices and, slightly overlapping, arrange them on a large hot serving dish. Pour the sauce over them and sprinkle with the coriander or parsley.

SERVES 4 TO 6.

Potato-Broccoli Pudding

3 medium-sized potatoes
1 bunch of broccoli (about 1½ pounds)
2 tablespoons of butter
1½ cups of chopped scallions or 2 medium-sized white onions, chopped
2 eggs
1 tablespoon of lemon juice
Salt and pepper to taste
1 cup of grated sharp Cheddar cheese

Boil the potatoes in their skins until tender, drain and dry over heat in a pot. Peel and put them through a potato ricer. Separate the broccoli, peel the stalks and cut into quarters or halves. Cook (florets and stalks), covered, in a small amount of boiling salted water until tender-crisp. Drain well. Melt the butter in a frypan and cook the scallions until soft. Place the eggs, lemon juice, salt and pepper and ½ cup of the cheese in a blender or food processor and process (or blend) for 10 seconds. Add the broccoli, potatoes and scallions and process (or blend) for 15 seconds, or until pureed. Pour into a deep buttered baking dish. Sprinkle the remaining ½ cup cheese on top. Bake in a preheated 350° F. oven for 30 minutes, or until just set and top is golden.

SERVES 4.

Potato-Carrot Fritters

These are an unusual accompaniment for fillets or broiled fish, lifting the meal into a conversation piece.

5 medium-sized potatoes, peeled and cubed
5 medium-sized carrots, scraped and sliced
1½ cups of flour
1½ teaspoons of salt
½ teaspoon of pepper
⅛ teaspoon of mace
⅓ cup of light cream
Vegetable oil

Boil the potatoes and carrots separately in salted water until tender, drain and dry over heat in a pot (reserve ⅓ cup of the cooking water from each). In a pot, mash together the potatoes and carrots, blending them well. With a wire whisk whip in the flour, salt, pepper and mace, gradually adding the reserved potato and carrot liquid. Finally beat in the cream. Place over low heat and cook, stirring constantly, for 6 minutes. Remove from heat. In a frypan, heat ¼ inch of vegetable oil. Using a tablespoon, dip out the potato-carrot mixture and drop into the hot fat. Cook over high heat, flipping the fritters to evenly brown them. Drain on paper towels and serve immediately.

SERVES 6.

Potato-Cauliflower Puree

6 large potatoes (3 pounds)
1 medium-sized head of cauliflower, broken up into
   florets
6 tablespoons of soft butter
Salt and pepper to taste
⅛ teaspoon of mace
About ½ cup of heavy cream
2 tablespoons of chopped parsley

Boil the potatoes in their skins until tender, drain and dry over heat in a pot. Drop the cauliflower into a pan of boiling salted water and cook until tender, about 10 minutes. Drain and dry thoroughly in the pan over heat, being careful not to burn it. Peel the potatoes and put them and the cauliflower through a potato ricer into a large warmed bowl. With an electric beater, beat in the butter, salt, pepper, mace and enough of the heavy cream to make a light, creamy mixture. Cook, stirring, over medium-low heat just enough to heat through. Taste for seasoning. Before serving, lightly sprinkle with the parsley.

SERVES 6 TO 8.

Champagne Potatoes

5 medium-sized potatoes, peeled and thinly sliced
2 medium-sized white onions, peeled and thinly sliced
Salt and pepper to taste
5 tablespoons of butter

3 tablespoons of champagne ⎫
2 tablespoons of heavy cream ⎬ BLENDED

3 tablespoons of bread crumbs
3 tablespoons of grated Parmesan cheese

Butter a 9-inch pie pan. Make a layer of potatoes and onions, interlacing them. Season with salt and pepper and dot with 2 tablespoons of the butter. Make a second layer and pour over the champagne-cream mixture. Sprinkle with salt and pepper, then with the bread crumbs and then with cheese and dot with the remaining 3 tablespoons butter. Bake, uncovered, in a preheated 350° F. oven for 50 minutes, or until the potatoes are tender and the top is golden. If top starts to brown before the potatoes are cooked, cover loosely with foil.

SERVES 4.

Potato Chips

One of the horsey set kept sending his fried potatoes back to the chef in a Saratoga, New York, restaurant, claiming that they were soggy. Finally the chef, an American Indian, became angry. He sliced the potatoes as thinly as he could and deep fried them until they were so crisp that they broke when touched with a fork. The diner was delighted, and thus, years ago, was born an American favorite, originally called "Saratoga Chips."

> 6 medium-sized baking potatoes, peeled and very thinly sliced
> Vegetable oil for frying
> Salt

The key to these chips is slicing them extremely thin, so that they are almost transparent. We use the thin-slicer on the Waring Food Processor, which is perfect. However, there are various kinds of slicers on the market which also thin-slice well. This is a must.

Place the thinly-sliced potatoes in a bowl of ice water for 1 hour. Drain and dry well in a cloth. Cook only one layer at a time, not overcrowding the frying basket, mini-fryer or bottom of the skillet. Potatoes must be completely immersed in the hot fat. Fry only until lightly brown and crisp. Test-fry a batch first. Drain on paper towels and sprinkle with salt. As we all know, these chips are also good cold.

SERVES 6.

Potato Cones with Mushroom Sauce

5 medium-sized potatoes
5 tablespoons of butter
2 egg yolks
Salt and pepper to taste
Pinch of nutmeg
½ cup of fine, dry bread
  crumbs

Paprika
½ pound of fresh mush-
  rooms, thinly sliced
1 teaspoon of cornstarch
1 cup of heavy cream
1 tablespoon of chopped
  fresh parsley

1 teaspoon of lemon juice

Peel the potatoes and boil in salted water until tender.
Drain and dry over heat in a pot, then mash them.
In a bowl, combine the mashed potatoes, 2 tablespoons of the butter, egg yolks, salt, pepper and nutmeg. Mix well. Cool. Make cone-shaped mounds
(about ⅓ cup of the mixture for each), shaping them
with your hands or using a pastry bag, and place them
on a buttered baking sheet. Sprinkle with the bread
crumbs and paprika. Bake in a preheated 400° F. oven
for 15 minutes or until golden.

While the cones bake, make the sauce. In a frypan,
heat the remaining 3 tablespoons butter and sauté
the mushrooms for 3 minutes. Remove them with a
slotted spoon and set aside. Mix the cornstarch with
the cream. Stir it into the pan the mushrooms cooked
in, mixing well. Then return the mushrooms to the
pan, add the parsley, lemon juice, salt and pepper
to taste. Simmer for about 3 minutes, or until the
sauce thickens. Serve the cones on top of the sauce,
giving each guest sauce along with cones.

SERVES 4.

Copenhagen Sugared Potatoes

Here's a favorite of the Danes, often served with their incomparable roast chicken. It has a distinctly different flavor, is quick and will be new to your guests.

16 small new potatoes
2 tablespoons of sugar
4 tablespoons of butter
1 tablespoon of warm water
2 tablespoons of minced parsley

Boil the potatoes in their skins until tender, drain and dry over heat in a pan, then peel. Over medium heat, in a saucepan, lightly brown the sugar. Add the butter and water, blending well. Add the potatoes, turning them to coat evenly, cooking and turning until they are sugar-browned. Sprinkle with the parsley.

SERVES 4.

Cottage Fried Potatoes

The French fried potato doesn't hold all the honors. Potatoes right out of the frypan are an international favorite. For a pleasant taste change, use bacon fat instead of butter and oil.

4 large potatoes
4 tablespoons of butter
1 tablespoon of olive oil
Salt and pepper to taste

Boil the potatoes in their skins until just cooked, drain and dry over heat in a pot. Peel and cut into ½-inch slices. Heat the butter and oil in a large frypan (you may have to have two fryings and more butter and oil) and brown the potatoes evenly, making them as crusty as you like. Season to taste with salt and pepper. Target: They should be soft and mealy inside and crisp on the outside.

SERVES 4.

Creamed Potatoes with Fresh Peas

This is a dish traditionally served with fresh salmon, either poached whole or salmon steaks grilled or sautéed. We also like to serve salmon loaf or salmon patties (made from canned salmon) with these creamy potatoes and sweet peas.

4 medium-sized new potatoes
1 pound of young, fresh peas, shelled (about 1 cup shelled), or 1 cup of frozen tiny peas
1 cup of heavy cream
½ cup of milk
1 teaspoon of salt
½ teaspoon of pepper
⅛ teaspoon of mace
¼ teaspoon of sugar

Boil the potatoes in their skins until tender, drain and dry over heat in a pot. Peel and cut into ¼-inch slices. Cook the peas in boiling salted water until tender and drain thoroughly. If using frozen peas, cook according to package directions. In a saucepan, combine the potatoes, cream and milk. Bring to a boil then reduce to a simmer. Season with salt, pepper and mace. Sprinkle in the sugar and stir without breaking up the potatoes. Simmer for 6 minutes. Add the peas while the potatoes and sauce are still simmering. Taste for seasoning.

SERVES 4.

Curried Potatoes and Peas

6 medium-sized potatoes
2 tablespoons of
   vegetable oil
1 medium-sized onion,
   finely chopped
1 teaspoon of curry
   powder
1 teaspoon of grated
   ginger

BLENDED:
¼ cup of tomato puree
½ cup of hot water
1 (10-ounce) package of
   frozen tiny peas,
   defrosted
Salt to taste
1 cup of yogurt

Boil the potatoes in their skins until tender, drain and dry over heat in a pot. Peel and cut into bite-sized pieces. In a large saucepan, over medium heat, heat the oil and cook the onion for 1 minute, or until it is soft. Stir in the curry powder and ginger. Cook 1 minute. Stir in the tomato puree–water mixture and simmer, uncovered, until it starts to thicken. Add the peas and simmer until the peas are tender-crisp. Add the potatoes, salt and yogurt and cook until heated through.

SERVES 6.

Czechoslovakian Potato Pudding

The Czechoslovakians serve this pudding filled with creamed vegetables, or simply serve it in thick slices as it is. We like the pudding ring filled with a mixture of creamed spinach and mushrooms.

4 large potatoes (2 pounds), peeled and finely grated (a food processor does this well)
2 medium-sized white onions, finely grated
4 eggs, beaten
2 tablespoons of minced parsley
1½ teaspoons of salt
½ teaspoon of pepper
2 tablespoons of melted butter mixed with 1 tablespoon of olive oil

Oil or butter a ring mold large enough to hold all of the ingredients. Place the grated potatoes in a sieve or strainer for 5 minutes to drain excess water. In a large bowl, place the potatoes, onion, eggs, parsley, salt and pepper. Blend well; spoon the mixture evenly into the ring mold. Dribble the melted butter and oil over the top. Place on a baking sheet in a preheated 400° F. oven for 1 hour, or until the top is crusty-gold. Gently loosen the sides with a table knife or spatula; invert on a warm serving platter.

SERVES 6.

Delhi Yogurt-Spiced Potatoes

Historians are still baffled as to how the potato, discovered by the Spaniards in Peru and brought to Europe, managed to get to India. The Indians may have been late in acquiring them, but they are ahead of many of us in their unique ways of cooking.

6 large potatoes (about 3 pounds)
2 tablespoons of butter
1 tablespoon of olive oil
1½ teaspoons of cumin seed
4 small white onions, chopped
½ teaspoon of hot Indian chili powder
Salt to taste
1½ cups of yogurt

Boil the potatoes in their skins until tender, drain and dry over heat in a pot. Peel and cut into ½-inch cubes. In a deep saucepan, heat the butter and oil. Stir in the cumin seed, cooking until they crack and break. Stir in the onion and chili powder. Blend in the potatoes, cooking over low heat, and turning constantly until they are coated. Remove from the heat. Season to taste with salt and blend in the yogurt. The Indians serve these potatoes chilled.

SERVES 6.

Diced Fries

4 tablespoons of butter
½ teaspoon of olive oil
4 medium-sized potatoes, peeled and diced
Salt and pepper to taste
3 tablespoons of bread crumbs (this is a French touch—
the potatoes become *sablées*, if crumbs are added)

Heat the butter and oil in a large frypan, then turn the heat low, add the potatoes, turning several times until they are well coated, season with salt and pepper and cook, turning occasionally with a spatula, until the potatoes are tender. Sprinkle on the crumbs 5 minutes before serving.

SERVES 4.

German Fries

These are also cooked like Cottage Fries (page 175), except minced onions are cooked in the butter and oil first, then the potatoes are added.

Steak Fries

These are cooked like Cottage Fries (page 175), except the potato slices are raw and ¼ inch thick. They are cooked, covered, and turned often with a spatula. Sometimes they are cooked with matching slices of raw onion. The trick here is patience: Fry over medium heat and don't try to rush the job or they'll not cook through.

Fried Potatoes au Gratin

6 tablespoons of butter
2 tablespoons of olive oil
6 medium-sized potatoes, peeled and cut into ¼-inch slices
Salt and pepper to taste
1½ cups of a medium-thick cream sauce mixed with 2 tablespoons of tomato puree
2 medium-sized ripe tomatoes, peeled, seeded, chopped and drained in a sieve for ½ hour
¼ cup of fine bread crumbs
¼ cup of grated Parmesan cheese

In a large frypan, heat 2 tablespoons of the butter and 1 tablespoon of the oil. Fry the potatoes, one layer at a time, until tender and golden on both sides. Add more butter and oil as needed. Drain on paper towels. Arrange the potato slices in a large, shallow baking dish, overlapping the slices if necessary, and sprinkling each layer with salt and pepper. Combine the cream-sauce mixture with the drained tomatoes and spoon over the top layer of the potatoes. Sprinkle with bread crumbs, then with the cheese. Dot with remaining butter. Bake in a preheated 400° F. oven for 25 minutes, or until top is browned.

SERVES 4 TO 6.

Potatoes Frigo

We call these tasty and unique potatoes "Frigo" in honor of David Frigo and his superb cheese shop at 46 Summer Street, Torrington, Connecticut, 06790, where (among other tasty items) we get two important ingredients, Gorgonzola and Asiago cheeses. The Frigo family virtually invented Asiago in Italy's Vicenza. Today, in Torrington they age this cheese for three years until it is golden, hard, nutty and, in our opinion, superior to Parmesan as a grating cheese. We like this with sautéed calf's liver, pink inside.

4 medium-sized baking potatoes
4 tablespoons of butter
⅓ cup of cream
¼ cup of crumbled Gorgonzola cheese
¼ cup of grated Asiago cheese

Boil the potatoes in their skins until tender, drain and dry in a pot over heat. Peel and cut into ½-inch cubes. In a shallow casserole, melt the butter and stir in the potatoes and the cream. Sprinkle with the cheeses. Bake, uncovered, in a preheated 350° F. oven for 15 minutes, or until heated through. Salt and pepper are not needed; the cheeses add the seasoning authority.

SERVES 4.

German Potato Fritters

1 small onion, minced
1 tablespoon of butter
2 cups of mashed potatoes
2 cups of finely chopped cooked leftover beef or lamb
(run it through a meat grinder)
1 egg white, stiffly beaten
Salt and pepper to taste
Vegetable oil

Sauté the onion in the butter and mix it with the potatoes and chopped meat in a bowl. Mix in the egg white, salt and pepper. In a frypan, pour about ¼ inch of oil. Heat. Cook tablespoons of the potato-meat mixture in the oil quickly until evenly browned.

SERVES 4.

Potato-Stuffed Green Peppers

4 medium-sized potatoes
(1½ pounds)
6 fat, firm green peppers
5 tablespoons of butter
1 tablespoon of oil
1 medium-sized onion,
finely chopped
½ teaspoon each of ground
coriander and mustard
seed
½ teaspoon of curry
powder
Salt and pepper to taste
2 teaspoons of lemon juice

Boil the potatoes in their skins until tender, drain and dry over heat in a pan. Peel and cut into ½-inch cubes. Cut a slice off the top of the peppers, trim the tops and finely chop them. Remove the seeds and white ribs from the pepper shells. Parboil the peppers in a large quantity of boiling water for 2 minutes. Drain and cool. In a frypan, heat 4 tablespoons of the butter and the oil over medium heat. Add the onion and chopped pepper tops and cook for 3 minutes. Add the potatoes and cook, turning often, until they are golden (about 6 minutes). Just before the potatocs are completely cooked, stir in the coriander, mustard seed, curry powder, salt and pepper. Stuff the peppers with the potato mixture, place them in a baking dish just large enough to hold them; sprinkle with the lemon juice and dot them with remaining butter. Pour about ¼ inch of water into the dish and bake, uncovered, in a preheated 350° F. oven for 20 minutes, or until heated through and peppers are tender.

SERVES 6.

Hungarian Potatoes and Mushrooms

7 medium-sized potatoes
6 slices of bacon
2 medium-sized onions, finely chopped
½ pound of fresh mushrooms, sliced
1 teaspoon of Hungarian paprika
¾ cup of sour cream
½ cup of cottage cheese
Salt and pepper to taste
2 tablespoons of chopped fresh parsley

Peel the potatoes and boil in salted water until tender but firm. Drain and dry over heat in a pot, then cut into ½-inch cubes. In a saucepan large enough to hold all ingredients, sauté the bacon until crisp. Pour off all but 2 tablespoons of fat. Drain and crumble the bacon and set aside. Add the onion to the saucepan and cook until soft. Add the mushrooms and cook for 2 minutes, or until crunchy-tender. Stir in the paprika, sour cream, cottage cheese, potatoes, bacon, salt and pepper and heat to a simmer. Transfer to a hot serving dish and sprinkle with the parsley.

SERVES 6.

Idahoes Arrabbiata

This is a seat-raiser; Arrabbiata means "raging." If wanted less hot, reduce the amount of red pepper flakes.

    3 tablespoons of butter
    3 tablespoons of olive oil
    2 garlic cloves, minced
    4 medium-sized Idaho potatoes, peeled and thinly sliced
    ½ teaspoon of oregano
    1½ teaspoons of hot red pepper flakes
    Salt to taste

In a large frypan, heat the butter and oil, and sauté the garlic for 1 minute. Add the potatoes, oregano, red pepper flakes and salt. Cook 5 minutes over medium heat, then turn potatoes. Cover and cook 5 minutes. Remove the cover and cook 10 minutes, turning the potatoes so they brown evenly. They should not be too crusty-brown, mealiness is desired, so do not overcook.

SERVES 4.

Indian Spiced Potatoes with Yogurt

    6 medium-sized potatoes
    ⅛ teaspoon of ground
      coriander
    ¼ teaspoon of black
      pepper
    1 teaspoon of cumin
    ¼ teaspoon of ground
      cardamom

    2 tablespoons of water
    1 small dry green or red
      pepper, crushed
    Salt to taste
    1 tablespoon of vegetable
      oil
    2 tablespoons of lemon juice
    ¾ cup of yogurt

Boil the potatoes in their skins until tender, drain and dry over heat in a pot. Peel and dice them. Combine the spices with the water, crushed pepper and salt, blending well. In a large frypan heat the oil. Add the spice mixture, lemon juice and potatoes. Cook until all are well blended. Remove the frypan from the fire and stir in the yogurt. Taste for seasoning, adding more salt, if necessary.

SERVES 4 TO 6.

Inca Spicy Potatoes with Cheese and Tomato

Peru's Incas were the first to cultivate potatoes in their Andes stronghold. They have various imaginative ways to serve them. This is one of our favorites.

6 large potatoes (about 3 pounds)
1 tablespoon of butter
1 tablespoon of olive oil
10 scallions (use half of the green tops cut into ½-inch lengths), chopped
4 ripe tomatoes, peeled, seeded and chopped

¼ teaspoon of ground cumin
¼ teaspoon of black pepper
1 teaspoon of salt
½ teaspoon of ground coriander
1 cup of grated Swiss cheese (Peruvians use *queso blanco*, but any mild white cheese will do)

Boil the potatoes in their skins until tender, drain and dry over heat in a pan. Set aside the unpeeled potatoes and keep warm. In a saucepan, heat the butter and oil and sauté the scallions for 3 minutes (they should be crisp). Stir in the tomatoes, cumin, pepper, salt and coriander, and simmer for 10 minutes. Add the cheese, stirring, until the cheese has melted. Peel the warm potatoes and quarter them. Spoon the spicy tomato-cheese sauce, very hot, over the potatoes.

SERVES 6.

Potato Kreplach

Filling

2 small onions, minced
1 tablespoon of butter
3 cups of mashed potatoes
½ cup of cottage cheese
1 egg yolk
1 tablespoon of chopped fresh dill or 1 teaspoon of
    dillweed
Salt and pepper to taste

In a frypan, over medium heat, cook the onion in the
butter until soft (do not brown it). Remove from
heat, cool slightly and stir in the potatoes, cottage
cheese, egg yolk, dill, salt and pepper.

Dough

2 cups of flour
2 medium-sized eggs
1½ teaspoons of salt
Warm water

Mound the flour on a pastry board and make a well
in the center. Break the eggs into the well, add the
salt and 2 tablespoons of water. Mix thoroughly and
knead into a smooth, firm dough, adding small
amounts of water, if too firm, or flour, if too soft.
Divide into two parts and allow the dough to rest for
½ hour, covered with a bowl. Roll the dough on a
floured board into ⅛-inch-thick sheets (or thinner).
Cut into 3-inch circles. Place a tablespoon of the
filling just off center in each. Moisten edges, fold
over and press edges together to seal. Cook in gently
boiling water, covered (as you do noodles). When
they rise to the top (about 7 minutes), they are
ready. Drain, then either brown them in butter or
serve with melted butter poured over. You can also

serve them with sour cream, or cooked in rich chicken broth and served as a soup with parsley sprinkled over the top.

MAKES ABOUT 25.

Potato and Leek Casserole

We like this with roast leg of lamb.

4 medium-sized potatoes, peeled and cut into ¼-inch slices
1½ cups of light cream
1 teaspoon of salt
3 large leeks (white part only), thinly sliced
Salt and pepper
⅓ cup of bread crumbs
3 tablespoons of butter

In a saucepan, place the potatoes, cream and salt; cover and simmer for 10 minutes until the potatoes are almost tender, just partially cooked. Shake the pan occasionally to keep the potatoes from sticking and scorching. Drain. Lightly butter a casserole and arrange layers of the potatoes and leeks, lightly seasoning each layer, and ending with a layer of potatoes. Sprinkle with bread crumbs and dot with the butter. Bake, uncovered, in a preheated 375° F. oven for 25 minutes, or until the potatoes and leeks are tender and the top is browned.

SERVES 4.

Lemon Dill Potatoes

2 pounds of very small new potatoes
3 tablespoons of butter
3 tablespoons of flour
1 cup of milk
1 cup of medium cream
2 tablespoons of strained lemon juice
Salt and pepper to taste
2 tablespoons of chopped fresh dill

Boil the potatoes in their skins until tender, drain and dry over heat in a pan. Make the sauce while the potatoes are cooking. In a saucepan, over medium heat, melt the butter. Add the flour and cook, stirring, until you have a smooth paste. Gradually add the milk and cream, stirring constantly until you have a smooth, medium-thick sauce. Stir in the lemon juice, salt and pepper. Peel the potatoes while they are still warm. Pour the sauce over them, sprinkle on the fresh dill.

SERVES 6.

Lleela's Potatoes and Yogurt

18 to 24 small new potatoes
2 tablespoons of vegetable oil
3 tablespoons of finely chopped green pepper
1 large garlic clove, minced
½ teaspoon of turmeric
½ teaspoon of cumin
¼ teaspoon of mace
Salt to taste
1 cup of yogurt
1 tablespoon of currants, cooked in oil until puffed and golden
2 tablespoons of coarsely chopped cashew nuts, cooked in oil until golden and crisp
2 tablespoons of chopped fresh coriander or parsley

Boil the potatoes in their skins until tender, drain and dry over heat in a pan. In a large saucepan, heat the oil and sauté the pepper and garlic for 1 minute. Stir in the turmeric, cumin and mace. Cook 1 minute. Stir in the potatoes and salt and cook 5 minutes to heat through. Stir in the yogurt and simmer 2 or 3 minutes. Just before serving, stir in the currants, cashews and coriander or parsley.

SERVES 6.

Lleela's Madras Potato-Onion-Tomato Mix

3 tablespoons of
  vegetable oil
2 medium-sized onions,
  chopped
1 garlic clove, chopped
6 medium-sized potatoes,
  peeled and cut into
  bite-sized pieces
3 medium-sized ripe,
  firm tomatoes, peeled,
  seeded and chopped

Salt to taste
Pinch of hot red pepper
  flakes
½ teaspoon of ground
  coriander
½ teaspoon of turmeric
1 teaspoon of mustard
  seeds
2 tablespoons of chopped
  fresh coriander or parsley

In a large saucepan, over medium heat, heat 2 tablespoons of the oil. Add the onion and garlic and cook for 3 minutes, or until soft. Add the potatoes, tomatoes, salt, red pepper flakes, ground coriander and turmeric. Simmer, covered, about 20 minutes, or until the potatoes are tender and the sauce has thickened. If the potatoes seem to become tender before the sauce thickens, remove the cover, raise the heat and cook off excess liquid. In a small frypan, heat the remaining 1 tablespoon oil. Add the mustard seeds and cook them until they pop. Stir them into the potato pan. Serve sprinkled with the coriander or parsley.

SERVES 4 TO 6.

Potatoes Madeira

This is a dish we enjoyed on the Portuguese island of Madeira, served with fresh mackerel cooked in tomato sauce. The flavor and the scent of the potatoes is unique, and is not the same if boiled with dry oregano.

8 medium-small new potatoes (2 per serving)
1 large bunch of fresh oregano
Salt and pepper
4 tablespoons of butter or more

In a pot, cover the potatoes and fresh oregano with water. Bring to a boil and cook until tender. Discard the oregano. Drain the potatoes and dry them over heat. Serve them in their skins, split, seasoned with salt and pepper and drenched with butter.

SERVES 4.

Maine Potato Dumplings

1 cup of mashed potatoes
1 cup of all-purpose flour
1½ teaspoons of salt
3 egg yolks, beaten

In a bowl, mix all ingredients thoroughly. Using a tablespoon, shape into balls the size preferred. Drop into boiling salted water and cook 10 minutes. Drain and serve with meat stew, the gravy spooned over the dumplings.

About 16 small dumplings.

Mashed Potatoes with Scallions

6 medium-sized potatoes
1 cup of minced scallions (use some of the green ends)
6 tablespoons of butter at room temperature
¼ teaspoon of nutmeg
Salt and pepper to taste
¾ cup of cream, heated

Peel the potatoes and boil in salted water until tender. Drain and dry over heat in a pot. Sauté the scallions in 1 tablespoon of the butter for 1 minute. Put the potatoes through a potato ricer into a large bowl. Mix in the remaining 5 tablespoons of butter, scallions, nutmeg, salt, pepper and enough cream to make the mixture light but not soupy. Whip well.

SERVES 4.

Mock Pomme Soufflé

Batter

1 cup of flour
1 teaspoon of baking powder
1 teaspoon of salt
½ teaspoon of pepper
½ cup of vegetable oil
1 cup of milk
2 egg yolks, lightly beaten
2 egg whites, stiffly beaten

Sift the flour, baking powder, salt and pepper into a bowl. Make a well in the center, add the oil and mix well. Pour in the milk and beaten egg yolks. Beat until smooth. Gently fold in the egg whites.

5 medium-sized potatoes, peeled and cut into ½-inch slices

1 cup of flour seasoned with 1½ teaspoons of salt, ½ teaspoon of pepper and ¼ teaspoon of dried oregano
Vegetable oil for deep frying

Cook the potato slices in boiling salted water for about 15 minutes. They should not be cooked through but should still hold their original shape. Drain and thoroughly dry over heat. Dredge the potato slices in the seasoned flour, then dip into the batter. Deep fry in the hot oil without crowding, until golden brown. Keep cooked potatoes warm in a 250° F. oven while the others are frying.

SERVES 4 TO 6.

Potato and Mushroom Bake

6 medium-sized potatoes, peeled and cut into ⅛-inch slices
½ pound of mushrooms, cut into ¼-inch slices and tossed with 1 tablespoon of flour
2 small white onions, finely chopped
3 tablespoons of finely chopped parsley
1 cup of grated Swiss cheese (reserve ¼ cup to sprinkle on top)
Salt and pepper to taste
1½ cups of medium cream
2 tablespoons of butter

Butter a shallow baking dish. Arrange a layer of potato slices, a layer of mushrooms, then a sprinkling of onion. Sprinkle the onion with some of the parsley and cheese, salt and pepper. Repeat the layers, making the top layer potatoes. Pour on the cream, sprinkle with the ¼ cup of cheese and dot with the butter. Bake in a preheated 325° F. oven for 45 minutes, or until the potatoes are tender and the top is golden. If top should brown before the potatoes are cooked, cover loosely with foil.

SERVES 4 TO 6.

New Potatoes, Swiss Chard and Chick-Peas

16 tiny new potatoes
¾ pound of Swiss chard,
  coarsely chopped (first
  remove the coarse
  middle rib)
1 cup of chicken broth
2 tablespoons of butter
1 medium-sized onion,
  chopped
1 garlic clove, minced

3 large, ripe tomatoes,
  peeled, seeded and
  chopped
Pinch of hot red pepper
  flakes
Pinch of oregano
1 teaspoon of sugar
Salt to taste
1 cup of cooked chick-peas
  (canned are good)

½ cup of grated Asiago or Parmesan cheese

Boil the potatoes in their skins until tender, drain and
dry over heat in a pot. Cook the Swiss chard in the
chicken broth until tender. Drain, saving the broth
and reserving the chard. In a large frypan heat the
butter and cook the onion and garlic for about 2
minutes, or until soft. Add the broth the chard cooked
in, tomatoes, pepper flakes, oregano, sugar and salt.
Simmer, uncovered, for 15 minutes, or until the sauce
has thickened. While the sauce simmers, remove a
band of skin from the center third of the potatoes,
leaving the skin on both ends. Stir in the potatoes,
chard and the chick peas and simmer 5 minutes, or
until heated through. Pass the cheese at the table.

SERVES 4.

Paprika-Cream Potatoes

6 tablespoons of butter

1 tablespoon of oil

6 medium-sized potatoes, peeled and cut into ¾-inch cubes

2 scallions (use a small part of the green end), finely chopped

Salt to taste

1 cup of sour cream
¼ cup of medium cream } BLENDED
1 teaspoon of paprika

In a large frypan, over medium heat, heat the butter and oil. Add the potatoes and salt, and cook, covered, for 15 minutes, or until tender and golden. As the potatoes cook, shake the pan often to prevent them from sticking. Stir in the scallions and cook one minute. Add the sour cream–cream–paprika mixture and blend well, but carefully. Heat to a simmer.

SERVES 4 TO 6.

Potatoes Parma

5 medium-sized potatoes

7 tablespoons of butter

Salt and pepper to taste

Pinch of nutmeg

2 tablespoon of minced fresh chives

½ cup of grated Asiago, Parmesan or any cheese of your choice

1 whole egg

Flour for dredging

2 eggs, beaten (for dipping)

Fine bread crumbs for dredging

1 tablespoon of olive oil

Peel the potatoes and boil in salted water until tender. Drain and dry over heat in a pot. Put the potatoes through a potato ricer into the pan they cooked in. Place on low heat to further dry out. Remove from heat and beat in 4 tablespoons of the butter, salt, pepper, nutmeg, chives, cheese, then the whole egg. When the mixture is cool enough to handle, form cylinders 2 inches long by 1 inch in diameter (oiling the palms of the hands makes this job easier). Dust the potato cylinders lightly with flour, dip into the beaten eggs, roll in bread crumbs and brown evenly in the remaining butter and the oil, adding more butter and oil if needed.

SERVES 4 TO 6.

Parmesan Potatoes

The Italians, probably the first Europeans to take the potato seriously, bring their unique imagination and flavoring techniques squarely to bear with the *patata* that they place next only to pasta. The Italians like these potatoes with their tender young roast lamb, delicately scented with rosemary.

6 medium-sized potatoes
4 tablespoons of butter
1 tablespoon of olive oil
1½ teaspoons of finely crumbled dry leaf sage
1 cup of grated Parmesan cheese
Salt to taste
¼ teaspoon of hot red pepper flakes

Peel the potatoes and cut into wedges. Boil in salted water until tender but still quite firm (what the Italians call *al dente*). Drain, dry over heat in a pot and keep warm. In a large frypan, heat the butter and oil; stir in the sage and sauté over medium heat until the butter is light brown. Add the potatoes, sprinkle in the cheese, salt and pepper flakes, turning the potatoes several times until they are well coated.

SERVES 6.

Peruvian Potatoes

6 large potatoes (about 3 pounds)
1 cup of olive oil
2 white onions, minced
1 teaspoon of salt
¼ teaspoon of black pepper
⅛ teaspoon of cayenne
½ cup of fresh lime juice

Boil the potatoes in their skins until tender. Drain, dry over heat in a pan, then peel. Put the potatoes through a potato ricer into a bowl and puree with an electric beater or a food processor. In another bowl, place the oil, onion, salt, pepper, cayenne and lime juice, blending well. Beat this sauce, gradually, a tablespoon at a time, into the potato puree, until the combination is right for your taste. In Peru these potatoes are topped with another sauce made of strips of red and green chilies (very hot to the tongue), sliced red onions, cooked in water until boiling, then drained with white vinegar, olive oil, to cover, added, plus salt and pepper. This is simmered for about 8 minutes, then the chili-onion mixture is poured over the sauced mashed potatoes where they are centered in a warm serving dish. The spicy potatoes are then surrounded by a garnish of cooked vegetables and fish. Use your own combinations. We like the spiced potatoes with the onion–lime juice sauce as is, and serve them with rare roast beef.

SERVES 6.

Potatoes with Pizzaiola Sauce

6 medium-sized potatoes

3 tablespoons of olive oil

1 garlic clove, chopped

1 small onion, chopped

1 tablespoon *each* of chopped fresh oregano and basil or 1 teaspoon *each* of dried oregano and basil

6 large ripe tomatoes, peeled, seeded and chopped, or 1 (1-pound, 12-ounce) can of Italian tomatoes, chopped

⅛ teaspoon of hot red pepper flakes

¼ cup of dry red wine

Salt to taste

8 tablespoons (1 stick) of butter

2 tablespoons of chopped broadleaf parsley

Boil the potatoes in their skins until tender, drain and dry over heat in a pot. Peel and cut into ½-inch slices. In a large deep frypan, heat 2 tablespoons of the oil and sauté the garlic and onion until soft. Stir in the oregano, basil, tomatoes, red pepper flakes, wine and salt. Simmer, uncovered, for 15 minutes, or until the sauce thickens. Meanwhile, heat 3 tablespoons of the butter and the remaining tablespoon of oil in a frypan and quickly brown the potato slices, a layer at a time, on both sides. Add more butter as it is needed. As the potatoes are browned, transfer them to the tomato sauce pan. When all have been browned and added, mix them gently but well with the tomato sauce. Simmer together for 2 minutes. Taste for seasoning. Serve on a hot serving dish with parsley sprinkled on top.

SERVES 6.

Polish Potatoes for Game Dishes

As the title indicates, the Poles use this unique preparation with duck, venison, rabbit and other kinds of game. We also serve them with roast veal.

7 medium-sized baking potatoes	1 tablespoon of chopped fresh dill
4 tablespoons of butter	1 generous tablespoon of capers, rinsed, dried and chopped
6 anchovies, drained, dried and chopped	
1 tablespoon of chopped broadleaf parsley	½ teaspoon of pepper
	½ cup of beef broth

Salt to taste

Boil the potatoes in skins until slightly undercooked, drain, dry over heat, peel and cut into ¼-inch slices. In a large frypan, melt the butter and add the potatoes. Cook over medium heat, turning with a spatula, until the potatoes are tender and golden. In a bowl, combine the anchovies, parsley, dill, capers, pepper and beef broth, blending well. Stir this into the potatoes, being careful not to break up the slices. Taste for seasoning, adding salt, if necessary. Heat through and serve hot.

SERVES 6.

Potato Ragout

This is a tasty potato stew, which comes in several versions in France. We like it with a veal or a pork chop.

8 slices of bacon, cut crosswise into ¼-inch strips
4 white onions, chopped
5 medium-sized round potatoes, peeled and cut into
   1-inch cubes
1 garlic clove, chopped
¼ teaspoon of oregano
¾ cup of beef broth
2 teaspoons of cider vinegar
Salt and pepper to taste

In a saucepan, sauté the bacon until golden. Pour off all but 3 tablespoons of fat. Add the onion to the saucepan and cook for 1½ minutes. Stir in the potatoes, garlic and oregano and cook for 1 minute. Add the broth, vinegar, salt and pepper. Cover and simmer for 15 minutes, or until the potatoes are tender and have absorbed the liquid. If potatoes become tender before liquid is absorbed, remove the cover, raise the heat and cook it off quickly.

SERVES 4.

Red Potatoes with Quick Hollandaise Sauce

Hollandaise Sauce

3 large egg yolks
2 tablespoons of lemon juice
½ teaspoon of salt
Dash of cayenne
8 tablespoons (1 stick) of butter, melted but not hot

Place the egg yolks, lemon juice, salt and cayenne in a blender container. Run on high for a few seconds, then switch off. Turn the blender on high again, and slowly pour in the melted butter. Taste for seasoning, then blend on high for another second or two.

18 to 24 small Red new potatoes
½ teaspoon of white pepper
4 tablespoons of butter, melted
4 tablespoons of minced parsley

Boil the potatoes in their skins until tender, drain and dry over heat in a pot. Remove a band of skin from the center third of the potatoes leaving skin on both ends. Season with the pepper, dip in the butter and roll in the parsley. Serve with the hollandaise sauce spooned atop.

SERVES 6.

Potatoes with Ricotta Cheese

6 medium-sized potatoes
4 tablespoons of butter
Salt and pepper to taste
2 tablespoons of chopped parsley
1 cup of slivers of cooked ham

BLENDED UNTIL SMOOTH:
2 cups of ricotta
1 egg yolk
¼ cup of cream
1 teaspoon of sugar
¼ teaspoon of cinnamon

Boil the potatoes in their skins until tender, drain and dry over heat in a pot. Peel and cut into ½-inch cubes. In a large bowl mix the potatoes while still warm with the butter, salt and pepper. Blend in the ricotta mixture, parsley and ham. Spoon into a buttered, shallow baking dish and bake in a preheated 400° F. oven for 20 minutes, or until heated through.

SERVES 4 TO 6.

Potatoes with Salt Pork

¼ pound of salt pork, cut into ¼-inch cubes
1 medium-sized onion, coarsely chopped
6 medium-sized potatoes, peeled and cut into ½-inch
    cubes
2 teaspoons of flour
Pinch of tarragon
Salt (optional) and pepper to taste
1 cup of chicken broth
2 tablespoons of chopped fresh parsley

In a large frypan, over medium heat, cook the salt
pork for 5 minutes, or until it is transparent. Pour off
all but 3 tablespoons of fat (if the salt pork does not
render that amount, add butter). Add the onion and
cook for 3 minutes, or until soft. Add the potatoes,
sprinkle them with the flour, tarragon, salt and pepper
and cook, stirring, for 3 minutes. Pour in the broth,
cover and cook over low heat for 20 minutes, or until
the potatoes are tender. If sauce becomes too thick
before the potatoes are tender, add small amounts of
hot broth. Sprinkle with the parsley before serving.

SERVES 4 TO 6.

Shirley Capp's au Gratin Potatoes

This is a respected dish around the Wingdale-Pawling area of New York State; Wingdale is where Mrs. Howard (Shirley) Capp has her famous game-bird farm "Birdcliff." Although we are very aware that Shirley Capp is the best of cooks, and are old friends, having bought her superb game birds for years, we first heard of her famous dish from a renowned restaurateur, Ralph Guidetti, chef and owner of that excellent inn, "Guidetti's," in Wingdale.

4 medium-sized potatoes
1 tablespoon of butter
1 tablespoon of flour
1 cup of milk
¼ pound of sharp
   Cheddar cheese, grated

Salt to taste
About ⅛ teaspoon of
   cayenne
Cream (optional)
⅓ cup of bread crumbs

Shirley says that the texture of the potatoes has a great deal to do with how much sauce is needed. If the potatoes are sticky, more is needed.

Peel the potatoes and boil in salted water until tender but not too soft. Drain, dry over heat in a pot and cool. Mince the potatoes and place in a shallow baking dish. In a saucepan, melt the butter, stir in the flour, blending until smooth, then add the milk, a little at a time, stirring so it does not lump. Add three-fourths of the cheese, seasoning with salt and cayenne to taste, stirring and simmering into a smooth sauce. Pour over the potatoes and mix in. If too thick, add a small amount of cream. Sprinkle with the remaining cheese and bread crumbs and bake in a preheated 375° F. oven for 35 minutes or until brown and bubbly.

SERVES 4.

Shirley Capp's Potatoes, Beans and Bacon

You must have your own garden, or know a gardener, for this recipe; the potatoes must be new ones, smaller than walnuts, and the green string beans baby ones, twice the thickness of match sticks.

6 slices of bacon
24 tiny new potatoes
1 pound of baby green beans
Salt and pepper to taste

In a large frypan or saucepan, fry the bacon until crisp, drain on paper towel and break it into ¼-inch pieces. Set aside. Wash the new potatoes well, leaving most of the moisture on them. Place the potatoes in the pan with the bacon fat, cover and cook for 5 minutes. Rinse the green beans, leaving most of the moisture on them and add them to the pan. Cover and cook over medium heat until both are tender and the beans still slightly crisp. If they don't have enough moisture to cook until tender, add small amounts of hot water. Before serving, stir in the bacon and cook, covered, for 2 minutes.

SERVES 4.

Shoestring Potatoes and Vermicelli

This may seem an unlikely combination, but we've enjoyed it several times in Rome. The potatoes are crisp in contrast to the pasta—the result delicious.

4 medium-sized potatoes, peeled and cut julienne
Vegetable oil for deep frying
12 ounces of vermicelli
8 tablespoons (1 stick) of butter, cut into small pieces
1 cup of grated Parmesan cheese
Freshly ground black pepper
Salt to taste

Deep fry the potatoes, a few at a time, in the vegetable oil until golden and crisp, drain on paper towels and keep warm in a 250° F. oven while the others are frying and the pasta is cooking. Cook the pasta in a deep pot of boiling, salted water until it is *al dente*, not soft but slightly resistant to the tooth. Drain and toss with the butter, cheese and a generous grinding of pepper. Sprinkle the potatoes lightly with salt, add them to the pasta and toss gently but thoroughly.

SERVES 6.

Potatoes with Small Pasta Shells

3 tablespoons of olive oil
1 large onion, coarsely chopped
1 garlic clove, minced
6 medium-sized potatoes, peeled and cut into ¾-inch cubes
1 (1-pound, 12-ounce) can of tomatoes

Pinch of cinnamon
½ teaspoon of dried basil
Salt and pepper to taste
½ pound of small pasta shells (maruzzini)
2 tablespoons of chopped fresh parsley
Grated Asiago or Parmesan cheese

In a large saucepan, over medium heat, heat the oil. Add the onion and garlic and cook until the onion is transparent. Add the potatoes and sauté for 10 minutes, stirring. Put the tomatoes into a bowl and break them up. Add the tomatoes, cinnamon, basil, salt and pepper to the potato pan and simmer, uncovered, for 20 minutes, or until the sauce thickens and the potatoes are tender. Meanwhile cook the pasta shells in boiling salted water. Drain well and add to the potato-tomato mixture. Simmer for 5 minutes, stir in the parsley and serve, passing the cheese at the table.

SERVES 6 TO 8.

Sour German Potatoes

7 medium-sized potatoes	Pepper to taste
4 slices of lean bacon, cut into ¼-inch squares	2½ cups of beef broth
1 large onion, chopped	3 tablespoons of white vinegar
3 tablespoons of flour	Salt (optional)
½ teaspoon of celery salt	2 tablespoons of chopped parsley
Pinch of thyme	

Peel the potatoes and boil in salted water until tender. Drain, dry over heat in a pot and cut into ¼-inch slices. In a saucepan, over medium heat, cook the bacon until it is golden. Add the onion and cook until transparent. Stir in the flour and cook over low heat, stirring constantly, until it is golden. Add celery salt, thyme and pepper. Slowly stir in the beef broth and cook, stirring, until the sauce is smooth and thickens. Add the vinegar and simmer, covered, for 7 minutes (if sauce gets too thick, add more broth). Taste for seasoning and add salt, if necessary. Add the potatoes to the sauce, mix well but carefully and heat to a simmer. Sprinkle with the parsley.

SERVES 6.

Spanish Garlic Potatoes

2 tablespoons of olive oil
2 tablespoons of butter
3 garlic cloves, minced
4 large potatoes, peeled and cut into ¼-inch slices
1 tablespoon of chopped chives
½ teaspoon of savory

1 cup of baby lima beans, fresh or frozen (if frozen, defrost but do not cook)
1 teaspoon of salt
½ teaspoon of pepper
¾ cup of hot chicken broth
3 tablespoons of finely chopped broadleaf parsley

In a large flameproof baking dish or casserole that will take the potatoes in one overlapping layer, heat the oil and butter and cook the garlic about 1 minute (do not brown it). Arrange the potatoes in one layer over the garlic, overlapping if necessary. Sprinkle with the chives and savory. Distribute the limas over the potatoes, sprinkle with salt and pepper and pour the broth around the edge of the vegetables. Cover tightly and bake in a preheated 325° F. oven for 45 minutes, or until the potatoes and beans are tender. Sprinkle with parsley before serving.

SERVES 4 TO 6.

Spanish Parsley Potatoes

3 tablespoons of butter
1 tablespoon of olive oil
1 medium-sized onion, chopped
1 medium-sized carrot, scraped and chopped
1 small green pepper, seeded, cored and chopped

6 medium-sized potatoes, peeled and cut into ½-inch cubes
Salt and pepper to taste
Pinch of saffron
Pinch of oregano
1 small bay leaf
¾ cup of chopped fresh broadleaf parsley

1 cup of chicken broth mixed with ½ cup of dry white wine

In a large frypan or saucepan, over medium heat, heat the butter and oil. Add the onion, carrot and green pepper and cook for 2 minutes, or until the onion is transparent. Add the potatoes, salt, pepper, saffron, oregano, bay leaf and parsley and cook for 2 minutes, stirring. Pour in enough of the broth-wine mixture to not quite cover the potatoes. Cover the pan and simmer for 15 minutes (shaking the pan occasionally), or until the potatoes are almost tender but still firm. Remove the cover and the bay leaf, raise the heat and cook off the excess liquid.

SERVES 4 TO 6.

Spicy Pakistani Potatoes

6 medium-sized potatoes	Pinch of turmeric
1 tablespoon of cooking oil	¼ teaspoon *each* of ground coriander, cumin, black pepper and cardamom
½ teaspoon of mustard seeds	Tiny pinch *each* of cinnamon, cloves, nutmeg and chili powder
1 green chili, seeded and chopped	2 tablespoons of lime juice
1 small white onion, finely chopped	2 tablespoons of chopped fresh mint or parsley
½ teaspoon of salt	

Boil the potatoes in their skins until tender, drain and dry over heat in a pot. Peel and put through a ricer. In a saucepan, heat the oil and cook the mustard seeds until they pop. Add the green chili and onion and cook for 2 minutes, or until they are soft. Add the salt and spices, mixing well. Stir in the lime juice, then the potatoes. Blend well and heat through. Taste for seasoning. Serve sprinkled with the mint or parsley.

Pass a bowl of curds or yogurt at the table as the Pakistanis do to cool this a bit.

SERVES 6.

Potatoes and Spinach Cochin Style

6 medium-sized potatoes

2 (10-ounce) packages
of fresh spinach or 2
(10-ounce) packages
of frozen chopped
spinach, cooked
according to package
directions

2 tablespoons of
vegetable oil

2 medium-sized onions,
chopped

1 teaspoon of grated
fresh ginger

Crushed red pepper flakes
to taste

Pinch of cinnamon

¼ teaspoon of ground
cardamom

Salt to taste

2 tablespoons of water

¾ cup of yogurt

1 teaspoon of chopped
fresh mint

2 tablespoons of lime juice

Boil the potatoes until tender, peel and cut into bite-sized pieces. If fresh spinach is used, cook each package separately. Remove tough stems and spoiled parts. Bring 4 quarts of water to a boil. Add one package of the spinach, pushing the spinach down into the water with a large fork. When water comes to a boil again, cook the spinach for 1 minute then remove with a fork and drain. Using the same water, cook the remaining package of spinach the same way. Thoroughly drain, then chop the spinach. Set it aside. In a large saucepan, over medium heat, heat the oil. Add the onion and ginger and cook for 3 minutes, or until the onion is tender. Stir in the pepper flakes, cinnamon, cardamom and potatoes. Sprinkle with salt, and add the 2 tablespoons of water and 2 tablespoons of the yogurt. Cook for 5 minutes, turning. Stir in the chopped spinach and cook for 2 minutes, or until the spinach is heated through. Stir in the remaining yogurt, mint and lime juice. Bring to a simmer and serve.

SERVES 6.

Steamed Potatoes with Caraway Seeds

24 to 36 tiny new potatoes (depending on size)
6 tablespoons of butter
1 small onion, minced
2 tablespoons of caraway seeds
Salt and pepper to taste
Paprika

Peel the potatoes and steam until tender but firm. Heat 2 tablespoons of the butter in a frypan. Add the onion and cook until soft but not brown. Stir in the potatoes, caraway seeds, salt, pepper and the remaining 4 tablespoons butter. Sprinkle lightly with paprika and sauté, turning, until the potatoes are slightly golden.

SERVES 6.

Stuffed Potato "Chops"

This is an impressive combination with a beef fillet. We also like it with a scallopini of chicken.

7 medium-sized potatoes
9 tablespoons of butter
Salt and pepper to taste
¼ teaspoon of nutmeg
2 tablespoons of chopped shallots
½ pound of chicken livers, coarsely chopped
3 medium-sized fresh mushrooms, chopped
Pinch of leaf sage
2 tablespoons of Marsala
2 teaspoons of flour
1 whole egg and 1 egg yolk, beaten
1 tablespoon of oil
Flour for dredging
1 egg, beaten, for dipping
Bread crumbs for dredging

Peel the potatoes and cook until tender in salted water. Drain and dry over heat in a pot. Mash with 4 tablespoons of the butter, salt and pepper to taste and the nutmeg. In a frypan, over medium heat, heat

2 tablespoons of the butter. Add the shallots and cook for 3 minutes, or until soft. Stir in the livers, mushrooms and sage and sauté until the livers are brown outside but pink inside. Stir in the Marsala, flour, salt and pepper. Raise the heat and cook quickly until the liquid has evaporated. Set aside and cool.

Beat the egg and egg yolk into the potatoes. Cool thoroughly. Lightly flour your fingers and make 12 chop-shaped patties about ½ inch thick and lay them on a lightly floured board or wax paper. Place one-sixth of the liver stuffing in the center of each of 6 of the "chops" and flatten it a bit. Lay another chop on top and press the edges together to seal in the stuffing. Cool.

When ready to cook, heat the remaining 3 tablespoons of butter and the oil in a frypan. Dredge the stuffed chops lightly in flour, dip in the beaten egg, then dredge with bread crumbs and evenly brown on both sides, adding more butter and oil, if needed.

SERVES 6.

Swedish Anchovy Potatoes

9 medium-sized potatoes (about 3½ pounds), peeled and cut into long thin strips
4 medium-sized white onions, thinly sliced
2 (2-ounce) cans of flat anchovy fillets, drained
½ teaspoon of pepper
1½ cups of medium cream
2 tablespoons of unsalted butter

Lightly butter a large baking dish and place a layer of potato strips, then one of onions. Spread half the anchovies over the onions and sprinkle with pepper. Repeat, ending with a layer of potatoes. Pour in 1 cup of the cream and dot with butter. Bake, uncovered, in a preheated 375° F. oven for 35 minutes. Add the remaining ½ cup of cream and cook for 10 minutes longer, or until the casserole bubbles and the potatoes are tender.

SERVES 6 TO 8.

Swiss Potato Balls

These are excellent served with just about anything and especially with cocktails if the balls are made bite-sized.

4 medium-sized potatoes	Salt and pepper to taste
4 tablespoons of soft butter	¼ pound of Gruyère cheese, cut into ½-inch cubes
2 large eggs, each egg beaten separately	Flour for dredging
Pinch of mace	Bread crumbs for dredging

Vegetable oil for deep frying

Boil the potatoes in their skins until tender, drain and dry over heat in a pan. Peel and while still hot, put through a potato ricer. Blend in the butter. Cool slightly and add one of the beaten eggs, mace, salt and pepper. Shape into balls the size of ping-pong balls (or smaller). Push a cube of cheese into the center and reshape the ball to completely encase the cheese. Roll the balls in flour, then dip into the remaining beaten egg. Coat well with bread crumbs and deep fry, without crowding, until golden. Drain on paper towels and keep warm in a 250° F. oven until all are cooked.

SERVES 4.

Swiss Potato Torte

Here's a simple but dramatic potato torte we had
served with roast veal in Geneva, Switzerland.

2 cups of shredded Swiss cheese
4 tablespoons of butter, cut into small pieces
1½ teaspoons of salt
½ teaspoon of pepper
⅛ teaspoon of dried marjoram
6 medium-sized potatoes (2 pounds), peeled and
  thinly sliced

Blend the cheese, butter, salt, pepper and marjoram.
Butter a 2-quart casserole. Place a thin layer of sliced
potatoes in the casserole, sprinkle lightly with the
cheese mixture. Keeping the layers thin (don't over-
lap the potatoes—the idea is to arrange as many
layers as possible), repeat the procedure, ending with
the cheese mixture. In a preheated 400° F. oven, bake,
covered, for 1 hour and 15 minutes, or until the potatoes are tender. Let the casserole stand, out of the
oven, for 10 minutes, or until all of the moisture is
absorbed. With a table knife or spatula, gently loosen
the potatoes from the bottom and sides of the casserole. Invert onto a serving plate and cut into wedges
at the table.

SERVES 4 TO 6.

Potatoes with Three Cheeses

For people who like potatoes *and* cheese, this is their dish.

   6 medium-sized potatoes
   4 tablespoons of soft butter
   ¼ pound of mozzarella cheese, cut into shreds
   ¼ pound of Gouda cheese, cut into shreds
   Freshly ground black pepper
   Salt (optional)
   ½ cup of grated Asiago or Parmesan cheese mixed
      with ½ cup of fine bread crumbs
   2 tablespoons of melted butter

Boil the potatoes in their skins until tender but still quite firm. Drain and dry over heat in a pot. While still warm, peel and cube them. In a large bowl, combine the potatoes, soft butter, mozzarella, and Gouda cheeses and a generous grinding of black pepper. Mix well, taste and add salt if necessary. Spoon into a large shallow baking dish. Sprinkle the top with the grated cheese–bread crumbs mixture. Dribble the melted butter over the top and bake in a preheated 450° F. oven for 10 minutes, or until the top is golden.

SERVES 6.

Tiny New Potatoes alla Ralph Guidetti

Over Wingdale, New York, way is a superb country restaurant, "Guidetti's," created and conducted in the now rare old Continental fashion. The owner, Ralph, is the chef; the efficient maître d' and overseer of customer contentment is B. J., the owner's attractive wife; the warm, intimate bar with the well-tended fireplace is majordomoed by skillful and friendly Jack Engstrom; the alert and effective waitresses, Betsy and Pat and waiter Randy are all friends of the owners and everyone else. Friendly is the wrap-up word for "Guidetti's"—and, incredibly, the food cannot be faulted. Ralph Guidetti is lucky. B. J. proves that. But also nearby are his friends, Lowell and Tom Judson, and their farm, where Guidetti goes when potatoes are being harvested and selects the finest of the smallest new potatoes he can find. In season, some lucky customers get them piping hot from the frypan with their drinks at the bar, then get a repeat later with dinner.

24 new potatoes, not larger than walnuts, washed but
   not dried, with some moisture left on them
4 tablespoons of olive oil
5 garlic cloves, peeled (do not cut up)
Salt and pepper
2 tablespoons of chopped broadleaf parsley

In a large frypan, over low heat, cook the wet potatoes, tightly covered, for 10 minutes, shaking the pan often to keep the potatoes from sticking (their moisture should help, but shake anyway). Add the olive oil and garlic, then sprinkle with salt and pepper to taste. Cover again and cook over low heat for another 20 minutes, or until the potatoes are tender. Continue shaking the pan. Sprinkle with the parsley. These are a delight; soft inside, golden skinned, and they are good with anything from a martini to a mackerel. We like them with Guidetti's wonderful striped bass.

SERVES 4.

Potato-Turnip Bake

This is a unique dish probably none of your guests will have had. Such is the personality of the potato that it can even hold its own with the authoritative turnip. We like this with a roast loin of pork.

5 medium-sized potatoes, peeled and thinly sliced
3 small turnips, peeled and thinly sliced
6 tablespoons of butter
1½ teaspoons of salt
½ teaspoon of pepper
1 cup of grated Asiago or Parmesan cheese
⅛ teaspoon of mace
¾ cup of chicken broth

Butter a baking dish or casserole. Arrange alternating layers of potato and turnip slices until half of them are used, dotting each layer with butter and seasoning with salt and pepper. Add half of the cheese, sprinkling it on evenly, then season with the mace. Continue layering, ending with potato. Sprinkle with the remaining cheese and dot with butter. Pour the chicken broth around the edge of the vegetables. Bake, uncovered, in a preheated 375° F. oven for 45 minutes, or until the top is brown and bubbling and vegetables are tender.

SERVES 4.

Turkish Potato Balls

6 medium-sized potatoes
3 tablespoons of butter
2 tablespoons of yogurt
¼ teaspoon of oregano
½ teaspoon of Lawry's
    seasoned salt
⅛ teaspoon of cayenne

2 tablespoons of fine dry
    toasted bread crumbs
1 whole egg and 1 egg yolk,
    beaten together
1 egg, beaten, for dipping
Bread crumbs for dredging
1 tablespoon of flour

Vegetable oil for deep frying

Boil the potatoes in their skins until tender, drain and
dry over heat in a pot, then peel. Mash the potatoes
while still hot with the butter, yogurt, oregano, seasoned salt, cayenne, flour and bread crumbs. When
slightly cooled, beat in the egg and yolk. Taste for
seasoning. Shape into balls the size of ping-pong balls.
Dip them in the beaten egg, then dredge with bread
crumbs and deep fry until golden. Drain on paper
towels and hold those that are fried in a 250° F. oven
while others are cooking. Serve while still crisp.

SERVES 4 TO 6.

Potato-Turnip Custard

3 large potatoes, peeled and diced
1 pound of turnips, peeled and diced
3 eggs
1½ cups of hot milk
2 tablespoons of melted butter
2 tablespoons of grated onion
Salt and pepper to taste

Cook the potatoes and turnips separately in boiling
salted water. Drain and dry over heat. Mash and mix
together. Cool slightly. In a large bowl beat the eggs.
Stir in the potato-turnip mash, the milk, butter, onion,
salt and pepper. Pour into a shallow baking dish. Set

the dish in a pan of hot water and bake in a preheated 350° F. oven for 30 minutes, or until set. Do not overcook.

SERVES 4 TO 6.

Potatoes with Vegetable Sauce

4 tablespoons of butter

1 tablespoon of olive oil

4 large potatoes, peeled and cut into ½-inch cubes

Salt and pepper to taste

1 small onion, chopped

1 garlic clove, chopped

1 small green pepper, seeded, cored and cut into thin strips

2 medium-sized ripe tomatoes, peeled, seeded and diced

½ teaspoon of sugar

½ cup of cut-up green beans

1 small zucchini, cubed (about 1 cup)

1 teaspoon of chili powder

Heat 2 tablespoons of the butter and the oil in a fry-pan over medium heat. Add the potatoes and sauté slowly, turning occasionally, until tender and golden. Season with salt and pepper. Set aside and keep warm.

In a saucepan melt the remaining 2 tablespoons of the butter and sauté the onion, garlic and green pepper for 2 minutes. Add the tomatoes, sugar and green beans and cook until the beans are crunchy-tender and the sauce has thickened. Stir in the zucchini, chili powder, salt and pepper and cook just until the zucchini is crunchy-tender. Transfer the hot potatoes to a warm serving dish and spoon the vegetable sauce over them.

SERVES 6.

Vernon Jarratt's Ciapotta

This from our friend, who owns Rome's famous "George's" restaurant. Mr. Jarratt remarks that this is a good dish if you and your guests are late in getting to the table, for it can be kept hot without any loss of flavor. We serve it with broiled fat sausages and a glass of ale.

5 medium-sized potatoes, peeled and cut into ¼-inch slices
4 tablespoons of butter
Salt and pepper to taste
5 medium-sized ripe tomatoes, peeled and cut into ¼-inch slices
4 white onions, thinly sliced and separated into rings

In a large casserole, layer the bottom with potato slices, dot with butter and season with salt and pepper. Arrange a layer of tomatoes and one of onion rings, dotting with butter and seasoning with salt and pepper. Continue the layering, buttering and seasoning, ending with buttered potatoes. Bake, uncovered, in a preheated 375° F. oven for 45 minutes, or until the potatoes are tender.

SERVES 4 TO 6.

Viennese Mustard Potatoes

7 medium-sized potatoes
6 tablespoons of butter
2 medium-sized white onions, chopped
3 tablespoons of flour
1½ cups of chicken broth
1 teaspoon of salt
½ teaspoon of pepper
¼ cup of Dijon-style mustard
¼ cup of bread crumbs

Boil the potatoes in their skins until tender, drain and dry over heat in a pan. Cut into ½-inch slices. In a saucepan, melt 3 tablespoons of the butter and sauté the onion until soft. Stir in the flour, mixing well. Add the broth, a little at a time, stirring. Season with salt and pepper. Bring to a boil, lower heat and simmer for 5 minutes. Stir in the mustard, blending well. Taste for seasoning. Butter a large baking dish and arrange the potato slices, overlapping, in a single layer. Pour the sauce evenly over the potatoes, sprinkle with the bread crumbs and dot with the remaining 3 tablespoons of the butter. Bake, uncovered, in a preheated 375° F. oven for 15 minutes, or until the sauce is bubbling and the potatoes are heated through.

SERVES 6.

Potatoes "Vol-au-Vent"

These are excellent served at a luncheon or a supper with an omelet or a piece of broiled fish.

6 uniform, long baking
  potatoes, peeled
3 tablespoons of melted
  butter mixed with 2
  tablespoons of oil
3 tablespoons of butter
¼ cup of chopped
  shallots
6 medium-sized
  mushrooms, coarsely
  chopped

1 tablespoon of flour
Pinch of cayenne
1 cup of heavy cream
1 cup of coarsely chopped
  cooked ham
Salt to taste
¼ cup of grated cheese
  (your choice)

Scoop out the inside of the potatoes lengthwise, leaving a ½-inch shell (a melon ball cutter is good for this). Cook the potato shells in boiling, salted water for 10 minutes. Drain and dry out in the pan over heat. Rub the outside with the butter-oil mixture and bake, hollow side down, in a preheated 425° F. oven for 20 minutes, or until golden and tender when pricked with the point of a knife.

While the potatoes are baking, make the filling. In

a frypan, over medium heat, melt the 3 tablespoons
of butter. Add the shallots and cook for 3 minutes,
or until soft. Add the mushrooms, cook 3 minutes,
then sprinkle in the flour and cayenne and mix well.
Slowly stir in the cream and cook until the sauce is
thick. Stir in the ham. Taste and add salt, if needed.

Fill the baked potato shells with the mushroom-
ham filling. Sprinkle the top with grated cheese and
lightly brown under the broiler.

SERVES 6.

Wyoming Camp Potatoes

In Wyoming thick beefsteaks are offered with these
potatoes.

5 slices of bacon
5 medium-sized potatoes, peeled and cut into ¼-inch
    slices
2 medium-sized white onions, sliced medium thick
1 (16-ounce) can of stewed tomatoes, chopped
1 teaspoon of salt
½ teaspoon of pepper
½ teaspoon of sugar
1 teaspoon of Dijon-style mustard

In a frypan, fry the bacon until crisp, remove, drain,
break into bits and reserve. Add the potatoes and
onion to the bacon fat, and cook for 10 minutes, turning frequently with a spatula. Add the tomatoes, salt,
pepper, sugar and mustard. Simmer for about 20
minutes until the sauce is thickish and the potatoes
are tender. Taste for seasoning. Sprinkle the bacon
over the top and serve very hot.

SERVES 4.

7

POMMES MARQUERITE   Serves 4

5 medium-sized potatoes, ——ed,
   quartered
1 teaspoon of
1 garlic clov
5 table   c
1/4 p
1 egg

Classics

Exactly what is a classic? The dictionary tells us that it means the first rank of Greek and Roman authors— Pliny, Socrates, Aristotle, et al.

In food it also refers to the highest rank. But classic also means "refined," and "famous."

The recipes that follow are certainly refined, in the best sense of the word. As dishes of the highest rank, they also are so famous that they have stayed with us for many years, with chefs of various countries and various times "refining" them.

Consequently, this is the "confident" chapter, one you can refer to and feel at ease with. Some of these recipes will be old friends because use and years have made them familiar. But they may have a new look; for example, there are a number of ways to prepare mashed potatoes (yes, they are classic), and each has its own name and own style. Here are French fries, also classic, and even, surprise, the humble Potatoes O'Brien, so well liked and respected in a number of countries outside of Ireland, its birthplace, that perforce it is a classic. And so is that American standby, Hashed Brown.

But there will be surprises here too. Classic ones. Read on!

Potatoes Anna
(Pommes Anna)

6 medium-sized potatoes (2 pounds), peeled
1½ sticks of butter, melted
Salt and pepper

Cut the potatoes into ⅛-inch slices. Place them in cold water for 3 hours. Drain and dry the potatoes with a cloth towel. Butter generously a deep glass or Pyrex casserole, 8 inches in diameter. Line the bottom of the casserole with a circular layer of overlapping potato slices; do the same on the sides forming a shell. Then layer remaining slices (they need not be so carefully arranged), spooning a little melted butter over each. Lightly salt and pepper each layer. The potatoes will come above the slices arranged on the sides of the casserole, but will settle as they cook. Bake, uncovered, in a preheated 400° F. oven for 1¼ hours, or until the potatoes are tender and the slices lining the dish are very brown. (You will be able to see this through the glass dish.) Remove from the oven and let rest for 10 minutes. Loosen the sides with a knife and invert onto a hot serving dish. It will look like a golden cake.

SERVES 4.

Berrichonne Potatoes

6 medium-sized potatoes,
    peeled and cut into
    balls with a melon
    scoop
5 tablespoons of butter
Salt
4 slices of bacon
2 medium-sized onions,
    chopped

⅛ teaspoon of dried
    tarragon
⅛ teaspoon of dried thyme
⅛ teaspoon of dried chervil
1 teaspoon of chopped
    fresh parsley

Parboil the potato balls in salted water for 7 minutes,
drain and dry them. In a large frypan, melt the butter
and sauté the potatoes until they are golden, shaking
the pan often so they do not stick. Salt lightly. In
another frypan cook the bacon until crisp. Drain, dice
and reserve. Discard two-thirds of the bacon fat and
sauté the onions until soft in the remainder. Put the
potato balls on a warm serving platter and sprinkle
them with the onions, bacon and herbs.

SERVES 6.

Château Potatoes

6 medium-sized baking potatoes
1 teaspoon of salt
8 tablespoons (1 stick) of butter, melted

Peel the potatoes and quarter them. Trim the sharp
edges so they look like small eggs. In a saucepan,
cover the potatoes with cold water, add the salt and
bring to a boil. Remove and drain then dry in the
pan over heat. Place the potatoes in a shallow, buttered baking dish and baste them with the melted
butter. Bake in a preheated 400° F. oven for 15 minutes, turn, then cook for another 15 minutes, or until
tender and browned.

SERVES 6.

Potatoes Chantilly

½ cup of heavy cream, stiffly whipped
1 teaspoon of salt
⅓ cup of grated Emmentaler cheese
2½ cups of mashed potatoes

Blend the whipped cream, salt and cheese. Evenly mound the mashed potatoes in a baking dish, masking it with the whipped cream mixture. Bake, uncovered, in a preheated 400° F. oven until the cheese melts and the potato mound is golden brown.

SERVES 4.

Potato-Chestnut Game Bird Puree

This French classic is usually served with game birds. We like it with roast baby pheasants.

1 pound of chestnuts
3 cups of beef broth
3 cloves of garlic, unpeeled
3 cups of freshly cooked mashed potatoes

6 tablespoons of butter
½ to ¾ cup of cream
1 teaspoon of salt
⅛ teaspoon of mace
4 shallots, chopped

Slash the chestnuts in one or two places and roast them on a tin in a preheated 425° F. oven for 8 minutes, or until the hulls crack. When cool enough to handle, peel off the outer shell and the inner layer of skin. In a saucepan, place the chestnuts, broth and garlic. Cover and simmer for 25 minutes, or until the nuts are tender and easily pierced with a fork. Drain them (discard the garlic) and push them through a sieve, or puree them in a food processor or blender. In a pot, place the chestnut puree, and beat in the potatoes, 5 tablespoons of the butter, ½ cup of cream, salt and mace. Add more cream and butter if mixture seems too heavy. Taste for seasoning. Sauté the shallots in the remaining tablespoon of the butter for 3 minutes, or until soft. Heat the puree over low heat, stirring, until heated through. Blend in the shallots. Serve immediately.

SERVES 6.

Potatoes and Chicken Romano

This is an Italian classic, nearly always paired with baked chicken, so we include that recipe.

Baked Chicken

6 chicken thighs	1 teaspoon of dried oregano
6 chicken drumsticks	1½ teaspoons of salt
5 tablespoons of olive oil	½ teaspoon of pepper
2 garlic cloves, halved	1 cup of fine bread crumbs
2 tablespoons of chopped broadleaf parsley, or 1 teaspoon of dried basil	Paprika

In a bowl, place all ingredients except the bread crumbs and paprika. With your hands, toss the chicken with the mixture, coating it well. Marinate for 2 hours.

Potatoes

6 medium-sized potatoes, peeled, quartered lengthwise and dried

On wax paper, spread the bread crumbs and dredge the chicken. Place in a large baking dish and sprinkle with paprika. In the bowl in which the chicken marinated, place the potatoes, tossing them well and coating them with the oil mixture in the bottom of the bowl. Place them around the chicken. Bake, uncovered, in a preheated 400° F. oven for 20 minutes. Turn the potatoes and cook for another 20 minutes.

SERVES 6.

Pommes Cocotte, Parisienne and Noisette

These classic little potatoes are almost a duplicate of another classic, *Rissolé*, so check that recipe for amounts and procedure (page 248). The difference is that *Rissolé* are boiled before browning in butter and *Cocotte, Parisienne* and *Noisette* are not. The *Cocotte* are sautéed raw in butter until golden. Classically, they are also shaped like olives, and are sometimes referred to as "olive potatoes."

Parisienne are a perfect small ball shape (as are *Rissolé*), are sautéed raw in butter and sprinkled with chopped parsley before serving. Sometimes the French sauté them in beef drippings.

Noisette are very small potato balls, the size of hazelnuts. They are also sautéed raw in butter, with much shaking of the pan.

The French insist that all three of these classics must be sautéed in "clarified" butter. Fine. But we do them in butter, period, and they are excellent— golden, soft and delicious.

Creamed Potatoes

This is a simple but delicious French classic.

    2 teaspoons of buttermilk
    2 cups of heavy cream
    4 large potatoes
    1½ teaspoons of salt
    ⅛ teaspoon of mace

The French heavy cream, *crème fraîche*, is almost twice as heavy as our heavy cream, due to the fact that it is aged and slightly fermented. We can almost duplicate it by adding 2 teaspoons of buttermilk to 2 cups of heavy cream, heating it until warm, then letting it stand at room temperature until it is very thick.

Boil the potatoes in their skins until tender but firm, drain and dry over heat in a pot. Peel the potatoes and cut into ¼-inch slices. Transfer the potatoes to a baking dish or casserole. Cover with the cream, then season with salt and mace. Bring to a boil on top of the stove, then bake, uncovered, in a preheated 300° F. oven just until the potatoes have absorbed most of the cream. Watch them carefully so the cream isn't absorbed too quickly and the potatoes burned. The French add more warm *crème fraîche* just before serving, but we like them as they come from the oven.

SERVES 4.

Potatoes Dauphine

6 tablespoons of butter
1 cup of water
1½ teaspoons of salt
1¼ cups of sifted all-purpose flour
4 large eggs
4 cups of mashed potatoes, seasoned with salt to taste
    and ½ teaspoon of mace
Vegetable oil for deep frying

In a deep saucepan, combine the butter, water and salt. Bring to boil and quickly stir in all of the flour. Reduce the heat to low and cook, stirring, for 2 minutes, or until the contents of the pan form a ball, pulling away from the side of the pan. Transfer the paste to a bowl and cool for 15 minutes. Beat in the eggs, one at a time. (This, now, is what the French call "*pâte à choux*," a paste which also is used for cream puffs, eclairs and profiteroles.) Add the mashed potatoes to the paste, blending well. Heat the oil in a deep fryer and drop in the potato mixture, a tablespoonful at a time. Do not crowd them in the fryer. Cook until they are golden and drain well on paper towels. Sprinkle with salt.

SERVES 6.

Note: See Potatoes Lorette (page 238). You can add the above *pâte à choux* to that recipe, roll into balls and deep fry.

Potatoes Dauphinoise

6 medium-sized potatoes
5 tablespoons of butter
1 garlic clove, peeled and crushed
Salt and pepper
1 cup of grated Gruyère cheese
⅛ teaspoon of nutmeg
1½ cups of milk

Peel the potatoes and cut into ⅛-inch slices. Soak in a bowl of cold water for 2 hours. Butter a shallow baking dish with 2 tablespoons of the butter. Rub the buttered dish with the garlic clove. Drain and dry the potatoes with paper towels. Arrange half of the potato slices in one layer, overlapping if necessary, on the bottom of the dish. Sprinkle with salt and pepper and half of the cheese. Place the remaining potato slices on top of the first layer and sprinkle with salt and pepper. Combine the nutmeg and milk and heat to a simmer. Pour the milk over the potatoes. Sprinkle with the remaining cheese and dot with the remaining 3 tablespoons of the butter. Bake in a pre-heated 400° F. oven for 45 minutes, or until the potatoes are tender, the milk absorbed and the top is golden. If the top starts to brown before the potatoes are cooked, cover loosely with aluminum foil.

SERVES 4.

Potatoes Delmonico

6 medium-sized potatoes
5½ tablespoons of butter
3 tablespoons of flour
1½ teaspoons of salt
2 cups of hot cream
4 hard-cooked eggs, cut into ¼-inch slices
5 tablespoons of grated sharp orange Cheddar cheese
⅔ cup of bread crumbs

Boil the potatoes in their skins in a small amount of water. Drain and dry over heat in a pan. Then peel and cut into ¼-inch slices. In a saucepan, melt 4 tablespoons of the butter and add the flour, stirring into a smooth paste. Blend in the salt and the cream, a little at a time, stirring over low heat into a thickish cream sauce. Butter a baking dish and alternate layers of potato slices and egg slices (bottom and top layers should be potatoes), masking each with the cream sauce and sprinkling with cheese. Sprinkle the bread crumbs atop and dot with the remaining 1½ tablespoons of the butter. Bake, uncovered, in a preheated 350° F. oven for 30 minutes or until bubbling and browned.

SERVES 6.

Duchess Potatoes

These mashed potatoes, into which eggs have been beaten, are sometimes served by the French just as they are, but more often they are used to decorate other dishes, often planked fish and beef, and also to rim creamed and cheese entrées. A pastry bag is used, the potatoes piped through while still warm and formed into any shape desired.

    4 large potatoes
    1½ teaspoons of salt
    ¼ teaspoon of nutmeg
    4 tablespoons of butter
    1 whole egg
    2 egg yolks

Boil the potatoes in their skins until tender. Drain and dry over heat. Then peel. Put the potatoes through a potato ricer into a bowl. Add salt, nutmeg and butter. With an electric beater, whip until very smooth. In another bowl, beat the egg and egg yolks until well blended. Mix the eggs with the potatoes, whipping until light and fluffy. They need finishing in the oven or the broiler. Form into mounds of any shape or size (or pipe through a pastry bag as the pros do) and in a preheated 425° F. oven brown lightly, or place quickly under the broiler for the same effect.

SERVES 6.

Piping Duchess Potatoes into Various Shapes

We've mentioned that experienced cooks pipe Duchess potatoes as a decorative border around various meat dishes. They also use the pastry bag and tube (we use a 14-inch bag with a large metal tube to fit) to form the potatoes into interesting and appealing shapes. After they have shaped the potatoes, they brush them with a glaze and bake them, uncovered, in a preheated 400° F. oven for 15 minutes, or until they are golden and the edges slightly brown. First, the glaze.

Glaze

1 egg
½ teaspoon of salt
1½ teaspoons of olive oil

In a bowl, combine all ingredients and blend thoroughly.

The French have names for the shapes, *petites pyramides*, which are mounded to form tiny pyramids; *rosettes longues*, which are fingers about 3 inches long; *doigts* that look like 3-inch pieces of rope, achieved by twisting the piping nozzle as you squeeze the potato through it; *couronnes*, resembling small crowns, made by holding the bag and tube vertically and swirling the little rings directly upon a baking sheet. *Petits pains* that look like small potato boats that are shaped by making a depression with the thumb and fingers; *galettes*, also hand-shaped, are round, flat cakes, usually with a pattern on top, a crisscross made with the blade of a table knife.

Working with a pastry bag and tube is fun cooking, and you certainly do not have to stay with the classic shapes. The technique isn't difficult; a few trial runs will not only make you an expert but encourage you to serve potatoes with interesting and imaginative shapes.

Abbreviated, here is the piping system: Spoon the Duchess potatoes into the bag (amount depends upon the number of potato shapes you wish to make), packing the potatoes as close to the tube as possible so that you will not have to exert too much pressure to send them through in a controlled stream. Twist the empty portion of the bag and hold it in place with your left hand. Cradle the bag in your right hand, resting your index finger on the top of the tube. The right hand squeezes the bag and guides the stream of potatoes from the tube.

All of the shapes should be piped directly upon a lightly floured baking sheet.

French Fries

One of the tastiest of all potatoes, and one of the most popular, this is most certainly a classic. Created by the French many years ago, this supposedly simple dish has several vociferous schools of procedure: They should be thin and crisp; no, they should be thick and mealy; better still, a midway French fry, not thin, not thick, crisp on the outside, mealy inside. Two things are certain: They shouldn't be soggy, and they should be piping hot and lightly salted. There are utensils that help, cutters that quickly cut a batch into the perfect size; the minifryers that save on time and on oil.

We like thin, crisp, but still slightly mealy French fries. Some believe that the potatoes to be fried should first be soaked in water. This probably came into popularity in the old days when potatoes were stored a long time and placing in water did soak out the excess sugar that develops from overlong storage. That sugar resulted in too-fast frying and soggy potatoes. This soaking is no longer necessary, nor does it aid in producing crisp fries.

We have several preferences that we think add to success. There'll be a lot of "shoulds" to follow, but they may help. Potatoes should be good firm, unblemished Idahoes. And only the center parts of the potatoes should be used. They should be cut uniformly into 3-inch-long, ⅜-inch-thick strips. They should be placed in a strainer or a sieve and *rinsed* under cold water and then very well dried on kitchen or paper towels. And, most important, they should be *double-fried*.

Frying twice, we find, insures crispness.

Amounts

3 large Idaho potatoes, peeled, cut (from the center) into 3-inch-long, ⅜-inch-thick strips, rinsed under cold water, dried thoroughly
Vegetable oil for deep frying
Salt

Method

Place 2 inches of oil, or enough to come up to the oil line on your fryer. Preheat 7 minutes (if you have a temperature control, it should be on medium or 325° F.) with the fry basket in for the last 3 minutes. A cold basket will quickly lower the temperature of the oil and throw timing off. Lift up the basket, place in the amount of potatoes that can be comfortably cooked at one time; we find 1½ cups about right for each frying. Cook for 3 minutes. This will seal the potatoes. Cool the potatoes for 20 minutes. (Take the fryer off heat, or turn off.) If you have a temperature control, set to 375° F., or raise to high, if no control, and heat the oil for 10 minutes. Remember to preheat the fry basket for a couple of minutes. Then cook the potatoes the second time for 4 minutes, or until browned the way you like them. Immediately drain well, serve immediately, or keep warm in a 225° F. oven until all are cooked. Salt just before serving. Do not salt in advance as it will make them less crisp.

SERVES 4.

Note: We seldom use the oil more than twice and strain it through double cheesecloth for storing, and *never* use it if it gets very dark, or foams while it is heating. Good luck!

And, although, "classic" French fries are eaten in certainly unclassic ways. The French remain true to form, preferring them crisp and brown with salt and pepper. The English like them with a light sprinkling of vinegar; the Dutch dip them in mustard-mayonnaise; in America many of us flood them in catsup.

Potato Fritters

This is a classic fritter the French claim to have developed. We don't doubt it. After they were pushed by Parmentier (who first had them in a German prison-of-war camp) into an appreciation of potatoes, the French have indeed accomplished marvelous things with them.

    4 medium-sized potatoes, grated
    5 tablespoons of flour
    1½ teaspoons of salt
    ½ teaspoon of pepper
    2 large eggs, lightly beaten
    2 tablespoons of vegetable oil
    Vegetable oil for frying

In a bowl, combine the potatoes, flour, salt and pepper and blend well. Stir in the eggs and 2 tablespoons of vegetable oil, mixing thoroughly. In a frypan, heat ½ inch of oil. It is hot enough when a small amount of the mixture dropped into it instantly sizzles. Keep the oil at this temperature. Drop heaping teaspoonfuls of the mixture into the hot oil. Stir each time before dropping into the oil. When the bottoms of the frying fritters are crisply golden turn them and brown the other side. Drain on paper towels and serve immediately.

SERVES 4.

Note: This can be converted into another recipe by grating the potatoes more finely, then forming the fritters into small balls, deep frying them, then draining well on paper towels.

Franconia Potatoes

Like many of the classics this is simplicity itself. It is used exclusively with roast meats. We like these with roast veal.

6 medium-sized potatoes
Roast beef, pork, veal or chicken

Boil the potatoes in their skins for 12 minutes, drain and dry over heat in a pot. Peel the potatoes and cut each in half. About 45 minutes before the roast is ready, circle it with the potatoes. At least three times during the final cooking of the meat, turn the potatoes and baste them well with the pan drippings.

SERVES 6.

German Potato Dumplings
(with cooked potatoes)

German potato dumplings are classic in both versions, this one using mashed potatoes and the one to follow using raw potatoes. With any variety of potato dumpling always cook one first to see if your mixture is right.

4 large baking potatoes
1½ cups of flour
1 large egg, beaten
1 teaspoon of salt

Boil the potatoes in their skins until tender, drain and dry over heat in a pot. Peel and mash. Then set aside to cool. In a bowl, place the cooled potatoes, flour, egg and salt, blending well. Knead with your hands until you have a smooth, elastic dough. If the dough is too soft and moist, add more flour, just a little at a time, until the dough is of the right consistency. Shape the dumplings into the size you desire, we like them ping-pong ball size. Lower them into boiling salted water and cook for 12 minutes. Take them from the water with a slotted spoon and drain well. The Germans sometimes split them, using two forks, and then serve them hot, drenched in melted butter and sprinkled with bread crumbs. Or they serve them with gravied dishes, stews, etc.

ABOUT 10 DUMPLINGS.

German Potato Dumplings
(with raw potatoes)

4 large baking potatoes, peeled and grated raw into a pot of cold water

2 large baking potatoes, boiled in skins, drained, dried over heat and mashed

1½ teaspoons of salt

Flour (optional)

15 (depending on the number of dumplings) toasted croutons

Drain the grated potatoes thoroughly, then place them in an absorbent cloth and carefully squeeze them dry. In a bowl, place the dry raw potatoes, the cooked mashed potatoes, the salt and, with your hands, knead until you have a smooth mass resembling dough. If too moist, add small amounts of flour until you can work it into a non-sticky dough. Roughly form small balls, pressing 1 toasted crouton into the center of each dumpling, then reforming it over the crouton. Cook in gently simmering salted water for about 15 minutes. Cook only one first to see if it is to your liking. These are good served with hot melted butter, but we like them with game stews, especially hare or rabbit with a dark, spicy gravy, some of which is spooned over the dumplings. The bland dumpling complements this type of dish beautifully.

About 15 dumplings (depending on the size of the dumpling made).

Gnocchi
(Italian Potato Dumplings)

This is a simple but elegant dish that few but sophisticated visitors to Italy will have had. It is often served
with a combination of melted butter, cheese and
tomato sauce. We prefer just the butter and cheese.

    4 large potatoes (about 2 pounds)
    1 teaspoon of salt
    3 egg yolks
    1½ to 2 cups of all-purpose flour
    6 quarts of water
    3 tablespoons of salt
    1 cup of melted butter
    1½ cups of grated Asiago or Parmesan cheese

Boil the potatoes in their skins until tender. Drain,
dry over heat in a pot, then peel. Put the potatoes
through a potato ricer onto a lightly floured pastry
board. When they have cooled, make a well in the
center, add the salt and egg yolks and mix thoroughly
together. Work in 1½ cups of flour, kneading into
a dough. Add additional flour to make a firm, smooth
dough that does not stick to your fingers. Divide the
dough into four parts. Roll each into a long cylinder
about ½ inch in diameter. Cut into 1-inch pieces.
Gently press the center of each with your thumb.
Cook in the 6 quarts of simmering water to which
the 3 tablespoons of salt have been added, a few at a
time so as not to crowd them, about 5 minutes. They
are ready when they rise to the surface. Remove with
a slotted spoon, drain well and transfer to a warm
serving plate. Spoon the melted butter over the
gnocchi and sprinkle with the cheese.

SERVES 8.

Hashed Brown Potatoes with Vinegar

This is a technique learned from our friend, the famous chef Antoine Gilly. Surprisingly, the addition of the vinegar helps both browning and flavor.

6 tablespoons of butter
1 tablespoon of white vinegar
6 medium-sized potatoes, peeled and cut into ¼-inch dice
1½ teaspoons of salt
½ teaspoon of pepper

In a large frypan, melt the butter, stir in the vinegar and the potatoes. Season with salt and pepper. Cook over medium heat. With a spatula, keep turning the potatoes until the desired degree of crustiness is attained. We like ours very crusty and brown. Some people prefer them more moist; it's all in the turning and timing.

SERVES 6.

Potatoes Lorette

This classic is usually made with the addition of *pâte à choux*, puff paste, which is quite complicated (see Potatoes Dauphine, page 227). This version is much easier and we think just as good.

6 medium-sized potatoes
4 tablespoons of butter
⅛ teaspoon of nutmeg
1½ teaspoons of salt
½ teaspoon of pepper
1 cup of grated Gruyère cheese
2 egg yolks
2 egg whites, stiffly beaten
Vegetable oil for frying

Boil the potatoes in their skins until tender, drain and dry over heat in a pot. Peel and rice them. Transfer the potatoes to a bowl and beat in the butter, nutmeg, salt, pepper, cheese and the egg yolks, one yolk at a time. Fold in the beaten whites. In a deep frypan or fryer, heat ¾ inch of oil until a bread cube browns quickly. Using 2 teaspoons, scoop out a spoonful with one and with the other push it off the filled spoon into the hot fat. Fry until golden, drain well on paper towels and serve immediately.

SERVES 6.

Potatoes Lyonnaise

This dish can be prepared either with potatoes first boiled in their skins or with raw slices. Both are excellent and simple. We prefer working with the raw slices.

    5 tablespoons of butter
    5 medium-sized potatoes, peeled and thinly sliced
    1½ teaspoons of salt
    ½ teaspoon of pepper
    3 medium-sized white onions, thinly sliced

In a deep saucepan or casserole, over low heat, melt 3 tablespoons of the butter and add the potatoes, salt and pepper. Cook, covered, for 15 minutes. In another smaller saucepan, heat the remaining 2 tablespoons of the butter and cook the onion until soft. Add the onion to the potato casserole, tossing them together. Cover and cook for 10 minutes, or until the potatoes are tender. Taste for seasoning, adding additional salt and pepper, if needed.

SERVES 4.

Potatoes Macaire

7 medium-sized Idaho potatoes
7 tablespoons of butter
Salt and pepper to taste

Bake the potatoes in their skins in a 400° F. oven for 1 hour. Scoop out the pulp and mash coarsely. Beat in 5 tablespoons of the butter, and season to taste. Form into 6 cakes or patties. In a frypan, melt the remaining 2 tablespoons of butter and brown the cakes evenly on both sides. Outside should be brown and crisp, inside soft and mealy. These are marvelous with meat loaf.

SERVES 6.

Potatoes Maître d'Hôtel

6 medium-sized potatoes
4 tablespoons of butter
2 cups of hot cream
½ cup of beef broth
¼ teaspoon of nutmeg
Pinch of cayenne
Salt to taste
2 tablespoons of finely chopped fresh parsley, chives, tarragon, thyme, basil or a combination

Peel the potatoes and halve them. Boil for 10 minutes in salted water, drain and dry over heat in a pot. Cut into ¼-inch slices. Melt the butter in a large frypan, add the potatoes and the remaining ingredients, except the herbs (the liquid should just cover the potatoes). Bring to a boil, cover and simmer for 15 minutes, or until the potatoes are almost tender. Remove cover and cook until sauce thickens. Transfer to a hot serving dish and sprinkle with the fresh herbs.

SERVES 4.

Pommes Marguerite

5 medium sized potatoes,
   peeled and quartered
1 teaspoon of salt
1 garlic clove, peeled
   and halved
5 tablespoons of butter

¼ pound of mushrooms,
   sliced
1 egg yolk
¼ cup of medium cream
2 tablespoons of chopped
   parsley

Paprika

In a saucepan, in 1 inch of water, cook the potatoes, tightly covered, with the salt and garlic for 15 minutes, or until tender. Meanwhile, in a frypan, heat 2 tablespoons of the butter. Add the mushrooms and cook for 1 minute over high heat. Set aside. When the potatoes are tender, discard the garlic, drain and dry the potatoes. Beat the potatoes with an electric beater until fluffy. Beat in the remaining 3 tablespoons of butter, the egg yolk and cream. Fold in the mushrooms and parsley. Taste for seasoning. Spoon into a buttered ovenproof serving dish. Bake in a preheated 375° F. oven for 15 minutes to heat through. Sprinkle lightly with the paprika.

SERVES 4.

Note: This may be prepared early in the day then heated in a preheated 375° F. oven for 45 minutes, or until thoroughly heated.

Potatoes Mont d'Or

Some of the classics have just slight variations, almost the same techniques but different cheeses and different methods of presentation.

5 medium-sized baking potatoes
1½ teaspoons of salt
½ teaspoon of pepper
⅛ teaspoon of mace
2 egg yolks
½ cup of warm heavy cream
2 egg whites, stiffly beaten
¼ cup of grated Swiss cheese

Peel the potatoes and boil in a small amount of salted water until tender. Drain, dry over heat in a pot, then rice them into a bowl. With a whisk whip in the salt, pepper, mace, egg yolks, one yolk at a time, then the cream. Fold in the beaten egg whites. Lightly butter an oval au gratin dish and spoon in the potato mixture, smoothing the top, cake-fashion. Sprinkle on the cheese. Bake, uncovered, in a preheated 350° F. oven for 15 minutes, or until the cheese has melted and the top is golden. Place under the broiler for a minute or two until crusty brown, but watch it closely.

SERVES 4.

Potatoes Nanette

5 tablespoons of butter
1 tablespoon of olive oil
6 medium-sized potatoes, peeled and cut into ¼-inch
 slices
1½ teaspoons of salt
½ teaspoon of pepper
1 tablespoon of finely chopped fresh chives
2 tablespoons of finely chopped broadleaf parsley
¼ cup of chicken broth

In a large frypan, heat the butter and oil. Add the
potatoes, sprinkle with salt and pepper and fry until
golden, turning, but do not cook until the potatoes
are soft. Place the potato slices in a baking dish,
sprinkle with the chives and parsley and moisten with
the chicken broth. Bake, uncovered, in a preheated
375° F. oven for 15 minutes, or until the potatoes are
tender.

SERVES 6.

Potatoes O'Brien

2 tablespoons of butter
1 small onion, finely chopped
1 small green pepper, cored, seeded and chopped
1 (4-ounce) can of pimientos, drained and cut into strips
Cooking oil
6 medium-sized potatoes, peeled and diced
Salt and pepper

In a frypan, over medium heat, melt the butter. Add
the onion and green pepper and cook until soft, do
not brown. Stir in the pimiento and set aside. In a
large frypan, heat ½ inch of oil. Add the diced potatoes and fry until golden and tender, turning occasionally. Drain and season with salt and pepper. Add the

onion mixture and toss together over high heat for 1 minute, or until heated through. Serve immediately.

SERVES 6.

Potatoes Paillasson

Here is another from Antoine Gilly, friend, teacher, and rated as one of France's four greatest living chefs. The rinsing is very important, otherwise the potatoes will stick and be too glutinous.

5 medium-sized potatoes, peeled and cut julienne
8 tablespoons (1 stick) of unsalted butter, at room temperature
Salt to taste

Carefully rinse the potatoes in two changes of cold water, wrap in a cloth towel and squeeze very dry. Use a heavy omelet or frypan with a cover. Melt 4 tablespoons of the butter and add the potatoes to the pan. Season to taste and cook, covered, over low heat for 20 minutes, or until the bottom is crisply golden. Flip it over; a plate slightly larger than the frypan placed over it helps, the pan inverted so the potato cake slides out on to the plate without breaking. Then it is a simple matter to slide it back into the frypan. But first melt the remaining 4 tablespoons of butter and lightly salt the potatoes. Cover the pan, and again, over low heat, cook for another 15 minutes, or until golden on the bottom.

SERVES 4.

Polish Potato Puffs

The Poles serve these with a mixture of sugar and sour cream. We like them with veal scallopini or chicken sautéed in garlic and dry vermouth.

7 medium-sized potatoes (about 2½ pounds)
2 tablespoons of butter
4 egg yolks
Pinch of nutmeg

4 tablespoons of sour cream
1 teaspoon of sugar
1 teaspoon of salt
4 egg whites, stiffly beaten
Vegetable oil for deep frying

Boil the potatoes in their skins until tender. Drain, dry over heat in a pot, then peel them. Put the potatoes through a potato ricer into a bowl. Thoroughly blend in the butter, egg yolks, nutmeg, sour cream, sugar and salt. Fold in the egg whites. Heat the oil in a deep fryer. Drop in spoonfuls of the potato mixture (about 4 or 5 at a time so they are not crowded). They are cooked when they are evenly browned, puffed and float to the surface. Drain on paper towels.

SERVES 6 TO 8.

Purée de Pommes de Terre
(Mashed Potatoes)

This all-time favorite, we all prepare our own way. But the French, as they do with many types of food, seem to make the best. We'll never forget one experience in Paris in the Berkeley Hotel, which had a small but elegant restaurant. As we sometimes do in Europe, we decided to make luncheon rather substantial and skip dinner. So we ordered loin lamb chops, new peas cooked with lettuce and mashed potatoes, a word the French refuse to use. "Mashed?" the waiter said, perplexed, until one member of this team said, "Pommes Purée." It seemed mere minutes later that two waiters wheeled in a table, the thick lamb chops in a chafing dish; drained, boiled potatoes in a copper pot. One waiter dried the potatoes again in the pot over the flame of another chafing dish, then warmed cream over the same flame, while the other waiter mashed the potatoes in the copper pot, adding salt, butter, then grated nutmeg into them. When the other waiter had the cream slightly scalded he took over, gradually adding the cream and vigorously whipping the potatoes until they almost resembled whipped cream. They were the best we have ever had. But what impressed us was the respect shown the potato—and the showmanship.

We prefer to boil the potatoes in their skins to retain the nutrients, but the French don't, at least with this recipe, which we asked for and promptly received, inasmuch as we saw most of it in action. We have increased the amounts.

5 medium-sized potatoes
1½ teaspoons of salt
5 tablespoons of butter
½ cup of medium cream
Nutmeg

Peel and cut each potato into three pieces. Place in a pot, cover with cold water and add the salt. Bring to a boil, then simmer for 25 minutes, or until the potatoes are tender. Drain and dry them in the pot over heat, being careful not to scorch them. Place them in a bowl and mash with a potato masher, or put them through a ricer. Gradually add the butter, whipping it in vigorously, then the cream, which has been quickly heated almost to the scalding point. After adding the cream gradually, and whipping it in, add the nutmeg and whip until the potatoes are creamy, fluffy and light.

SERVES 4 TO 6.

Bombay Puris

On our four trips to India, we confess one of the consistent visions that flashed before our eyes as we jetted that 10,000 miles was not the Taj Mahal, but the golden, crisp, hot puffed potatoes called *puris* or *pooris*. An Indian classic, *puris* are as ubiquitous in that subcontinent as the sacred cow.

2 large baking potatoes	SIFTED TOGETHER:
3 tablespoons of butter	2 cups of all-purpose flour
1 large white onion, minced	⅔ cup of whole wheat flour
Yogurt	⅓ teaspoon of pepper
Water	1½ teaspoons of salt
Vegetable oil for frying	⅓ teaspoon of ground cardamom
	1 teaspoon of cumin

Boil the potatoes in their skins until tender, drain and dry over heat in a pot. Peel and then mash without adding liquid or seasoning. In a large bowl, combine the potatoes, butter and onion and blend well. Stir in the sifted flour and seasonings. Add small amounts of yogurt and water, working the mixture with your hands into a pliable dough. The addition of the yogurt with the water makes the *puris* crisper. When the dough is pliable and elastic, cover with a damp, wrung-out kitchen towel and let the dough set in the bowl for 40 minutes. On a lightly floured pastry board, with lightly floured rolling pin, roll the dough into a ¼-inch sheet. With a cookie cutter, cut into 2½-inch circles. Deep fry the *puris* in oil heated to 360° F., completely immersing them and gently pressing them down in the oil with a spatula. This assists in puffing them. When puffed and golden remove and drain on paper towels. These glorified potato chips, unlike ours, are served hot.

MAKES ABOUT 30.

Rissole Potatoes

5 medium-sized potatoes, peeled and cut into balls with
a melon scoop.
5 tablespoons of butter
1½ teaspoons of salt

Parboil the potato balls in salted water for 7 minutes,
drain and dry. In a deep frypan, melt the butter, add
the potatoes and cook until they are an even golden
brown color, shaking the pan frequently so they don't
stick. Season with salt and serve immediately.

SERVES 4.

Potatoes Rösti

6 medium-sized potatoes (about 2 pounds)
12 tablespoons (1½ sticks) of butter
Salt and pepper

Boil the potatoes in their skins for 15 minutes. Peel
the potatoes and grate them on the medium blade of
a hand grater (so they come out in thin strips ½ inch
by 1½ inches). Cook each potato separately or make
one large *rösti*. If you cook them separately, melt 2
tablespoons of butter in a 6-inch frypan over medium
heat. Add the grated potato and mix it well with the
butter, then season with salt and pepper to taste.
Lower the heat and cook for about 10 minutes, or
until the bottom is golden. Shake the pan from time
to time so the potatoes do not stick. Place a plate over
the pan, turn the pan over so potatoes fall out, then
slide them back into the pan and brown on the other
side. Hold the cooked potatoes in a warm oven until
all are cooked. To make one large *rösti*, use a large
frypan and proceed as above using all of the potatoes
and 8 tablespoons of butter.

SERVES 6.

Potatoes Savoyarde

Cook as for Potatoes Dauphinoise (page 228) substituting chicken broth for the milk. Use less salt as the chicken broth may supply enough, but taste for seasoning and adjust accordingly.

Snow Potatoes

5 medium-sized Idaho potatoes, peeled and each cut
    into 8 pieces
4 tablespoons of butter
1½ teaspoons of salt
Boiling water

In a deep saucepan, place the potatoes, butter and salt. Add boiling water to the depth of ¼ inch. Cover and cook over medium heat for 3 minutes. Remove the cover and cook until all of the water has evaporated. Put the potatoes through a ricer and serve immediately with a dollop of soft butter on top.

SERVES 4.

Note: If, when the water has evaporated, the potatoes are not quite tender enough, add a very small amount of boiling water and continue to cook.

Pommes Soufflées

Some of us may consider this classic not worth the effort, or the gamble, for both are involved, as is patience, luck and exactly the right potatoes, sliced precisely and cooked in hot oil of exact temperatures. But these potato "balloons" are dramatically different and will place you as a host in that same category. Suggestion: Do not attempt this dish for the first time when you are expecting guests. These are trial-and-error potatoes; if at first you don't succeed—but you know that cliché. It helps to have two deep fryers (the mini fryers work well if not overloaded) with temperature controls; if not, two deep saucepans and a deep-frying thermometer.

6 medium-sized Idaho potatoes (make certain they are solid, perfect potatoes)
Vegetable oil for deep frying
Salt

Take your time and peel and cut the potatoes into rectangular lengthwise slices (there are excellent, in-expensive potato slicers on the market), cutting with the grain, into 3-by-1½-inches-and (*exactly*) ⅛-inch-thick slices. Place the potato slices in ice water until chilled, then drain and dry very well on a cloth towel. Heat the oil (enough to completely submerge 6 slices of potatoes; never cook more at one time) in one fryer to 285° F.; to 400° F. in the other. Heat should be medium in the first, high in the second fryer. Fry 6 slices in the lower heat for 3 minutes, then remove to paper towels to drain and cool for 5 minutes.

Place the cooked, cooled slices in the very hot oil. If everything is working well they will almost immediately puff into balloons. The extreme heat will have caused instant expansion, but the brown skins will not burst or even crack. As soon as they are brown, a matter of seconds, lift the slices out with a slotted spoon, or better still, take the wire cooking basket out and drain on paper towels. Sprinkle with salt and serve immediately.

SERVES 6.

Note: The first cooking stage can be done hours ahead. Also, if the potato balloons collapse after the second cooking as they are draining on paper towels, don't despair. Try cooking them again very briefly in the 400° F. oil just before serving. Usually they repuff.

Straw Potatoes

4 medium-sized potatoes, peeled and cut into long, thin
    sticks (about the size of a wooden match stick)
Vegetable oil for deep frying
Salt

Soak the potato sticks in cold water for 1 hour. Drain
and dry well with a cloth towel. Deep fry, a few at a
time, for about 4 minutes, or until they are golden.
Drain on paper towels and keep those that are cooked
warm in a 225° F. oven while others are frying. When
all are cooked, sprinkle with salt and serve immediately. These are sometimes called "match stick" potatoes.

SERVES 4 TO 6.

8

Bakers and Pancakes

Bakers

Monuments to the appeal and versatility of our favorite potato—the baked-in-its-skin mealy beauty that has no equal—are the intriguing restaurants that are opening using the baked potato, not only as the main attraction, but as the meal.

Franchised "Potato Pit" restaurants and others are now having a successful run in California and elsewhere, serving baked potatoes with tempting toppings ranging from avocado and cheese to rare steak and various seafood and chicken combinations. There also are several "baked potato" restaurants in Europe.

The concept behind the unique restaurants started with a question. Does a potato taste better than a roll? No contest! A baked potato as a base, or even by itself, tastes better than practically anything.

In the restaurants, a huge Idaho, baked to perfection and wrapped snugly in foil to keep it piping hot (see comments on pages 7 and 8 as to the advantages of foil in potato cookery), arrives at your table, split, neatly spread with the topping of your choice. You dip into it with fork, and there it is, two in one: a nice tender piece of pink steak and underneath the mealy, buttery, moist baked potato, all in one forkful. A stroke of genius!

The Scandinavians offer baked potato halves mixed with various fishes and shellfish. Their tiny tender shrimp with butter and fresh dill on top of a baked potato are superb.

Just about anything goes. It's fun and rewarding to experiment.

We've found that scooping out the baked potato pulp and mashing it with butter, then blending in finely-chopped, garden-fresh scallions, before returning it to the shell and heating it for a few minutes, adds unique flavor and zest to the potato.

One of the best potato treats we've ever had involved baked potatoes that were filled with creamy mashed filling (from the pulp) and topped with caviar.

We all bake potatoes, probably the most ancient system of all, in our own ways. But it pays to use Idahoes (Long Island Russets and Maine Kennebecs are also superb), blocky potatoes, first choice, about a half-pound apiece, with no pronounced taper that will overcook. Wash well and dry and pierce the skin (eat the skin after it is baked; it's good for you and delicious!). There are numerous suggestions: Use a nail and leave it inserted, it will conduct heat and so the potato will cook evenly. Piercing the skin in several places allows the steam to escape and also prevents the potato from bursting. Some make an incision on the top center of the potato. Some rub the skin with oil to give it a shiny texture. Others use foil, no fuss, its own container, even server, keeping the potato hot longer.

And, remember that the baked potato can also be the repository for other types of cooking. Bake a few extra and have them later, peeled, then hash browned, cottage fried, minced in cream, au gratin, even mashed.

A reminder: a medium-sized potato (three per pound) bakes in about 60 minutes at 400° F. Bake on the oven rack or even a cookie sheet, but never on the bottom of the oven itself, for that will produce too soft potatoes. Bakers are done when they feel soft when pinched.

But bake potatoes your own way; you've probably been doing it about as long as you've been using a knife and fork.

Following are some innovative toppings for that mealy marvel that could be new and interesting.

For Dieters

Freshly ground coarse black pepper and salt
Seasoned salt, seasoned pepper
Snipped parsley, dill, watercress or chives
Chopped drained pimiento
Low-calorie salad dressing
Low-calorie cheese shreds with thin, sliced sweet Spanish onion or green onion
Whipped butter (fewer calories per serving)
Lemon butter
Hot skim milk or chicken broth seasoned with herbs
Low-calorie sour cream
Yogurt
Cottage cheese combined with chives, dill, pimiento or tomatoes
Marinated mushrooms
Mock sour cream (cottage cheese whipped in a blender)

For Non-Dieters

Roquefort butter (see our version, Potatoes Roquefort, page 269)
Sour cream, plain or with chives
Avocado, mashed with sour cream (see our Baked Potato with Avocado Sauce, page 257)
Whipped cream cheese with chives

Cheese sauce
Chopped chives
Shredded Cheddar cheese
Diced ham and cheese
Clam Chowder (see Easy New England Chowdered
    Potatoes, page 260)
Shrimp creole
Sloppy Joe style
Creamed or curried chicken
Chopped beef and onion, or creamed chipped beef
Sausage meat and scallions
Chili sauce
Sliced sausage or frankfurter
Nuggets of Gorgonzola cheese buried in the potato
Sauerkraut and strips of corned beef
Chopped ham and egg, or bacon and egg, or crisp
    bacon bits
Poached egg, topped with hollandaise or béchamel
    sauce
Stews: lamb, beef, chicken, canned or homemade
Melted sharp cheese
Turkey and cheese sauce
Parmesan cheese, blended with butter, chopped
    garlic and parsley
Cheddar cheese and fresh tomato

And ad infinitum! Baked potato meal ideas are as
limitless as the fertile human brain.

We have, however, an offering of complete recipes
for those who haven't the time nor the inclination to
create their own baked potato combinations.

Remember to wrap *all* baked potatoes in foil to keep
them at their best—hot. Also see pages 7–8 where we
discuss how cooking potatoes in foil preserves Vitamin C.

Antoine Gilly's Stuffed Baked Potatoes

4 large baking potatoes
1 tablespoon of chopped fresh chives
1 teaspoon of chopped fresh tarragon
½ teaspoon of salt
½ teaspoon of pepper
⅛ teaspoon of nutmeg

2 tablespoons of shallots, minced and simmered for 5 minutes in 2 tablespoons of butter
¼ cup of heavy cream
1 small package of Liederkranz cheese
2 tablespoons of bread crumbs

Wrap the potatoes in aluminum foil and bake in a preheated 400° F. oven for 1 hour, or until cooked. Take the potatoes from the oven, and, laying them the long way, cut off and save the tops. Remove the pulp with a spoon and place the empty potato shells on a baking dish. In a bowl, mash the potato pulp, mixing in all ingredients (except the bread crumbs) one by one, to make a puree. Check seasoning. Fill the potato shells with the puree and sprinkle with the bread crumbs. Bake in a preheated 450° F. oven for 5 minutes, or until heated through. Replace the tops and serve.

SERVES 4.

Aunt Edie's Roasted Potatoes

from Barbara M. Valbona

4 medium-sized baking potatoes, unpeeled
2 garlic cloves, minced
1½ tablespoons of vegetable oil
Salt and pepper
1 tablespoon of oregano
1½ tablespoons of paprika

Scrub the potatoes, dry and cut into eighths lengthwise. Place in a casserole. Sprinkle with the remaining ingredients. With your hands roll *all* ingredients until potatoes are thoroughly coated. Bake in preheated 400° F. oven for one hour or until the potatoes can be pierced easily with fork.

SERVES 6.

Baked Potatoes with Avocado Sauce

You can really get elegant with a baked potato. It has an affinity for the most unusual sauces (see Baked Potatoes with Pesto, page 61).

6 medium-sized baking potatoes, scrubbed and baked
2 tablespoons of lemon juice
1 small ripe avocado, peeled, pitted and diced (do this at the last minute)
12 tablespoons of unsalted, soft butter
½ teaspoon of garlic salt
Salt to taste

While the potatoes are baking prepare the sauce. Place the lemon juice and avocado in an electric blender container and blend into a puree. Spoon into a bowl, add the butter and garlic salt and whip into a smooth blend. Taste for seasoning and add salt, if needed. Spoon over piping hot, split baked potatoes. We like this with a broiled chicken, but no dessert afterward!

SERVES 6.

Bacon-Stuffed Potatoes

4 large baking potatoes, scrubbed
4 slices of bacon, each rolled tightly
Melted butter
Salt

After the potatoes have baked for about 35 minutes, in one end of each, with a vegetable corer, core out a tubular opening large enough to accommodate the roll of bacon, saving the end pieces removed from the potatoes. Insert a bacon slice into each potato, replacing the end and bake until the potatoes are soft, about 15 minutes longer. Cut the potatoes halfway through and serve with melted butter and salt.

SERVES 4.

Potatoes à la Boursin

This is a recipe from the French Boursin cheese country.

4 medium-sized baking potatoes, scrubbed and baked
4 tablespoons (about) of Boursin herb and garlic cheese

Cut the potatoes in half lengthwise. With a fork, mash the potatoes right in the skins. Press 1 tablespoon of Boursin cheese into one half of each potato; replace the other half potato, pressing together, sandwiching the cheese between the halves. Wrap well in foil and bake in a preheated 400° F. oven for 10 minutes.

SERVES 4.

Crab-Stuffed Baked Potatoes

Here is a tasty, fast one, with the stuffing ready before the potatoes are baked.

2 tablespoons of grated onion
¼ cup of heavy cream
1 (10-ounce) can of frozen condensed cream of shrimp soup
⅛ teaspoon of cayenne
½ cup of grated Cheddar cheese
1 (7-ounce) can of crabmeat, cleaned and flaked
4 medium-sized long baking potatoes, scrubbed and baked
Salt to taste

In a saucepan, combine the onion, cream, shrimp soup and cayenne. Over low heat, stirring, cook for 6 minutes. Add the cheese, stirring until it has melted.

Stir in the crabmeat. Split the potatoes lengthwise, reserving the 4 best shells, and scoop out the pulp. Rice the pulp into a bowl and, a little at a time, mix in one-half of the soup-cheese-crabmeat sauce. Taste for seasoning. Spoon the mixture into the potato shells. Place on a cookie sheet, spoon over the remaining seafood sauce and bake in a preheated 450° F. oven for 10 minutes until heated through.

SERVES 4.

Baked Potatoes Stuffed with Creamed Cabbage

6 medium-sized, long baking potatoes, scrubbed and baked
5 tablespoons of butter
3 cups of finely shredded, tender green cabbage

1 garlic clove, minced
½ teaspoon of caraway seeds
Salt and pepper to taste
2 teaspoons of lemon juice
½ teaspoon of brown sugar

½ cup of sour cream

While the potatoes are baking, prepare the cabbage. In a frypan, melt 2 tablespoons of the butter. Add the cabbage, garlic, caraway seeds, salt and pepper. Cover tightly and steam until the cabbage is tender and the liquid has cooked off. Stir in the lemon juice, brown sugar and sour cream. Heat through but do not boil.

Cut a thin slice from the top of the potatoes lengthwise. Scoop out the pulp (reserve the shells) and mash it with the remaining 3 tablespoons of butter, salt and pepper. Return two-thirds of the mashed pulp to the potato shells (the remainder can be used in another recipe). Place on a baking dish and spoon the cabbage onto the potatoes. Bake in a preheated 400° F. oven for 15 minutes, or until thoroughly heated.

SERVES 6.

Easy New England Chowdered Potatoes

6 medium-sized baking potatoes, scrubbed and baked
3 tablespoons of butter
2 (8-ounce) cans of minced clams, drained
½ teaspoon of salt
Paprika
2 (8-ounce) cans of frozen New England clam chowder

Cut a large X in the top of each potato, fold back the skin and remove the pulp. Reserve the shells. In a bowl mash the pulp with the butter. Add the clams and salt and blend well. Taste for seasoning. Spoon the mixture back into the potato shells. Sprinkle with paprika. Bake on a cookie sheet in a preheated 400° F. oven for about 15 minutes, or until heated through and golden on top. Meanwhile, heat the soup according to label directions. Serve the soup in a sauceboat to be spooned over the potatoes.

Serves 6.

French Country-Style Stuffed Baked Potatoes

3 large baking potatoes, scrubbed and baked
1 cup of finely crumbled Gruyère cheese
2 tablespoons of heavy cream
3 tablespoons of butter
½ cup of minced cooked ham
½ teaspoon of salt
½ teaspoon of pepper

Cut the baked potatoes in half lengthwise and spoon out the pulp. Reserve all shells. In a bowl, combine the potato pulp, ½ cup of the cheese, cream, 2 tablespoons of the butter, ham, salt and pepper and blend well. Spoon the mixture into the 6 potato half shells and place on a cookie sheet. Sprinkle on the remain-

ing ½ cup cheese and dot with the remaining tablespoon of butter. Bake in a preheated 400° F. oven for
10 minutes, then place under the broiler until crusty-
brown. One filled potato half shell for each guest,
along with a nice fat, pink fillet of beef merits raves.

SERVES 6.

Garlicky Stuffed Bakers

Sophisticated cooks have discovered that large amounts
of garlic do not overwhelm, but instead impart a
memorable, even slightly sweet, flavor.

10 garlic cloves, unpeeled
4 tablespoons of butter
1½ tablespoons of flour
1 cup of light cream
Salt and pepper to taste
2 large baking potatoes, scrubbed and baked
2 tablespoons of heavy cream
1 tablespoon of chopped chives

Place the garlic in a small saucepan, cover with water
and cook for 3 minutes. Drain the garlic, cool slightly
and peel. In another saucepan, melt 2 tablespoons of
the butter, add the garlic and, over low heat, cook
covered, for 6 minutes, or until tender (do not burn
it). With a slotted spoon, remove the garlic and reserve. Stir the flour into the pan the garlic cooked in,
stirring into a smooth paste. Add the light cream,
gradually, stirring into a smooth, thickish sauce. Season with salt and pepper. In a blender, place the
sauce and the garlic, blending thoroughly. Split the
baked potatoes, remove the pulp, keeping the shells
intact. Rice the pulp into a bowl, whip in the remaining 2 tablespoons of the butter, the garlic sauce and
the heavy cream. Taste for seasoning, then stir in the

chives. Spoon equal amounts into the shells. Bake in a preheated 400° F. oven for 10 minutes, or until heated through. Brown under the broiler, if desired.

SERVES 4.

B. J. Guidetti's Stand-Up "Kiev" Nude Bakers

How to make a potato carry the dinner conversation. This unique presentation turns the trick.

4 large baking potatoes, peeled
8 tablespoons (1 stick) of butter, half soft, half hard
Salt and pepper

Stand the potatoes up vertically, cut a small slice off the underside of each so the potatoes stand solidly upright. With a vegetable corer scoop a nickel-sized hole to the center of each potato. Push as much as possible of the hard butter into each cavity. Rub the outside of the potatoes well with the soft butter. Salt and pepper to taste. Bake standing upright, uncovered, in a preheated 375° F. oven for 40 minutes, or until the potatoes are tender and crisp.

SERVES 4.

Hash-Stuffed Bakers

4 medium-sized long
  baking potatoes,
  scrubbed and baked
1 cup of chopped cooked
  meat (leftover beef is
  ideal)
¼ cup of minced celery
  (scrape the celery
  before mincing)
2 scallions(white part
  only), minced
1 teaspoon of salt
½ teaspoon of pepper
1 tablespoon of finely
  chopped broadleaf
  parsley
3 tablespoons of beef broth
1 teaspoon of A1 Sauce
3 tablespoons of grated
  Asiago cheese

Cut the potatoes in half lengthwise. Scoop out the
pulp, reserving the 4 best shells, and rice into a bowl.
Add the meat, celery, scallions, salt, pepper, parsley,
beef broth and A1 Sauce, blending thoroughly. Taste
for seasoning. Spoon into the potato shells, sprinkle
with the cheese and bake in a preheated 400° F. oven
until hot and top is golden.

SERVES 4.

Ichabod's Baked French-Fried Slices

This specialty of Ichabod's Restaurant in Canton,
Connecticut, is so unique and delicious that some
people come just for the potatoes.

4 medium-sized baking potatoes, scrubbed and baked
Vegetable oil for deep frying
Salt and pepper to taste

While the potatoes are in the last stage of the baking
(still firm, not soft) heat 2 inches of oil until a cube
of bread sizzles and browns quickly. Keep the oil at
that heat. Cut the unpeeled potatoes into ⅓-inch
slices. Fry the slices quickly, just until they crust and
are golden. Drain on paper towels, season to taste

with salt and pepper and serve immediately. The customers at Ichabod's seem to like these with fillet of sole.

SERVES 4 TO 6.

Jean's Shrimp-Stuffed Potatoes
with Poached Eggs

6 medium-sized long baking potatoes, scrubbed and baked
8 medium-sized shrimp, cooked until they just turn pink, and coarsely chopped
5 tablespoons of butter
⅓ cup of grated Parmesan cheese
Salt and pepper to taste
6 eggs, poached, drained and trimmed

Cut the potatoes lengthwise and remove the pulp, reserving the 6 best shells. Rice the pulp into a bowl, add the shrimp, butter, one-half of the cheese, salt and pepper, blend thoroughly. Spoon the mixture back into the 6 reserved shells and bake in a preheated 375° F. oven until the top starts to turn golden. With the back of a tablespoon, make a depression in the center of each potato. Place a poached egg in each and sprinkle the remaining cheese on top of the egg. Bake for another 2 minutes, then place under the broiler until golden.

SERVES 6.

Ken's Baked New Potato Surprise

Usually new potatoes are not baked. Here's a surprisingly delicious exception from a friend. We like to surround standing ribs of roast beef with these delicious morsels.

24 small, but not tiny, new potatoes, washed, dried and rubbed with olive oil
2 teaspoons of salt

Cut the potatoes in half and sprinkle with salt. Bake in a preheated 450° F. oven until the potatoes are tender, puffed and browned.

SERVES 6.

Jerry's Low-Cal Mock French Fries

Here's an easy one with practically no calories, a baked potato French-fried looking and tasting, without being French fried.

4 medium-sized baking potatoes
2 egg whites, beaten until frothy
Salt

Scrub the potatoes and cut each into 8 pieces lengthwise, then dry. Dip the potato pieces in the egg white to lightly coat. Place on a lightly oiled baking sheet, not touching, and sprinkle generously with salt. Bake in a preheated 425° F. oven for 40 minutes, or until golden-crisp and tender. Serve right from the oven.

SERVES 4 TO 6.

Baked Potatoes with a
Madras Spicy Yogurt Topping

Here is a topping that will make the potato jump out of its skin.

1 tablespoon of vegetable oil	¼ teaspoon of cayenne
½ teaspoon of mustard seeds	½ teaspoon of ground cumin
¼ teaspoon of curry powder	1 garlic clove, minced
1 cup of yogurt	1 teaspoon of ground ginger
2 tablespoons of chick-pea flour	Salt to taste
	6 medium-sized baking potatoes, scrubbed and baked

In a frypan heat the oil. Add the mustard seeds and curry and cook until the mustard seeds pop. Stir in the yogurt, flour, cayenne, cumin, garlic, ginger and salt. Stir well and simmer 5 minutes. Split the hot potatoes and spoon on the yogurt topping.

SERVES 6.

Norma Jean Maxwell's Buttered Bakers

This may seem lavish, but it is worth it. These bakers have made "Prissy" Maxwell a famous hostess.

4 large baking potatoes, scrubbed, dried and pierced in several places
8 tablespoons (1 stick) of soft butter
Salt and pepper

Rub the skin of the potatoes well with the butter and sprinkle with salt and pepper. Bake, uncovered, on a cookie sheet in a preheated 375° F. oven for one hour or until the potatoes are soft to the squeeze. Eat the entire potato, skin and all.

SERVES 4.

Baked Potatoes with Pesto

We enjoyed this surprise dish in Genoa on our last visit, not only reminding us that Italians don't always eat pasta, but that they were among the first in Europe to discover the potato. It may seem like a lot of work to prepare pesto just as a topping for potatoes, but the leftover pesto can be frozen and used with pasta, and these potatoes will instantly make you a famed host.

1 recipe of Pesto (page 61)
3 large baking potatoes, scrubbed and baked

You can easily make the pesto with a blender while the potatoes are baking. When the potatoes are cooked to your liking, the skins crisp, remove them, cut them into halves lengthwise. Remove the pulp and rice it, then return it to the 6 half shells. Spoon a big dollop of pesto on each potato half. Served very hot with a nice veal chop or breast of chicken scallopini, you'll have a meal to remember. The entrée should be very simple—this potato is rich!

Serves 6.

Pigs in a Poke

from Bruno M. Valbona

4 large baking potatoes, scrubbed
1 package "Brown 'N Serve" sausage
Salt and pepper

With a vegetable corer, core two holes through each potato the narrow way. Stuff these holes full of sausage meat. Add salt and pepper to taste and wrap the stuffed potatoes in aluminum foil (shiny side in).

Bake in a preheated 375° F. oven for 45 minutes, or until done. Serve immediately from the oven.

Leftover sausage and potato cores can be combined with a little oregano, salt, pepper and garlic powder, wrapped in foil and baked along with the "Pigs"—it makes excellent snacking.

SERVES 4.

Note: Bruno Valbona and his wife, Barbara, are that rarity in couples, both superb cooks who have studied under the best of French and Italian chefs. Bruno Valbona is also Vice President of Research and Development at Waring, and responsible for many of their products, including their Food Processor, which we consider the best.

Bakers with "Red" Caviar and Sour Cream

Few of us can afford the classic gray caviar from the sturgeon. But these "red" fish roe are very tasty and almost affordable.

1 cup of sour cream
1 scallion (white part and a little of the green), minced
½ teaspoon of salt
½ teaspoon of pepper
4 medium-sized baking potatoes, scrubbed and baked
4 to 6 teaspoons of red caviar

In a bowl, combine the sour cream, scallion, salt and pepper and blend. Take the hot potatoes from the oven and split them in half lengthwise. Spoon the sour cream mixture onto the potatoes and top with 1 to 1½ teaspoons of red caviar.

SERVES 4.

Potatoes Roquefort

6 large baking potatoes
½ cup crumbled Roquefort cheese, firmly packed
About ½ cup of heavy cream
2 small whole scallions, minced
Salt and pepper to taste

⅓ cup of fine dry bread crumbs ⎫
½ garlic clove, minced ⎬ MIXED
3 tablespoons of melted butter ⎭

Scrub the potatoes and bake them in preheated 400°
F. oven for 40 minutes, or until easily pierced with a
fork. Cut off the tops of the potatoes lengthwise and
scoop out the pulp, reserving the shells. Put the pulp
through a potato ricer. Beat in the cheese and enough
cream to make the potatoes light and fluffy. Mix in
the scallions, salt and pepper and spoon the potato
mixture back into the shells, mounding it. Sprinkle
the bread crumb–garlic-butter mixture over the tops
and bake in a preheated 350° F. oven for 20 minutes,
or until crusty-brown.

SERVES 6.

Spinach-Filled Baked Potatoes

Here, again, is an entire vegetable course served in one baked potato shell. This can be prepared ahead, but if it is placed in the oven cold it will take longer to heat.

6 medium-sized long baking potatoes, scrubbed and baked

8 tablespoons (1 stick) of soft butter

1 teaspoon of salt

½ teaspoon of pepper

1 teaspoon of dillweed

1 (10-ounce) package of fresh spinach, cooked and chopped, or 1 (10-ounce) package of frozen, chopped spinach, defrosted

3 tablespoons of chopped shallots cooked in 2 tablespoons of butter

6 tablespoons of grated sharp Cheddar cheese

Cut off the tops of the potatoes lengthwise. Scoop out all of the pulp leaving the shells intact. Mash the potato pulp with the butter, salt, pepper, dillweed, blending thoroughly. Squeeze all the liquid from the spinach and add the spinach and shallots to the potato mixture, mixing well. Taste for seasoning. Spoon the mixture into the shells and bake on a cookie sheet, uncovered, in a preheated 400° F. oven for 20 minutes, or until heated through. Remove from the oven and sprinkle 1 tablespoon of cheese on top of each potato. Place under the broiler until the cheese has melted and top is golden.

SERVES 6.

Bakers with Sour Cream Stuffing

This is the all-time favorite of just about everyone. But it is not a simple matter of dolloping sour cream atop a baked potato.

3 large baking potatoes
5 tablespoons of softened butter
1 teaspoon of salt

2 egg yolks
½ cup of sour cream } BLENDED

Rub the potatoes with oil and bake in a preheated 400° F. oven until tender, about 45 minutes. Split the potatoes lengthwise and carefully scoop out the pulp, reserving the 4 best shells. Rice the pulp into a bowl, and while the potatoes are still hot, whip in 3 tablespoons of the butter and the salt. Beat in the egg yolks–sour cream mixture, whipping into a smooth puree. Taste for seasoning. Mound into the reserved shells and place on a cookie sheet. Dot with the remaining 2 tablespoons of the butter and run under a broiler until golden.

SERVES 4.

Baked Potatoes Stuffed with Oysters

6 long baking potatoes, scrubbed and baked
5 tablespoons of butter
1 tablespoon of minced shallots
¼ pound of mushrooms, coarsely chopped

1½ tablespoons of flour
Salt to taste
1 cup of heavy cream
1 teaspoon of Worcestershire sauce
Pinch of cayenne
12 fresh small oysters

3 tablespoons of grated cheese (your choice)

While the potatoes are baking, prepare the stuffing. In a frypan, heat 2 tablespoons of the butter. Add the shallots and cook for 1 minute, or until soft. Add the mushrooms and cook 1 minute longer. Sprinkle in the flour and salt and cook, stirring constantly, until the flour is well mixed in. Gradually stir in the cream, Worcestershire sauce and cayenne and cook, stirring, until you have a medium-thick smooth sauce.

When the potatoes are cooked, cut a thin slice from the top lengthwise. Scoop out the pulp, reserving the shells, and mash the pulp with the remaining 3 table-spoons of butter and salt to taste. Spoon two-thirds of the potatoes back into the shells (the remainder can be used in another recipe). Add the oysters to the pan with the mushroom sauce and simmer until the edges curl and they become plump. Place the potatoes in a baking dish. Spoon the mushroom-oyster sauce onto the potatoes in the shells. Sprinkle cheese on top and place in a preheated 425° F. oven for 10 minutes, or until heated through and top is golden.

SERVES 6.

Vegetable-Stuffed Baked Potatoes

Here is the vegetable course in one unique presenta-tion.

    4 medium-sized long baking potatoes, scrubbed and
      baked
    1 cup of Cream-Cheese Sauce (see page 273)
    ½ cup of chopped cooked carrots
    ½ cup of cooked baby lima beans
    ¼ cup of chopped, cooked sweet red pepper
    ½ teaspoon of salt
    ⅓ cup of bread crumbs
    2 tablespoons of butter

Cut the potatoes in halves lengthwise. Scoop out the pulp, reserving the 4 best shells, and rice it into a bowl. Stir in two-thirds of the sauce and all of the cooked vegetables and salt. Taste for seasoning. Spoon the mixture into the potato shells. Spoon on the remaining sauce. Sprinkle with bread crumbs, dot with butter and place in a preheated 400° F. oven until heated through and top is golden.

Cream-Cheese Sauce

Makes about 1 cup.
    2 tablespoons of butter
    2 tablespoons of flour
    1 cup of light cream
    1 tablespoon of light sherry
    ¼ cup of grated sharp Cheddar cheese
    Salt and pepper to taste

In a saucepan, melt the butter and stir in the flour, stirring until it becomes a smooth paste. Over low heat, gradually blend in the cream, stirring until the sauce becomes thick and smooth. Whisk in the sherry and cheese and stir until the cheese melts. Season with salt and pepper.

SERVES 4.

Pancakes

It is believed that the Germans created the first potato pancake. Certainly they made it a classic and a favorite worldwide. It appears here rather than in the chapter with the rest of the classics because the pancake, too, is versatile and comes in a number of versions. There are almost as many ways to prepare German potato pancakes as there are varieties of potatoes. Each section of Germany has its own touch.

We have assembled here all those that we have eaten in Germany and some interesting pancakes from other countries.

Serving potato pancakes with any meal always causes comment. They are unique; but many of us do not cook them because we consider them complicated. Actually, they are simplicity itself. But there are some steps to be taken when you prepare raw potato pancakes that will insure success.

Peel the potatoes last and do the other steps first. Potatoes, once peeled, will darken if they are exposed to the air for any length of time. One sure way to avoid this is to peel and then grate the potatoes into water. But always make certain they are well drained then squeezed dry, preferably in a kitchen towel.

In a bowl, lightly beat the eggs or yolks that will be used, then add the flour, salt, pepper and any other ingredients, such as onion. Also beat the egg whites (if they are beaten separately), and heat the oil or other fat in a griddle or frypan and have it ready. In short, do everything you can in advance, so when the potatoes are grated they can quickly be beaten into the other ingredients and fried right away.

Potato pancakes are like pasta and soufflés; they should be cooked and served immediately. The guests wait for the pancakes, not vice versa. We like to conscript a willing guest who wants to learn the pancake technique. He stays with the frypan proudly turning out pancakes while we deliver them piping hot and crisp to the table.

The pancakes can be kept warm in a low oven until the whole batch is cooked, and they will be good. But there is no substitute for speed of service.

These crispy cakes are as addictive as peanuts, so be sure you make enough.

All Saints' Day Pancake

This is served in various Catholic sections of Ireland on the eve of All Saints' Day.

8 medium-sized baking potatoes, peeled, grated and
squeezed dry in a kitchen towel
1¼ cups of flour
1½ teaspoons of salt
½ cup of light cream
4 tablespoons of butter
¼ cup of light brown sugar
4 tablespoons of melted butter

In a large bowl, combine the potatoes, flour and salt and mix well. Add the cream gradually, blending until the mixture holds together. Let set for 45 minutes. In a frypan, large enough to hold the potato mixture in one large, thick pancake, melt the butter. Add the potato mixture, shaping it into a large cake with a spatula. Cook over medium-low heat for 20 minutes (using a spatula to keep pancake from sticking to the bottom of the pan), or until the underside is crusty brown. Turn and cook until the entire pancake is crusty brown. Serve sprinkled with brown sugar and melted butter.

SERVES 6.

Pancakes with Beef Broth

8 medium-sized baking potatoes, peeled and grated into
a bowl of cold water
1 cup of cold beef broth
2 eggs
1 cup of flour
1½ teaspoons of salt
½ teaspoon of pepper

Soak the potatoes in the water for 10 minutes, drain and squeeze dry in a kitchen towel. In a bowl, combine the potatoes, broth, eggs, ½ cup of the flour, salt and pepper. Beat well, mixing thoroughly. The batter should approximate that of ordinary pancake batter. If too thin, add small amounts of the remaining flour until the batter is of the proper consistency. Grease a pancake griddle and spoon on enough of the batter to make medium-sized cakes. Cook until crisply golden brown on both sides.

SERVES 6.

German Pancakes with Boiled Potatoes

4 large baking potatoes, peeled
Juice of 1 lemon
2 medium-sized potatoes, boiled and mashed (about 1⅓ cups)
2 eggs, beaten
1½ teaspoons of salt
¼ cup of light cream
Vegetable oil for frying

Grate the raw potatoes into a bowl half filled with water to which the lemon juice has been added (the lemon juice prevents the potatoes from discoloring). Remove the potatoes, but do not discard the liquid. Squeeze the moisture from the potatoes in a kitchen towel. Pour the liquid from the bowl, but retain any starchy residue that has collected in the bottom. In a large bowl, combine the grated potatoes, mashed potatoes and the potato starch. Add the eggs, salt and cream, and vigorously beat into a batter. In a frypan, heat ½ inch of oil. Add the batter, a tablespoon at a time, to form the size pancake desired. When firm and golden brown underneath, turn and cook until the other side is done. Drain on paper towels. Serve immediately.

SERVES 4 TO 6.

Bombay Potato Cakes

5 medium-sized potatoes
1 tablespoon of soft butter
1 teaspoon of salt
½ teaspoon of cayenne or to taste
½ teaspoon of turmeric
7 tablespoons (or more) of rice flour
Vegetable oil for deep frying

Peel the potatoes and boil in salted water until tender. Drain, dry over heat in a pot, then mash them. In a bowl, combine the potatoes, butter, salt, cayenne, turmeric and the 7 tablespoons of rice flour and mix well. It must hold together as a firm dough; add more flour, if necessary. Heat at least 2 inches of oil in a deep fryer or deep pan. Pinch off large enough balls of dough that, when flattened, will make 2-inch cakes. When the oil is hot enough to quickly brown a bread cube, slide the cakes into it, one at a time, cooking several at a time without crowding. Fry for 2 minutes, or until golden brown and slightly crusty on both sides. Remove with a slotted spatula or spoon and drain on paper towels. Serve immediately.

SERVES 4.

Potato Cheese Cakes

5 medium-sized baking potatoes, peeled, grated and
    squeezed dry in a kitchen towel
½ cup of sour cream
½ cup of grated sharp Cheddar cheese
2 tablespoons of melted butter
1 teaspoon of salt
½ teaspoon of pepper
Vegetable oil for frying

In a bowl, combine all the ingredients, blending well. In a large frypan (one that can go under the broiler) heat 3 tablespoons of oil. Add the potato mixture, 1 tablespoonful at a time, and press into cakes with a spatula. Cook over medium heat until golden brown and crisp underneath. Do not turn the cakes. Sprinkle them lightly with oil and place under a broiler until they are golden brown and crisp on top.

SERVES 4.

Copenhagen Cakes

These small Danish potato cakes are sometimes served with fruit preserves or maple syrup, but they are most often offered with roast meat.

1 egg
1 cup of milk
½ cup of flour
2 tablespoons of melted butter
1 teaspoon of salt
½ teaspoon of pepper
4 medium-sized baking potatoes, peeled and cubed
Vegetable oil

Combine the egg, milk, flour, butter, salt and pepper in a blender jar. Blend on high for 30 seconds. Gradually add the potato cubes, until everything is blended into a thickish smooth batter. Coat a frypan with oil, heat over medium heat and cook the cakes, 1 tablespoonful for each. Cook until crisply golden brown on both sides. These are rather "soft" cakes with a different and delightful flavor.

SERVES 4.

French Pancakes

5 medium-sized baking potatoes, peeled and finely
   shredded

½ cup of light cream
2 tablespoons of melted butter
1 tablespoon of olive oil
2 tablespoons of beer
2 large eggs   BEATEN TOGETHER
1 cup of flour   UNTIL WELL BLENDED,
1½ teaspoons of salt   THEN STRAINED INTO
½ teaspoon of pepper   A LARGE BOWL
⅛ teaspoon of cayenne

Vegetable oil for frying

Blend the potatoes with the batter in the bowl. Heat
about ¼ inch of oil in a deep frypan and add the
batter by the tablespoonful to the size cake desired.
Cook on both sides until crisply golden brown.

SERVES 4 TO 6.

German Sour-Cream Cakes

8 medium-sized baking potatoes, peeled, grated and
   squeezed dry in a kitchen towel
2 eggs, lightly beaten
3 tablespoons of flour
1½ teaspoons of salt
⅓ cup of sour cream
6 tablespoons of vegetable oil

In a bowl, combine the potatoes, eggs, flour, salt and
sour cream. Beat together until well blended. Using
two frypans, over medium-low heat, heat 3 tablespoons of oil in each. Spread half of the potato mixture in each, shaping into ½-inch-thick cakes with
a spatula. Cook until golden brown on the bottom,
cut each cake into quarters and brown on the other
side.

SERVES 8.

Green Mashed-Potato Pancakes

3 medium-sized potatoes
Salt and pepper to taste
2 tablespoons of heavy cream
1 egg, lightly beaten
2 tablespoons of finely chopped fresh chives
2 tablespoons of finely chopped fresh parsley
4 tablespoons of butter
1 tablespoon of vegetable oil

Peel the potatoes and boil in salted water until tender. Drain and dry over heat in a pot. Put the potatoes through a potato ricer into a bowl. Add the salt, pepper, cream, egg, chives and parsley, blending thoroughly. Shape the mixture into 4 cakes (or more, depending on the size you prefer). Heat the butter and oil in a large frypan over medium heat and cook the cakes until golden brown on both sides.

SERVES 4.

B. J. Guidetti's Grandmother's Pancakes

See page 213–14 for background on the Guidettis. B. J.
says that her grandmother had three musts: 1. Large
black iron skillets. 2 Bacon fat. 3. Potatoes must be
grated on the fine grater used for hard cheese, or else
the pancakes won't have the lacy crispness around the
edges. Grandmother also said that if you grated a
little of your skin into the potatoes, don't worry, it
adds authenticity.

> 5 large baking potatoes, peeled and grated on the fine
>   grater
> ½ large onion, grated
> 1 tablespoon of flour
> 1 egg, lightly beaten
> 1 teaspoon of salt
> Pepper to taste
> Bacon fat (1 tablespoon for each frying, replenish when
>   necessary)

In a bowl, combine all the ingredients, except the
bacon fat. Blend well. Melt the bacon fat over
medium heat and fry 3 or 4 pancakes at a time, using
a heaping tablespoon of batter for each pancake,
pressed down with a spatula. B. J. uses two black iron
frypans and cooks all pancakes quickly, until they are
brown on both sides and the edges lacy-crisp. She
serves them with applesauce. Her cooking trick: When
B. J. sees the grayish hue of the pancakes turn white
she knows it is time to flip them over and cook them
on the other side.

ABOUT 18 PANCAKES.

Potato Latkes
(Jewish Potato Pancakes)

4 large baking potatoes, peeled, grated and squeezed
   dry in a kitchen towel
1 large white onion, grated
2 eggs, beaten
3 tablespoons of matzo flour
½ teaspoon of baking powder
1½ teaspoons of salt
½ teaspoon of pepper
½ cup of vegetable oil

In a large bowl, blend the potatoes and onion. Stir in
the eggs. Add the flour and baking powder, salt and
pepper and mix thoroughly. Have the oil heated in a
frypan. Drop the potato mixture in by the tablespoonful, press into cakes with a spatula and cook until
golden brown and crusty on both sides. Drain on
paper towels. Serve with meat dishes with applesauce
on the side.

SERVES 4 TO 6.

State of Maine's Potato Pancakes

Try a poached egg on these potato cakes. Excellent!

1½ cups of sifted flour
2 egg yolks
1½ cups of milk   } BEATEN TOGETHER IN
1 teaspoon of salt   A LARGE BOWL

1 tablespoon of melted butter
3 medium-sized potatoes, peeled, grated and squeezed
   dry in a kitchen towel
2 egg whites, stiffly beaten

Gradually stir the flour into the egg yolk–milk bowl,
then blend in the melted butter and potatoes. Fold in
the egg whites. Drop the potato batter by the table-

spoonful onto a hot greased griddle. Cook until golden brown on both sides.

SERVES 4.

Moscow Mashed Potato Cakes

6 medium-sized potatoes
6 tablespoons of butter
2 egg yolks
Salt and pepper to taste
1 small white onion,
  finely chopped

6 medium-sized fresh
  mushrooms, finely
  chopped
1 teaspoon of flour
1 whole egg, beaten
About ¾ cup bread crumbs

Peel the potatoes and boil in salted water until tender. Drain and dry over heat in a pot. Mash the potatoes while still hot. Beat in 2 tablespoons of the butter, egg yolks, salt and pepper. Cool. Shape into flat 3- or 4-inch cakes.

In a frypan, melt 2 tablespoons of the butter. Add the onion and sauté for 1 minute. Add the mushrooms, sprinkle with the flour, salt and pepper and sauté quickly, stirring, to allow moisture to evaporate, without overcooking the mushrooms. Place a spoonful of the filling off center on each potato cake, fold over. Press the edges together. Brush with the beaten egg and dust with the bread crumbs. Heat the remaining 2 tablespoons of the butter in a frypan and cook the cakes until golden brown on both sides, being careful in turning to keep the cakes intact. Add more butter as needed.

SERVES 4.

Leftover-Potato Pancakes New England Style

We like these with pork chops and stewed pears.

½ cup of bread crumbs
½ cup of light cream
3 cups of leftover mashed
  potatoes
1 small onion, grated
2 egg yolks, lightly
  beaten

1 teaspoon of salt
½ teaspoon of pepper
Pinch of nutmeg
Pinch of dried thyme
3 tablespoons of bacon
  drippings (or use butter,
  but bacon fat is better)

In a large bowl, place the bread crumbs and blend with the cream; let stand for 1 hour. Add the potatoes, onion, egg yolks, salt, pepper, nutmeg and thyme to the bread crumb bowl and blend well. In a large frypan, heat the bacon fat and drop in 1 heaping tablespoonful of the potato mixture for each cake, flattening with a spatula. Fry over medium-high heat until one side is brown and crisp. Turn and repeat the procedure (add more fat if necessary).

SERVES 4.

Plain Potato Pancakes

8 medium-sized baking potatoes, peeled

2 egg yolks
2 tablespoons of flour ⎫ BEATEN TOGETHER
1½ teaspoons of salt ⎬ IN A LARGE BOWL
½ teaspoon of pepper ⎭
2 egg whites, stiffly beaten
Vegetable oil for frying

Grate the potatoes, as quickly as possible, into a strainer, over a bowl. With the back of a spoon, press as much liquid out of the potatoes as you can. Immediately blend the grated potatoes with the egg yolk mixture. Pour off the liquid that has collected in the bowl where the potatoes drained, but save any starchy residue that has collected in the bottom. Add this to the potato–egg yolk mixture, blending well. Fold in the egg whites. In a deep frypan, over medium heat, have ½ inch of oil heated. Place 1 heaping tablespoon of the potato mixture for each pancake. Press down with a spatula, forming a cake. Fry, turning once, so each side is golden brown and crispy. Drain on paper towels. Serve immediately.

SERVES 6.

Quick Potato Cake with Skins

6 medium-sized baking potatoes, scrubbed
3 small white onions, grated
1½ teaspoons of salt
½ teaspoon of pepper
Vegetable oil for frying

Grate the unpeeled potatoes and squeeze dry in a kitchen towel.

In a bowl, combine the potatoes, onion, salt and pepper and mix well. In a large frypan, have sufficient oil heated to prevent the cake from sticking. Spread the potato mixture evenly forming one large cake, about ½ inch thick. Cover, cook over medium-low heat, until the bottom is brown and crisp. Turn (if necessary, add more oil and heat before returning the pancake to the pan) and brown the other side. If the cake breaks up during this turning, don't be concerned as you can reshape it with a spatula. Cook until the bottom is crisp and brown.

SERVES 4 TO 6.

Rhinelander Potato-Onion Cakes

1½ cups of milk

6 medium-sized baking potatoes, peeled

3 small white onions, finely chopped ⎱
2 large eggs, beaten
½ cup of flour   ⎰ BLENDED IN A
1½ teaspoons of salt   LARGE BOWL
½ teaspoon of pepper

Vegetable oil for frying

Place the milk in a large bowl and grate the potatoes into it. Drain well and add them to the bowl with the onions and other ingredients. Mix thoroughly. Heat ½ inch of oil in a deep frypan. Drop the batter in by the tablespoonful to make the size cake desired. Press into cakes with a spatula and brown on both sides until crisp. Drain on paper towels. Sprinkle lightly with salt and serve immediately.

SERVES 4.

Variations

Apple pancakes: Omit the onion and substitute 1 large, peeled, chopped apple. *Another flavor touch:* Add 2 tablespoons of chopped broadleaf parsley to the batter. In some sections of Germany potato pancakes are served with crisp bacon, sometimes the whole slice, sometimes in bits. Also some German recipes insist that potato pancakes be fried in bacon fat. It does make a delicious difference.

Russian Potato Cakes

1 egg, beaten
6 medium-sized baking potatoes, peeled, grated and
   squeezed dry in a kitchen towel

¼ cup of warm water ⎫
1 package of dry yeast ⎪
1 teaspoon of sugar   ⎬ BLENDED TOGETHER IN A
1 teaspoon of salt   ⎪ LARGE BOWL
½ cup of flour   ⎭

Sour cream

Add the egg and potatoes to the bowl containing the
yeast mixture, and blend well. Set aside in a warm
place for 10 minutes to rise. Cook on a greased pancake griddle, forming the cakes the size you prefer.
Cook until crisply golden brown on both sides. Serve
with sour cream on the side.

SERVES 4 TO 6.

Potato-Zucchini Pancakes

5 medium-sized baking
   potatoes, peeled and
   grated into a bowl of
   cold water
2 medium-sized zucchini,
   peeled and grated
1 small white onion,
   grated

3 eggs, lightly beaten

BLENDED
3 tablespoons of flour
½ teaspoon of baking
   powder
1½ teaspoons of salt
½ teaspoon of pepper

Vegetable oil for frying

Drain the potatoes and place them, the zucchini and
onion in a kitchen towel and squeeze dry (the object
to wring as much moisture from the vegetables as
possible). In a bowl, combine the vegetables, the eggs
and blended flour, mixing well. Lightly oil a pancake

griddle (which is best) or a frypan. Spoon a heaping tablespoon for each pancake onto the griddle or in the pan, press into cake shape with a spatula, and fry on both sides until crisp and brown.

SERVES 6 TO 8.

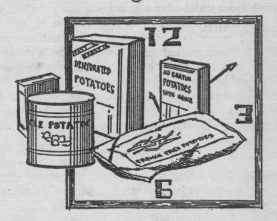

Processed Potatoes

Today potatoes are so popular and so much in demand that the busy housewife does not even have to peel and cook them. Processors have thought up so many ingenious ways to precook and package potatoes, that we hereby, partly through the courtesy of the state of Idaho, offer a short, but we hope helpful, chapter on these numerous appealing potato products found on grocery shelves.

To follow: Thoughts on cooking and serving, plus a quick reference chart, and some ideas to stir the imagination.

All processed potatoes have instructions and suggestions on the packages, and your own imagination will also serve you well in offering these quickie potatoes in unique ways.

They are a decided boon for the busy or working

housewife. The authors were served crusty, tasty hashed brown potatoes with a delectable pot roast of beef at a friend's home while at work on this book. We both remarked about how good the potatoes were, and how expertly our hostess managed to get them *just* right, never an easy task with hashed browns.

The hostess smiled and thanked us. A couple of days later in a telephone conversation she told us that the hashed browns were dehydrated.

Processed potatoes have come a long way in a short time. With their consistent high quality no one need feel any qualms about serving any variety.

Dehydrated Instant Flakes:

Preparation—Add to boiling or hot water depending on package directions, with milk, butter and salt.

Time—1 to 3 minutes.

Serving Suggestions—Mashed potatoes, potato patties, Chantilly potatoes, Duchess, Shepherd, soup rosettes and other decorative trim squeezed from a pastry tube, *gnocchi*, vichyssoise, soufflés, cheese puffs, hors d'oeuvres and for any recipe that calls for mashed potatoes.

Or use directly from package for thickening gravies, sauces, breading, for biscuits, pancakes, doughnuts, quick and yeast breads.

Dehydrated Diced:

Preparation—With salt and sugar, add to boiling water then either simmer 10 minutes or soak overnight.

Time—10 to 15 minutes.

Serving Suggestions—Stews, home-fried potatoes, hashed browns, hashed-in-cream, O'Brien potatoes, casseroles, salads, soups, chowders, creamed potatoes, scalloped and au gratin, lyonnaise.

Dehydrated Shredded:

Preparation—Use as diced or to reconstitute as raw shreds, add with sugar and salt to boiling water, soak for 30 minutes, drain.

Time—10 to 15 minutes (30 minutes for soaking).

Serving Suggestions—hashed browns, hashed-in-cream, soups, potato pancakes, O'Brien potato bread, hash and to extend and keep meat loaf and meatballs moist and tender.

Dehydrated Scalloped with Sauce Mix:

Preparation—Add boiling water, seasoning mix and bake.

Time—45 minutes.

Serving Suggestions—Delmonico potatoes, hot German potato salad, casseroles, add any combination of meat, fish or fowl, vegetables and garnish.

Dehydrated Au Gratin with Sauce Mix:

Preparation—Add boiling water, sauce mix and bake, covered.

Time—45 minutes.

Serving Suggestions—Use in casserole combinations.

Canned Small Whole Peeled Potatoes

Basic Method—Use as an ingredient, fry or roast.

Time—already fully cooked.

Serving Suggestions—Use in stews, for every kind of fried potatoes, deep fry whole or roast.

Frozen French Fries (straight cuts, crinkle cuts, thin cuts, slim crinkle cuts, shoestrings, wedge cuts):

Basic Method—Preblanched to brown in deep fryer, oven or in skillet.

Time—3 to 15 minutes, depending on size.
Serving Suggestions—Hors d'oeuvres, salads, stews, casseroles, snacks.

Frozen Hash Browns, Southern Style:

Basic Method—Heat in oven or skillet or use directly from freezer as ingredient.
Time—10 minutes.
Serving Suggestions—Stews, home-fried potatoes, hashed brown potatoes, hashed-in-cream, O'Brien potatoes, casseroles, salads, soups, chowders, creamed potatoes, scalloped and au gratin potatoes, lyonnaise potatoes.

Frozen Hash Browns (shredded, shredded and scored):

Basic Method—Heat in oven or skillet or use directly from freezer as ingredient.
Time—5 minutes.
Serving Suggestions—Hashed browns, hashed-in-cream, soups, potato pancakes, O'Brien potato bread, hash and to extend and keep meat loaf and meatballs moist and tender.

Frozen Potato Rounds (Tots, Logs, Gems, etc.):

Basic Method—Heat in oven, deep fryer or skillet.
Time—2 to 15 minutes.
Serving Suggestions—Suitable for any meal, snack or hors d'oeuvres.

Frozen Cottage Fried:

Basic Method—Heat in oven, deep fryer, skillet or as ingredient.
Time—2 to 15 minutes.
Serving Suggestions—For every style of fried potato, for scalloped, au gratin and casseroles.

Frozen Patties (triangles, round):

Basic Method—Heat in oven, deep fryer, skillet or barbecue grill.

Time—3 to 15 minutes.

Serving Suggestions—Fry or grill or use as base for open-face broiled sandwiches.

Frozen Small Whole Peeled:

Basic Method—Heat in water or oven; fry or use as ingredient.

Time—Pre-cooked.

Serving Suggestions—Use in stews for every kind of fried potato, deep fry whole, roast or heat and serve with lemon butter, parsley, chives, etc.

As with the baked potato, your imagination can use the processed potato in all kinds of intriguing ways:

Use instant mashed potatoes to make baked eggs in potato nests, cover a stew, as a base for creamed dishes.

Make a potato cake with frozen potato rounds and shredded hashed browns, mixed with eggs, heavy cream and Swiss cheese.

Make an interesting potato and chicken or beef loaf with frozen hashed browns and crinkle-cut French fries, mixing the hashed browns with the cooked chopped meat, along with onion, seasonings and cream, and line the loaf pan with the French fries, then pour in the mixture.

Use crushed potato chips instead of bread crumbs for dredging seafood and chicken. Much tastier than bread crumbs.

Use potato sticks to top creamed dishes, or include them in an omelet filling.

Dip chicken-to-be-fried in beaten egg then instant potato flakes.

Cover a casserole with potato tots during the last 15 minutes of baking time.

Use shredded hashed browns as the base for potato pancakes.

Potato salad is easy with reconstituted dehydrated diced potatoes.

Serve frozen French fries as an appetizer with an interesting dip such as guacamole.

Top country fries with creamed eggs or fish.

Carry on. The serving process for processed potatoes is endless.

The processed potato people are turning out new products so fast that it is difficult to keep up with them. But new, at least to us, as we write this book, are thick, steak-cut French fries, thick-sliced cottage fries, stuffed baked potato puffs, mashed potato balls, shoestring potatoes in butter sauce, sliced potatoes in butter sauce, bite-sized potatoes with peas in bacon-cream sauce, diced potatoes in a sour cream sauce. Some of these products come in the convenient "no clean-up" plastic cooking pouches.

There is no question, the Incas who first developed the potato, have all turned over in their graves—with envy.

Potato Sweets

We hope, as with any satisfying book, this surprise ending will please.

Potato sweets? Yes, and we don't mean sweet potatoes either, as they really aren't potatoes.

The potato is such a marvel that in many cases it can be substituted wholly, or in part, for flour in making cakes, cookies, doughnuts and other desserts. Its semisweet mealy goodness melds magnificently with dessert ingredients.

Not long ago we were fortunate enough to be invited to a seder. One of the highlights was cooked by a chef from Israel: The best macaroon cookies we have ever tasted. Slyly, he told us that they were made with potatoes. We were surprised, but knowing the remarkable alchemy of the potato that converts even a chocolate cake into a moist delight, we didn't doubt his word. Our disappointment was that he wouldn't relinquish his recipe. We've been more generous. Here is our entire potato dessert repertoire.

Chocolate Potato Cake

1 cup of cold mashed
    potatoes
2 cups of all-purpose
    flour
1 teaspoon of baking soda
1 tablespoon of double-
    acting baking powder
½ cup of soft butter

2 cups of sugar
4 large eggs
¾ cup of buttermilk
1 teaspoon of vanilla
1 teaspoon of salt
4 squares (4 ounces) of
    unsweetened chocolate,
    melted

In a large bowl, place all of the ingredients, except
the chocolate. With an electric mixer, at low speed,
mix until well blended, occasionally scraping the bowl
with a spatula so that the mixture is completely
blended. Beat at medium speed for 4 minutes. Add
the chocolate and mix until it is thoroughly blended
into the mixture. Butter a 13-inch by 9-inch baking
pan; pour in the batter and bake in a preheated
350° F. oven for 45 minutes, or until a toothpick
pushed into the center emerges clean. Let stand for
10 minutes; remove from pan and cool the cake on a
wire rack.

Or bake in three 9-inch layers for 20 minutes, or
until toothpick emerges clean.

ABOUT 10 SERVINGS.

Potato Chocolate Drops

½ cup of shortening
1 cup of brown sugar, firmly packed
½ cup of cold mashed potatoes
1 egg, beaten
2 squares (2 ounces) of unsweetened chocolate, melted
1 teaspoon of vanilla

SIFTED TOGETHER
1½ cups of sifted flour
½ teaspoon of salt
½ teaspoon of baking soda
¾ cup of buttermilk
½ cup of chopped nuts (your choice)
Chocolate icing (optional)

In a large mixing bowl, cream together the shortening and sugar. Beat in the potatoes, egg, chocolate and vanilla until well blended. Add the flour mixture to the batter alternately with the buttermilk, blending until smooth. Stir in the nuts. Drop well-rounded teaspoonfuls of dough onto greased cookie sheets. Bake in a preheated 400° F. oven for 10 minutes. Swirl the chocolate icing over the tops while still warm, if desired.

MAKES ABOUT 3 DOZEN.

Potato Coffee Cake

This must be assembled the day before you wish to serve it.

½ cup plus 1 teaspoon
  of sugar
1½ teaspoons of salt
2 packages of dry yeast
  dissolved in ½ cup of
  warm water
1 cup of warm milk
½ cup of shortening
1 cup of mashed potatoes
  (they must be freshly
  cooked and
  unseasoned)

2 eggs, lightly beaten
9 cups of flour
  (approximately)
½ cup of soft butter
1 cup of coarsely chopped
  white and dark raisins
½ cup of coarsely chopped
  pecans

BLENDED
1 cup of sugar
1 teaspoon of cinnamon

1 egg white, beaten just until frothy

Add the 1 teaspoon of sugar and ½ teaspoon of the salt to the yeast and water and let rise in a warm place (an oven heated to its lowest temperature then turned off as soon as heated makes an excellent warm place) for 10 minutes. In a large bowl, combine the yeast mixture, the remaining ½ cup of sugar and teaspoon of salt, the milk and shortening and mix well. Stir in the potatoes and the eggs and then gradually stir in 5 cups of the flour, mixing well after each addition. Sprinkle ½ cup of flour onto a pastry board. Place the dough on it and knead for 10 minutes adding more flour until you have a non-sticky, smooth, flexible dough. Butter a bowl, drop the ball of dough into it, turn it over so the entire ball is buttered. Cover and refrigerate overnight.

Lightly flour a pastry board and a rolling pin and roll the dough out into a ½- or ¾-inch-thick rectangle. Spread with the soft butter. Sprinkle on the raisins and pecans and the sugar-cinnamon mixture. Starting on the short side, roll up like a jelly roll, stretching the dough a bit while rolling, and seal the edge. Bring the ends together to make a ring and place sealed edge down, in a buttered ring mold. Brush the top with the egg white and let rise in a warm place for about 1 hour, or until it doubles in volume. Bake in a preheated 375° F. oven for 40 minutes, or until top is golden.

SERVES 10 OR MORE.

Down East Custard Pie

1 medium-sized potato
2 tablespoons of butter
¾ cup of sugar
2 egg yolks, beaten
½ cup of milk
Juice and grated rind of ½ lemon
2 egg whites, stiffly beaten
1 partially cooked 9-inch pastry shell

Boil the potato in its skin until tender, drain, dry over heat in a pot then peel.

Mash the potato with the butter, whipping until smooth. Cool. In a bowl, combine the cooled potato, sugar, egg yolks, milk, lemon juice and rind. Blend thoroughly. Fold in the egg whites. Pour into the pastry shell and bake in a preheated 400° F. oven for 25 minutes, or until set.

SERVES 6.

Dora's Jam-Filled Dumplings

6 medium-sized potatoes
½ cup of butter
½ cup of fine bread crumbs
½ cup of brown sugar
¼ teaspoon of cinnamon

½ cup of sifted flour
2 egg yolks
1½ teaspoons of salt
⅛ teaspoon of mace
15 teaspoons of apricot or raspberry jam

1 egg white, beaten until frothy

Boil the potatoes in their skins until tender, drain and dry over heat in a pot. Peel the potatoes and rice them into a mixing bowl.

In a small saucepan, melt the butter. Add the bread crumbs and cook until they are golden. Remove from the heat and cool thoroughly. With a fork, stir in the brown sugar and cinnamon until well mixed. Set aside.

In the mixing bowl with the potatoes, whip in the flour, then the egg yolks, one at a time. Whip in the salt and mace until everything is well blended and you have a smooth dough. Cover and refrigerate for 2 hours, or until the dough is thoroughly chilled. Lightly sprinkle a pastry board with flour and using a floured rolling pin, roll the chilled dough out into a 9- by 15-inch rectangle. Cut the dough into 3-inch squares, place a teaspoon of the jam on each square just off center; fold them diagonally, brush the edges with beaten egg white and pinch together sealing the jam inside. Cook the dumplings 4 or 5 at a time (do not crowd them) in gently boiling, salted water, lowering them into the water with a slotted spoon. Cook about 5 minutes, or until the dumplings surface. Keep your eye on them so they do not stick to the bottom of the pot or to each other. Remove with a slotted spoon onto a hot serving dish. Stir the butter–bread crumbs–sugar mixture again with a fork to blend well and sprinkle it over the dumplings while they are still hot. Serve immediately.

MAKES 15 DUMPLINGS.

Potato Doughnuts

All ingredients should be at room temperature.

1 cup of freshly riced potatoes
3 tablespoons of butter
¾ cup of sugar
2 tablespoons of baking powder
¼ teaspoon of cinnamon   } SIFTED TOGETHER INTO
3 cups of sifted flour   A MIXING BOWL
½ teaspoon of salt
2 eggs, beaten
¼ cup of milk   } WELL BLENDED
1 teaspoon of vanilla
Vegetable oil for deep frying
Confectioners' sugar

Add the potatoes and butter to the mixing bowl with
the dry ingredients, and with a pastry blender cut
them in until the mixture has the consistency of coarse
crumbs. Add the egg-milk-vanilla mixture and blend
well. Lightly flour a pastry board and knead the
dough well (if it is too soft to handle, refrigerate for
a half hour). Roll it out to a ½-inch thickness; cut
with a floured 2½-inch doughnut cutter. Heat the
deep fat (enough to submerge 6 doughnuts; don't
cook too many at one time) to 375° F. Slide the
doughnuts in, one at a time, using a spatula. Cook for
1 minute on each side, or until golden on both sides.
Drain, cool and sprinkle with confectioners' sugar.
Don't waste the dough you cut out to make the holes;
fry them after the doughnuts are cooked; they are
tasty little snacks.

MAKES ABOUT 20 DOUGHNUTS.

Potato-Frosted Cake

1 (18½-ounce) package of cake mix (your choice)
1 cup of freshly mashed, unseasoned potatoes
¼ cup of butter at room temperature
3 (3-ounce) packages of cream cheese, at room
   temperature
¾ cup of sugar
2 teaspoons of vanilla
1½ cups of walnut meat halves

Bake the cake according to package directions. In a bowl, whip together the potatoes, butter, cream cheese, sugar and vanilla. The mixture should be very smooth. Evenly spread the potato frosting on the cake, decorating it with the walnuts pushed into the sides.

SERVES 6 TO 8.

Helen's Potato-Molasses Cookies

½ cup of dark molasses
½ cup of butter
⅓ cup of brown sugar
1½ cups of freshly
   cooked riced potatoes
1 cup of chopped
   walnuts
Confectioners' sugar

SIFTED TOGETHER:
2 cups of flour
½ teaspoon of baking
   soda
2 teaspoons of baking
   powder
½ teaspoon of ginger
½ teaspoon of cinnamon
½ teaspoon of salt

In a double boiler, over hot water, combine the molasses and the butter, beating until heated through and the butter is melted. Pour into a bowl and beat in the brown sugar. Add the sifted, dry ingredients and mix well. Beat in the potatoes until the mixture is smooth and well blended. Stir in the walnuts. Drop from a spoon onto a buttered cookie sheet and bake in a preheated 375° F. oven for 10 minutes. Sprinkle with confectioners' sugar.

MAKES ABOUT 50 COOKIES.

Potato Pudding with Lemon Sauce

This is a rather tart, piquant dessert, excellent after a dinner of roast pork, roast goose or any rich meat.

4 egg yolks
⅓ cup of sugar
2 tablespoons of lemon juice, strained
1 tablespoon of grated lemon rind
1 cup of freshly mashed, unseasoned potatoes
½ cup of chopped blanched walnuts
4 egg whites, stiffly beaten

In a bowl, beat the egg yolks until thick, smooth and lemony in color. Beat in the sugar, then the lemon juice and rind. Whip in the mashed potatoes. Stir in the walnuts. Fold in the egg whites. Place ½ inch of water in an 8-inch cake pan. Bring to a boil on top of the stove. Line the bottom of a 6-cup charlotte mold with buttered wax paper and butter the sides of the mold. Pour the potato mixture into the mold. Place the mold in the cake pan with the boiling water and bake in a preheated 350° F. oven for 40 minutes. Remove from oven, cool 8 minutes; carefully run a knife around the edges of the pudding and unmold onto a serving plate. Remove the wax paper. Serve with lemon sauce (below).

SERVES 6.

Lemon Sauce

Makes 1 cup

¼ cup of sugar
1 cup of warm water
1½ tablespoons of cornstarch
3 tablespoons of butter
2 tablespoons of strained lemon juice
¾ teaspoon of grated lemon rind
Pinch of salt

In the top of a double boiler, combine the sugar, water and cornstarch, blending well. Cook over very hot water, stirring until the base sauce has thickened. Take from the heat and gently beat in the butter, lemon juice, lemon rind and salt.

Maine Potato Candy

¾ cup of cold, unseasoned mashed potatoes
4 cups of confectioners' sugar
4 cups of chopped shredded coconut
1½ teaspoons of vanilla
½ teaspoon of salt
4 squares (4 ounces) of baking chocolate

In a bowl, blend well the potatoes and sugar. Add the coconut, vanilla, and salt and blend well. Press into one large, or two small pans so the candy will be ½ inch thick. Melt chocolate over hot water. As soon as it has melted pour it evenly over the top of the candy. Cool and cut into squares.

For variation, make haystacks by forming white mixture into cones 1 inch high. Allow to stand, uncovered, for 20 minutes. Dip the base of each cone in melted chocolate; place on wax paper until the chocolate hardens.

MAKES ABOUT 100 SMALL HAYSTACKS.

Maine Devil's Food Cake

½ cup of milk
4 squares (4 ounces) of
    bitter baking chocolate
1 cup of plain, hot
    mashed potatoes
1 cup of shortening
2 cups of sugar
4 egg yolks

SIFTED TOGETHER:
2 cups of sifted cake flour
1 tablespoon of baking
    powder
¼ teaspoon of salt
1½ teaspoons of vanilla
4 egg whites, stiffly beaten

Heat the milk and chocolate together over hot water, stirring well until the chocolate is melted. Remove from the heat. Stir in the potatoes, blending well. In a large bowl, cream the shortening and 1¾ cups of the sugar until light and fluffy. Blend in the potato-chocolate mixture, then add the egg yolks, mixing well. Gradually stir in the sifted dry ingredients. Add the vanilla and stir until you have a smooth, well-mixed batter. Gradually beat the remaining ¼ cup of sugar into beaten egg whites. Fold into the cake batter and pour into three 8-inch layer cake pans lined with wax paper. Bake in a preheated 350° F. oven for 30 minutes or until toothpick comes out clean. When slightly cool, invert on a rack and remove the wax paper. When cold spread your favorite frosting between each layer and over the top and sides.

Potato Orange Cake

This is surprisingly light and of exactly the right taste and texture to serve with that homemade ice cream you've been meaning to make. The orange flavor is subtle.

4 eggs
1 cup of sugar
1 teaspoon of baking powder
½ cup of potato starch
½ teaspoon of salt
2 tablespoons of orange juice
Grated rind of half the orange

In a bowl, whip the eggs until thick and smooth, then beat in the sugar until the batter "ribbons." Sift in the baking powder and potato starch; add the salt and blend well. Thoroughly mix in the orange juice and rind. Butter a 9-inch round cake pan, line it with wax paper (cut a circle for the bottom and strips for the sides), butter the wax paper. Pour in the cake batter and bake in a preheated 325° F. oven for 15 minutes. Turn the heat up to 350° F. and bake 15 minutes or until set. Turn out on a rack, remove the paper and cool.

SERVES 4.

Potato Pecan Snowballs

½ cup of butter or margarine, softened
1 cup of confectioners' sugar
¼ cup of cold mashed potatoes
2 tablespoons of milk
1 teaspoon of vanilla
¼ teaspoon of salt
1¾ cups of sifted flour
1 cup of chopped pecans

In a large mixing bowl, cream together the butter and ½ cup of the confectioners' sugar. Add the mashed potatoes, milk, vanilla and salt, blending thoroughly. With a wooden spoon, stir in the flour and pecans until blended. Shape into 1-inch balls. Bake on greased cookie sheets in a preheated 350° F. oven for about 20 minutes. Cool slightly, then roll in remaining ½ cup confectioners' sugar.

MAKES ABOUT 3 DOZEN.

Jane's Potato Torte with Orange Icing

⅔ cup of cream
5 squares (5 ounces) of bitter baking chocolate
2½ cups of sugar
1½ cups of butter, at room temperature
5 egg yolks
1½ cups of cold riced potatoes
1½ teaspoons of vanilla
¼ cup of Grand Marnier

SIFTED TOGETHER:
2 cups of sifted flour
2½ teaspoons of baking powder
½ teaspoon of cinnamon
1½ cups of chopped almonds
2 tablespoons of grated orange rind
5 egg whites, stiffly beaten

Over hot water in a double boiler heat the cream and chocolate, stirring until the chocolate has melted. In a large bowl, cream the sugar and butter. Beat in the egg yolks, one at a time. Beat in the potatoes, then the chocolate-cream mixture. Beat in the vanilla, Grand Marnier, flour mixture, almonds and orange rind. The mixture should be smooth and very well blended. Fold in the egg whites and pour into an unbuttered 10-inch spring-form mold. Bake in a preheated 350° F. oven for 1¼ hours, or until toothpick comes out clean. Cool in the mold. Remove from mold, invert and ice. Our friend Jane uses a butter frosting. We like an orange icing (see below).

Orange Icing

    4 tablespoons of orange juice
    1 tablespoon of lemon juice
    1½ cups of sugar
    ½ teaspoon of grated orange rind
    2 egg whites

Place all ingredients in the top of a double boiler and beat with a wire whisk until well blended. Over rapidly boiling water continue a constant beating for 6 minutes, or until it is of a spreadable consistency.

SERVES 8.

Index

ABOUT THE AUTHORS

If, as has been said, MARIA LUISA SCOTT and JACK DENTON SCOTT are the foremost and most formidable team of cookbook authors in the country, they have won that honor with honest and impressive credentials.

For over a decade they worked and learned with their friend, Antoine Gilly, one of the four greatest living French chefs. Gilly, who has cooked for such notables as King George V of England, the Prince of Wales, and Prime Minister Lloyd George, also authored a book with the Scotts, *Feast of France*, which the *Wall Street Journal* called one of the best cookbooks ever written. For his contribution to that book, Jack Denton Scott was awarded the Prix Litterari of the Paulée de Meursault. He is also a Commandeur Associé of the Commanderie des Cordons Bleus de France.

The Scotts spent some ten years researching and writing *The Complete Book of Pasta*, the first book of its kind. It has since become a classic, and was pronounced a favorite by such culinary experts as Julia Child, Helen McCully, Michael Field, James Beard and Craig Claiborne. Other highly acclaimed cookbooks by the Scott team include *Informal Dinners for Easy Entertaining; Cook like a Peasant, Eat like a King* and *Mastering Microwave Cooking*. They are also major contributors to the *Great Cooks' Guides*. Jack Denton Scott has published some thirty-five books, including novels, travel and natural history books, and juvenile books.

The Scotts have been around the world more than a dozen times and have collected recipes from every country they have visited. They live in Washington, Connecticut.

KITCHEN POWER!

☐	12207	**COOKING WITH HERBS AND SPICES** Craig Claiborne	$2.50
☐	13414	**SOURDOUGH COOKERY** Rita Davenport	$2.25
☐	13019	**MASTERING MICROWAVE COOKING** Scotts	$2.25
☐	12777	**PUTTING FOOD BY** Hertzberg, Vaughan & Greene	$2.95
☐	12278	**LAUREL'S KITCHEN** Robertson, Flinders & Godfrey	$3.95
☐	12263	**YOGURT COOKERY** Sophie Kay	$2.25
☐	11888	**CROCKERY COOKERY** Mable Hoffman	$2.25
☐	13168	**THE COMPLETE BOOK OF PASTA** Jack Denton Scott	$2.25
☐	13250	**MADAME WU'S ART OF CHINESE COOKING**	$2.25
☐	13558	**BETTER HOMES & GARDENS BLENDER BOOK** The Dworkins	$2.25
☐	12186	**BETTER HOMES & GARDENS HOME CANNING COOKBOOK**	$1.95
☐	13833	**BETTER HOMES & GARDENS NEW COOKBOOK**	$3.50
☐	13626	**BETTY CROCKER'S COOKBOOK**	$2.95
☐	10538	**AMERICA'S FAVORITE RECIPES FROM BETTER HOMES & GARDENS**	$1.50
☐	12309	**THE ART OF FRENCH COOKING** Fernande Garvin	$1.75
☐	12199	**THE ART OF JEWISH COOKING** Jennie Grossinger	$1.95
☐	12316	**THE ART OF ITALIAN COOKING** Mario LoPinto	$1.75

Buy them wherever Bantam Bestsellers are sold or use this handy coupon:

Bantam Books, Inc., Dept. KP, 414 East Golf Road, Des Plaines, Ill. 60016

Please send me the books I have checked above. I am enclosing $_____
(please add $1.00 to cover postage and handling). Send check or money order
—no cash or C.O.D.'s please.

Mr/Mrs/Miss _____

Address _____

City _____ State/Zip _____

KP—8/80

Please allow four to six weeks for delivery. This offer expires 12/80.